The Theatre Student

ORGANIZATION AND MANAGEMENT
OF THE NONPROFESSIONAL THEATRE

The Theatre Student

ORGANIZATION AND MANAGEMENT OF THE NONPROFESSIONAL THEATRE

including backstage and front-of-house

Jim Cavanaugh

PUBLISHED BY
RICHARDS ROSEN PRESS, INC.
NEW YORK, N.Y. 10010

Standard Book Number: 8239–0259–5
Library of Congress Catalog Card Number: 72–75222

Dewey Decimal Classification: 792

Published in 1973 by Richards Rosen Press, Inc.
29 East 21st Street, New York City, N.Y. 10010

First Edition
Manufactured in the United States of America

For Kathleen and Brennan

The philosophies and techniques outlined in this book could not have originated with one person; they have been developed in communion with the thousands of teachers, directors, casts, crews, boards, students, and audiences with whom I have been fortunate enough to work and to whom I am indebted for a lifetime of friendship, challenge, and exciting theatre.

ABOUT THE AUTHOR

JIM CAVANAUGH has worked in Theatre—professional and nonprofessional—virtually all his life. His teens were spent at his local community theatre, at 19 he was program director of a network radio station, and from 1952 to 1954 he directed the Heidelberg (Germany) Little Theatre when off duty from his job as the Russian translator for H.Q., U.S. Army Europe. Since then, he has stage-managed on Broadway, directed Off-Broadway, handled nearly every job in nine seasons of summer theatre, managed community theatres for ten years, and is now happily in the world of college theatre.

Mr. Cavanaugh studied directing with Lee Strasberg at the American Theatre Wing, then attended Goodman Memorial Theatre in Chicago, where he received his B.F.A. with honors in directing. After several years of theatre work in New York, he signed on as managing director of the Rochester (Minn.) Civic Theatre, directing more than seventy-five productions between 1960 and 1967, quadrupling the membership, and building a quarter-million-dollar theatre building with funds raised entirely within that town of 40,000 people. He was next named executive director of the Omaha (Neb.) Playhouse, one of the oldest and most famous community theatres in the country.

He is past president of the North Central Theatre Association, immediate past member of the Board of Trustees of the National Theatre Conference, and in his second three-year term as board member of the American Community Theatre Association, which he has twice served as convention program chairman. In 1969 he was chairman of ACTA's Monaco Festival, held in five American cities prior to sending a community theatre entrant to the World Amateur Theatre Festival in Monte Carlo; he is currently community theatre editor of the *Educational Theatre Journal.*

Now assistant professor of Theatre Arts at Mount Holyoke College, South Hadley, Massachusetts, Mr. Cavanaugh is director of its Laboratory Theatre, teaches acting and directing, and is founder–producer–director of the Mount Holyoke College Summer Theatre. His interest is in training students for whom the Theatre will be an avocation; his efforts are directed toward the communication of the joys and rewards that good Theatre—professional and nonprofessional—can and must bring to participant and audience alike.

Photographs by MICHAEL FEINSTEIN, Mount Holyoke College Photographer

CONTENTS

9

PREFACE

Manage or Flop—this frighteningly accurate admonition served as title and spur of a panel assembled by Dr. Walter H. Walters, Dean of the College of Arts and Architecture of the Pennsylvania State University, at a recent convention of the American Theatre Association. It was Dean Walters' thesis that responsibility is an artistic validity in itself, to which we panel members addressed ourselves, proving and reproving his point, even occasionally surprising one another in the simple reality of some of the proof.

Much of the material in this book was touched on in that session, whose designation is the unwritten subtitle of each succeeding chapter. If I were not afraid the words would lose their punch with repetition, I would remind you at the top of each page: manage or flop. Too many potentially good performances, and potentially productive theatres—educational, community, professional—do indeed flop, daily, as a direct result of the sin of poor management, natural child of poor organization.

It is a shameful truth that nonprofessional theatre, especially, is too often sustained not by the discrimination but by the chauvinism of its audience, intent on seeing familiar faces in unfamiliar situations. It is a happier truth that the introduction of good plays, well produced, can lengthen the life of a theatre—for a time. But, no matter how fine the script, how beautiful the production, how artistically inspired the troupe, how sincere your reasons for establishing a theatre, *you will flop* if you fail to set out with the firm belief that Organization is an art equal to Acting, Directing, Design, and the other more obvious of the theatre arts, with a strong and well-defined structure and with your entire group committed to following the precepts of that structure in every aspect, in every department, in every moment of your theatre work.

It is the purpose of this book:

● to challenge you in each area of theatre with the need for a matrix within which you may move with a direction, not merely an enthusiasm (though please do not discount the perpetual need for enthusiasm) and

● to provide you with the blueprints for building such an organization for the better running and more certain continuation of your nonprofessional theatre.

Most students attracted to the theatre during their undergraduate days will not earn a very large part—if any—of their lives' income in the professional theatre; I earnestly hope, however, that, properly stimulated and inspired by their early leaders, they will always want to be associated with theatre of some sort. That theatre will almost certainly turn out to be nonprofessional: school, church, club, neighborhood center, or community. And the success of that theatre will depend not so much on the quality of the onstage work—as stated, the audience of a nonprofessional theatre is regrettably often less conscious of quality than it should be—as on the strength and depth of its organization and management. And good management will very likely even help to raise the quality!

Jim Cavanaugh

FOREWORD

The examples given and recommendations made in this book have been deliberately aimed to help organize and manage every sort of nonprofit theatre: schools and colleges (both student-run clubs and faculty-run departments), community and children's theatres, settlement house and neighborhood groups, and one-time producing organizations, such as churches or social-action committees.

If a particular area of discussion appears not to apply to you, by all means skim it—but then come back to it after you have found the meat you seek. I believe you will find, with a minimum of elision or addition, aid for your needs, too, in each segment of this book.

Part 1

THE BASIC THEATRE ORGANIZATION

The man selling neckties out of a battered suitcase on the corner may carry a superior tie, but unless he begins to work under a definite regimen he will shortly be out of business (was he ever *in* business?). Or, and perhaps worse, he will be condemned to the same corner at the same level of productivity for life. John Wanamaker, legendary department store founder who began by tramping through early Pennsylvania with his merchandise on his back, added a *system* to his popularity and found himself the head of an empire. Some of today's finest firms began in a pushcart, a kiosk, or a ruck-sack . . .

. . . and added to their belief in their product—organization.

The current cry (from some would-be artists) that to organize the arts is to sterilize them is as far from the facts as the old-fashioned concept that truth and beauty and an artistic idea were all a theatre needed to survive.

Remember this scene from late-night television movies?:

"Hey, gang! I've got a great idea! We'll raise the money by putting on a show!"

"Swell! Sally's uncle has that old barn . . ."

"Yeah! And my dad'll let us use all those old costumes in our basement!" (They run off, like Stephen Leacock's horseman, in all directions at once.)

Wow! Not only do they earn the money to help the poor widow (or whatever), but Billy's dad brings a famous Broadway producer to the show, and the entire production, put together in three and a half days, is transported to New York, where all the kids become stars overnight. Even the funny little guy who can't do anything right.

Well, that works in the old movies, but don't count on it as you begin your community theatre or start a drama club, or stage a one-time play to make money, celebrate an event, or contribute to your community's creative or social-action life.

Do, please, establish your group and do put on your play—put on many. There is a pleasure to be given and received between the stage and the auditorium that can be found nowhere else, and you should experience that pleasure. And share it. Any town in today's world with a population of more than 1,000 is culturally barren without its own community theatre or equivalent; any high school without a regularly scheduled program of drama is not preparing its students for tomorrow's even more artistically aware, communication-oriented life; any college whose campus does not boast at least one student-run nondepartmental theatre organization is not part of the 1970's; and the successes—whatever one's political belief—of the recent Moritoria for Peace and the government's response have surely and lastingly proven the uses of theatrical techniques, well organized, in communicating social or political messages on the broader stage of a city, a state, or a nation.

Having said all this, I must now take a step back and caution you: If you intend to produce more than one play, be sure your community *wants* more than one. If your plan is to establish a permanent theatre group, be very sure that a theatre group can be supported by a willing and ever eager public. High on the list of reasons for the demise of nonprofessional theatres is a fact that, however sorrowfully, must be faced: Some communities just don't want and just don't think they need a theatre. (From here on I shall use the word "community" in its fullest sense, to refer not only to a city but to a neighborhood, a collection of several towns, a high school, a college, or an organization—any congregation of people who share or who could share a cultural life.)

Be very sure that the stirrings within the founding devotees—"We need a theatre!"—are shared in the community at large, or that the community can be shown *why* it needs a theatre. Be sure, too, that, once shown, the people of the community will support the beginnings and the continuation of your group, even after the novelty has worn off. Discussion with local leaders—teachers, ministers, elected officials, newspaper, radio, and TV people—will give you a chance to hear qualified opinions on the likelihood of your success and will give them a chance to hear your serious, well-organized ideas as to why you believe such an activity is needed, and how—with neatly drawn budgetary facts and figures—it could be sustained.

A prime way to prove to yourself that you have not fostered an in-group designed by and for the founding fathers is to outline at the beginning the ways you will involve the community in the theatre. Probably most of the organizers are creative people—actors, a director or two, possibly a designer—and there is no question but that *they* will be bringing their talents and energies to each play for the first year or so. But, in addition, the front of the house must be staffed, publicity campaigns mounted and followed up, tickets must be sold, money accounted for, and so on. Literally dozens of people can and should work on every major production; that number will move up into the hundreds when a musical or a classic is scheduled.

Tell the community leaders of this broad need for involvement, and point out that it covers all educational and economic backgrounds; people of all ages and with all degrees of theatrical experience (beginning at 0) will be sought, brought into the group, and will contribute as they gain from your theatre. Convince them that you will avoid the common—and usually correctly applied—stigma carried by nonprofessional theatres: that they are cliques of arty people looking for a place to show off. Listen to your own speeches, then, and do involve the entire community from the first day. The founders will grow tired, graduate, or move to another town before long, and, even while they are working with you, they must not hold all the talent, the power, the jobs in their few hands. A gratifyingly successful rule I made and adhered to at one theatre I ran said: "At least half of the cast for each play will be composed of people who have never acted with this theatre before." The public grew to realize that we meant it, and that they would be honestly considered for roles; even more, that this same philosophy pervaded offstage departments, that all doors were open to all comers. We were believed because *we* believed, and the theatre prospered. The entire community was involved constantly; the theatre never became the plaything of a few but continued in fact as a communitywide group. Whether that town really needed that theatre in the early days will never be known, but the town needs the theatre now, and knows it; it has known it for some time. And the feeling is joyously mutual.

Most communities will respond as beautifully as that one. Some will not. Some may never provide the atmosphere or the audience for a continuing nonprofessional theatre. Find that out, if you can, before you get too deeply involved, and avoid the broken heart that accompanies the realization that everyone doesn't feel about the theatre as you do.

If you are lucky and get the support of the community leaders, or at least find that they're not against you, go to it. Start your theatre. Hang on to the sense of fun those kids had transforming Uncle Dan's barn into a pleasure palace; hang on to the drive for expression and creativity that you know must find its outlet on the stage; hang on to the sure knowledge in your heart that your community needs this theatre; and keep, by all means, the message you want to share by theatrical means. Without these heartfelt motivations, form and structure are empty.

But please—to all these intentions, add: Organization.

Organization won't stunt your creativity—it will provide an arena within whose visible limits you can grow; it won't suck all the fun out of theatre—it will relieve you of at least some of the burdens and remove hidden obstacles so that despair and disappointment won't destroy the fun; it won't dilute your statement—it will clear away annoying debris so that the message will stand out more sharply.

Organization need not be complicated; follow the procedures in this book and in those listed in the Bibliography that best apply to your situation. Every theatre is different, but most problems stem from common roots. Moving ahead with a plan as you cast your show or establish your group will show you specifically where you're going; more to the point, it will show how you're going to get there. You'll protect yourself from the common route of ad-libbing your way to failure.

All right, I'll say it: Manage or Flop.

Chapter I

THE CHAIN OF COMMAND

When arriving as new director of a theatre, I make it a point to accept all existing rules, at least for the first show, on the premise that there is a reason for each tradition—even if obscure—and not wishing to make new-broom changes until giving each system a chance to work on its home ground.

My first play at a large community theatre was the behemoth Gypsy, *with 19 sets, 60 performers, and a running crew of 25. Musicals ran twenty-two nights at this theatre; running crews were flexible within that time. Prop girls, grips, flymen, makeup crews, electricians, and the like worked as many or as few performances as they wished. The assumption was that the actors' onstage glory gave them more stake in showing up night after night than did the unsung backstage workers' gloryless toil.*

I disagreed—believing that a smooth production needs a pattern filled not only by the same actor saying the same line at the same moment of each performance, but also the same crewman throwing the same switch or zipping the same zipper at the same moment each night. But I bought the plan. It was my first play there.

On closing night I was passing through the backstage area during the busy second act, when the chief prop girl, who hadn't worked the show for several nights, ran up to me with an armload of spears for the first burlesque-house scene. "Oh, thank God!" she gasped. "Where do these damn things go?"

Closing night. Twenty-two performances. Prop chief.

Needed? Firm and show-long chain of command.

* * *

Creation by committee was a common penchant of the American arts until the recent wave of management-wise producers, devotees, and arts councils took command, but the midair arm-flailing that accompanies decision by lucky accident still contributes heavily to the death of many nonprofit artistic organizations. The desire to create seems to transcend the need to name and

follow leaders; too many sensitive people cavil at giving or taking orders even when that sensitivity obviously delays or otherwise harms the work in progress. A commune may be the great leveler, but it won't get a show on. A headless body, however agile each working part might be, however willing, cannot produce. At least not in the arts.

There must be a leader.

There must be a line of leaders.

A clearly defined chain of command must exist in the executive organization of any theatre and in the production staff of each specific show, with every board member, crew member, cast member, and committee member fully aware of the chain, of who his superiors are, who his subordinates, and of just what responsibilities, rights, and limits he has in that chain, that organization, and that show. Each leader must know his own and his team's privileges and duties, and he must be in attendance. Constantly. Leading.

"I assumed someone else would handle it," or "I didn't know that was part of my department" are lines that must not be found in the minds or mouths of anyone in your organization. The assuming of *anything* is taboo; responsibilities must be made known to all and must be fulfilled on time, and reported as fulfilled immediately to the crew head or committee head, who will report the completion in turn to his superior.

Delegation and limiting of authority on the governing board and on the production crews are often difficult to accomplish, especially in a long-established group in which the founding fathers (somehow always called the Old Guard) have held sway so many years that their embrace of their theatre has become a stranglehold. The Old Guard (or the equally grabby and rightfully proud incorporators of a new and fast-growing theatre) must be persuaded—by legislation if necessary—to let others join in the decision-making, or, even more profitably, to step aside for a show or a season after a stated length of time in power to share the joys and the troubles with new, sometimes younger, surely fresher minds and hearts. In a school theatre, with leaders graduating each year, this continuing grooming of new artistic and managerial commanders is a must. It should be as obvious a must to postgraduates in their theatres.

Each year or each play, all committees of the Board and of the production staff should include at least a few new members who will learn from the experienced workers and be ready to take command in the normal course of time or in case of illness, overload, or revolution, all of which occur in the best of theatres. Their accumulated experience and eventual move into leadership after a few shows, or a year or so on a committee of the Board, is your surest and strongest way to forge an effective chain of command. And to survive.

CHAIN OF COMMAND IN THE PARENT PRODUCING ORGANIZATION

A nonprofit theatre should be set up organizationally the same as any club—with officers, di-

rectors, and strong committee chairmen. (See Figure 1.)

Boards and committees will be discussed at length in Chapter III, but note now that the basic duties of the members of a Theatre Board are exactly the same as the duties of their opposite numbers on any Board or committee of any nonprofit organization. The main difference lies in the need, with us, for even stronger and more interested leaders at the head of each chain of command.

The makeup of the Board and its committees should include a few people chosen not for their organized minds but for their inventiveness and creativity and ability to move beyond organization in search of beauty, innovation, and challenge; it is then up to the theatre leadership to channel those imaginative minds into each specific problem at hand. Their opinions are the living justification of the inclusion of artistic people in the business of theatre management. They must be listened to. But two dangers exist and must be watched for and avoided by the leader: creation by committee, on the one hand, as struc-

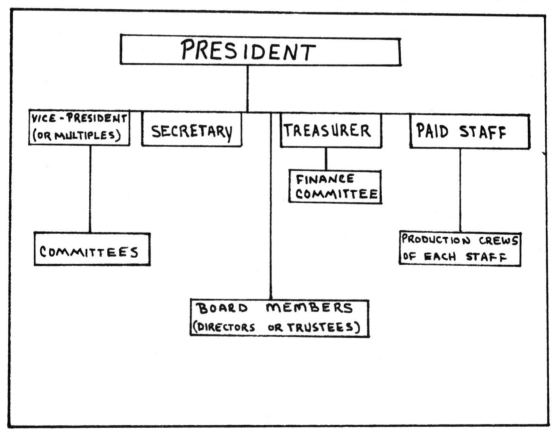

FIG. 1. Organizational Setup of a Nonprofit Theatre

ture meets flair and both are compromised into an empty solution; and creation by the loudest voice, as the artist, knowing he is there for his unique point of view, insists in growing volume that the only path is his, of beauty; or the businessman, not always sold on the value of artists out of their ateliers, tromps down hard and loud on the seemingly impractical suggestions. The eventual wearing down of the tired ear by the bombastic voice, from whichever side, can result. So can walkouts. The leader must exercise his leadership and see that the contributions of the artist are indeed used when of use and that hurt feelings are soothed before a creative worker is lost to that theatre forever.

The artist on an administrative Board may feel hemmed in by the chain and believe that he can better contribute with no tangible structure to inhibit him. Help him to achieve the feeling of freedom but do not for a moment forget that we must all have that matrix, that limit, that chain of command, visible or invisible.

CHAIN OF COMMAND IN PRODUCING A PLAY

Just as a Roberts-Rules Board is necessary to guide the parent producing organization—the theatre—so is a strong and creative chain of command, in the form of a production staff, needed to ramrod the living reason for all this organization—the show. (See Figure 2.)

Any work of art stems from the creative genius of the artist. In the theatre, the prime artist is the playwright, from whose viscera-*cum*-brain has sprung the play. Everyone who contributes to the bringing to life of his play is, therefore, a re-creative artist, creative in his own artistic field but dedicated to the vitalization of the artistic work of the playwright. At the head of this team of re-creative artists, and leader of the production staff, is the director.

In the nonprofessional theatre, the director is also generally the *de facto* producer of the play, drawing his power and his finances from the overall producer, the money provider: the Board of

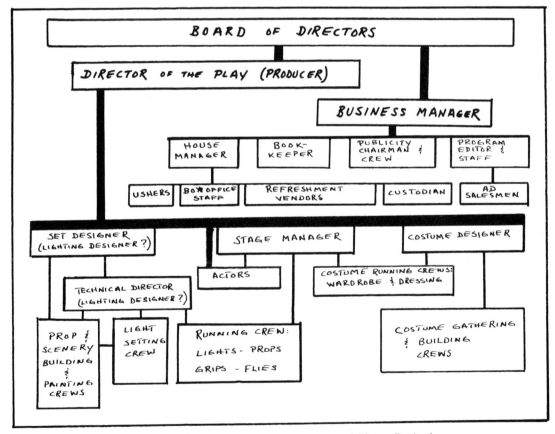

FIG. 2. Chain of Command of a Nonprofessional Theatre Production
Note the dual lines in some areas, especially to distinguish between leadership of preparation crews and of running crews.

Directors; and answerable, in turn, to them on all matters of theatre policy set or approved by them and passed on to him for execution.

Beyond those limits, the advice and consent of the Board, the director/producer is the unquestioned leader of the play. Until such time as he misuses his leadership, the director has full freedom to lead, to put into dramatic living form his concept of the playwright's original art work. He supervises each element, okaying each step made by each department head on the team of artists, craftsmen, and administrators that make up the production staff.

THE DIRECTOR AND HIS PRODUCTION STAFF

Long before casting, the director/producer meets with his designers, giving them his concept of how the play is to be done and aiming them

---

DREAM Production Meeting Checkpoints

Production Meetings are held each Monday at 12 Noon in the Green Room, including Monday, May 10. BE ON TIME. Bring your Assistant if you like.

Unless otherwise indicated, each of the assignments listed below *is* to be COMPLETED by the time of Production Meeting, not quitting time that night.

Remember the Rule of Three if you get behind on these due dates: There are only three possibilities to get you back on schedule: 1) Simplify
                                                                      2) Add personnel
                                                                      3) Work longer hours.
                                                    We will only accept #1
if you have been working to your full capacity since production began, for the chief reason for falling behind schedule is usually the classic American dream of completion by Opening Night. We aim to be completed by 3 days before Tech Rehearsal, and therefore urge that no one attempt to compromise this schedule by adapting it to life, liberty and the pursuit of working-hour happiness. The happiness - and it can be a big one - should come thru doing your creative work well on this beautiful play. That's working-hour happiness in a big way Do your toughest work now, while you're fresh; not later when you're pressed and tempers flare. Eat the Broccoli first.

MON APR 12 -   Scenery: Overhead sign built, painted, hung.
                          Throne platform in the process of being installed.
                          Hillocks (including short stair platform) completed - method of
                                  stabilizing them in place devised.
                          Bower platform and escape safely completed and installed.
                          All ceiling hardware installed; all flies hung; swinging ropes
                                  safely usable.
                          Pageant wagon abuilding; or wheels frantically sought.

                Props, Sound, Publicity, House Management, Costumes, Lighting under way.

MON APR 19 -   Scenery: Complete anything hanging-over from last checkpoint. Plus:
                          Bower (Hammock) installed and safe.
                          Throne platform, stairs and escape completed and safe.
                          Basic pageant wagon (no decor needed) complete, moveable and safe.
                          Decor (columns, etc) beginning in the shop.

                Props: Actual swords and scabbards here and able to be worn and used.
                          Actual canes usable.
                          Practical pan-pipes usable (and the actual method of carrying them
                                  on his person now usable);
                          Puck's toy here and usable.

                Publicity: Outdoor signs at Lab Theatre repainted permanently.
                          Program format approved and basic cast and crew list initialled.
                          Draft approved of highschool letters. Begin printing them.
                          Poster (if there is one) format approved - order them
                          5-college calendar information due by today.

                House Management: Tickets ordered.
                                   Plan for securing amphitheatre approved.

                Fontaine: Sound plot approved; sources being scoured.
                          At least one horseback rehearsal conducted.

                Tony: Sound system in Amphitheatre fully checked and approved - proper
                          tapedeck approved and available (Inform Fontaine of track-taping).
                          Speakers checked, etc . . .

                Vicki: Makeup design approved by Jim and Joan. Plot delineated.

MON APR 26 -   Scenery: All complete: Furniture
                                        Flowers
                                        Torches (including mechanics for lighting & dousing)
                                        Netting on stairs (hillocks) and throne.
                            Decor cannot be set into amphitheatre today as originally scheduled
                            because of Spring Weekend concerts next weekend. But don't let this
                            slow you down - - complete them in the shop so they'll be totally
                            ready to install a week from today.

              Props: Tools for Mechanicals usable.
                        Bottom's 3 flowery pieces usable.
                        Books and scripts usable.
                        Burgomask instruments usable.

              Publicity: Full campaign in the works - ads ordered.
                                        Posters going up.
                                        Highschool letters mailed.
                                        Dorm activities scheduled.
                                        Pins/badges made.
                                        Choragos courted.
                                        Weekly calendar to have weekly item.
                                        Letters to Summer Theatre mailinglist.
                                        Confirm photo call with Mike & Kris.

              House Management: Letters to Complimentary Ticket list sent.
                                 Usher and Box Office sign up sheets up.

              Costumes & Makeup: Plan ahead:
                        Dress Parade (No makeup): This Wed, Apr 28, 7 pm: (4 Lovers,
                                                                          Puck, Oberon,
                                                                          Titania, Bottom.)
                                  Publicity Photos (Outdoors): This Fri, Apr 30 - Check in 3 p.m. or
                                           earlier for costume and makeup.
                                  Dress Parade - entire costume plot - Wed May 5, 7 pm.

              Fontaine: Sound fully taped, spliced and leadered.

              Tony: Tape playable at nightly rehearsals (no maintenance men - US.)

MON MAY 3 -   Tomorrow is 3 days before Tech, and EVERYTHING is to be finished. Lest there
              be confusion, I repeat: EVERYTHING US TO BE FINISHED - every prop, every nail,
              every zipper, every gel (check with the Chief Lighting Designer) every letter
              mailed . . . EVERYTHING.   Any work done now is to repair damage or to add
              things that have just been discovered to be needed. All finishing touches are
              COMPLETED BY NOW. Save strength and energy for correcting errors, not the
              jobs we've always known had to be done.   LOOK FOR TROUBLE IF THIS ISN'T SO?

WED MAY 5 - Dress Parade - everyone in everything. 7 p.m. (or earlier) checkin.

FRI MAY 7 - Tech/Dress - everything except full costumes (but we'll need some pieces, like
            Pyramus/Thisbe additional costumes, etc.). All running crews and Lab Theatre staff
            check in at 3, and be ready to go at 3:15 - - if you can't be ready in 15 minutes,
            check in at noon or whatever time you need to.   TD & Set Designer sit with
            directors during entire rehearsal for consultation and notes. Break for dinner
            at 5:30; pick up again at 7 - - until completion.

SAT MAY 8 - FULL DRESS WITH EVERYTHING EXCEPT MAKE UP. Ready to start rehearsal at 1:30 -
            call your crews whatever time before that necessary to go. Joan, join Tony and Bill
            in sitting with us for rehearsal.   Work till dinner. Reconvene at 7.

FIG. 3. Checkpoints—or Do List—for the Production Staff

This production schedule of checkpoints was used on a recent college production of A Midsummer Night's Dream.
*The stress on completion three days before Technical Rehearsal is deliberate, and is implemented on each play. The common
goal of finishing the production in time for opening night must not exist in a well-managed theatre. The actors must have the
opportunity to wear, handle, and step on every part of the production throughout dress rehearsal, or they will be insecure in their
movements—and their concentration—on opening night. The director must see everything that will exist, in its place, in time
to make corrections or adjustments if necessary. And the three-day grace period allows time for repair or replacement when the
unexpected happens.*

*As the performances were all given outdoors, in the afternoon, the references here to lighting design were inserted jokingly,
to add some fun to a serious list of needs and dates.*

toward a common goal, so each creative leader is working within the same style of production, within the same budget, and with a common set of deadlines. Weekly production meetings begin shortly before auditions, including each department head, and, possibly, his assistant; the production staff, in other words.

It is at these production meetings that one of the most important—and hardest to instill—facets of a strong director manifests itself: the ability to delegate authority. The charismatic one-man-show that many directors make of themselves is often necessary to galvanize a group to form, to re-form, to pull itself out of a slump, to be ready to open; and it is a valid way of work. But even the most egocentric me-first director must realize—must be made to realize, possibly—that he is not alone in his caring for the play, in his desire to work hard to accomplish his goal, or in his ability to work hard. He is, after all, just a link in that chain and, though the chief link, not at all indispensable. Should he get sick, someone will carry on the play if the director has shared the leadership duties and decisions, or at least delegated a certain amount of authority to subordinates. This is true only if the director truly cares for the play, not merely for the renown he is achieving for himself in producing the play. If the latter, he is in trouble, and so is the theatre. No one can run the whole show, nor should he.

One of the strongest condemnations I ever heard in this respect was the remark made by one regional repertory director about another: "He won't let the wardrobe mistress buy a spool of thread unless he's with her to approve the color." Engage talented and responsible department heads, and, within the limits of the concept, the budget, and the schedule, give them their heads. Then check their progress at the weekly production meeting, comparing it with the prestated list of deadlines each one has agreed to earlier as fair and achievable checkpoints. (See Figure 3.) A mimeographed list of these checkpoints, once each department has accepted them as meetable, must be given to everyone as soon after the first full production meeting as possible, and referred to at each successive meeting, in order to stop trouble or lateness when it occurs, not meet it unexpectedly at dress rehearsal. Immediate corrections are possible, when discussed with all present; perhaps one of the other leaders will have an idea where to find that elusive prop, or a suggestion on solving a problem in another area, or crew personnel who can be lent to a needy department for a few days. Talking out troubles at production meetings, where the collective brain may be picked, helps each area. Which helps the play.

THE RULE OF THREE

It is at these meetings that the Rule of Three mentioned in the sample schedule in Figure 3 may be exercised most effectively. Over the years I have learned that when a department of a play begins to lag, there are only three possibilities open to its leader to restore it to the level of progress of the rest of the production, the level necessary for a successful play and a continuing organization. If a project is behind schedule, you may:

(1) simplify the project; and/or
(2) add personnel to the project; and/or
(3) work longer hours on the project.

There are no additional possibilities.

Anything looser than this weekly (in summer theatre, daily) production meeting, or the firm application of the Rule of Three when necessary, will allow mistakes to occur, to be compounded, and then to become irrevocably locked into your artistic work. In some theatres where there are no production meetings, director and designer become strangers, each in his own bailiwick, passing occasionally in the hall or talking briefly in a noisy shop or sewing room. Misunderstandings and half-understandings develop, creation by accident (occasionally by malice) sets in, and the artistic product is determined without the discipline and careful control that must be present at its inception and at every moment right through closing night and the striking of all sets and costumes.

The designers in their turn must not be content to present plans for a masterwork and walk away; they are leaders of their artistic areas and must be on the scene whenever possible to answer questions of their crews, to show the way, and to assure themselves that the translation from sketch to stage is achieved properly and with an economy of time, labor, and money. The color rendering of the sets or of the costumes is a contract between designer and director (my current designer likes to say)—a visual contract of what is expected and what is to be delivered. And if that delivery requires that the designer join his crew and grab a hammer or a sewing machine, then so be it. Beware the designer who proffers lovely drawings with the proviso that he not have to be around for construction. He has no place in your chain of command and no loyalty to your show. You do not need him.

Each crew member, each actor, each department head works better knowing where he belongs on the chain, knowing that unless he fills his slot with all that is in him, a work of art will not emerge, a flop is imminent.

Chapter II

CONSTITUTION AND BYLAWS

"We, the people of the United States, in order to form a more perfect union, establish justice, insure domestic tranquility, provide for the common defense, promote the general welfare, and secure the blessings of liberty to ourselves and our posterity, do ordain and establish this Constitution for the United States of America."

Every constitution need not be as beautifully worded as that *Constitution, but each should be forged with the same urgency, the same love, and the same attention to detail that has made that document the strong guide it has been.*

* * *

Having decided on the structure of your chain of command, your next step is to make your decision official by setting down on paper a clear statement of that chain, together with your other feelings, ideas, and beliefs as to what your theatre is and what it is meant to accomplish, in the same way the framers of the U.S. Constitution set about clarifying the status and the purpose of their new organization. As they found, so you will very likely find, the best form for this statement of intent is that of constitution and bylaws. Some groups combine these two documents into a single constitution, which is perfectly legitimate and may suit your theatre best; but in fact the two have separate functions and work together, reflecting different approaches to the need for organizing.

The constitution defines your reason for being; the bylaws make sure you stay that way.

What *is* your reason for being? Are you in existence for the purpose of producing plays, period? Do you plan to add to the cultural life of your community? Are you primarily a social group seeking recreation? Do you want to change public opinion through the medium of theatre? All are fine goals for a new theatre; you must select yours and state clearly for yourself and for those who follow just what the goals of the founding fathers of your theatre are.

AUDIENCE-ORIENTED OR PARTICIPANT-ORIENTED?

Some excellent theatres have flopped as their third or fourth season bumped to an opening over the battling bodies of board members, some crying that the season was too audience-oriented, some equally upset that it was too participant-oriented. This constant argument need not exist if your theatre decides before the first play is produced which orientation is best for you.

An audience-oriented theatre, as its name implies, has the box office squarely in mind in the selection of plays and the staging of those plays. It knows, or learns about, the tastes of its audience and then gears itself to those tastes. It recognizes the need for public support, in approval and in ticket buying, and sets its policies accordingly. (It need not go as far as one community theatre that spent quite a bit of time at a board meeting discussing a letter from a long-time patron, who suggested that the theatre adopt a policy of producing plays written only prior to 1956. This meeting took place in 1968.)

A participant-oriented theatre, on the other hand, knows that it must attract talented workers in all fields, and that it will neither find nor keep the best theatre people by producing one silly box-set comedy after another; that it must vary its fare to provide fine acting roles, interesting sets to be designed, ideas to be considered and offered to the audience through the dramatic medium, and meat for all volunteers to find nourishing; and that the participant find some ego-satisfaction in what he does. This is not to damn the theatre worker who travels somewhat on ego, as long as it does not affect his work or his offstage relations with his co-workers. A modicum of ego is necessary for a good performance, nearly always. (One community saw its volunteer actors form themselves into a guild, threatening to withhold their bodies from the stage unless the theatre provided them with beer money. An organization can, it seems, become *too* participant-oriented.)

A BLENDING OF THE TWO

It is probably obvious that I feel that a combination, a blending, of the two—of audience and participant awareness—is what most theatres need. A workable balance is possible if every theatre accepts the fact that without the help of talented theatre craftsmen it will produce rotten evenings, and that a play may appeal to a broad audience without being pap. A season may offer plays of lightness with fun parts to play and happiness for tired businessmen, complemented by plays of substance for thinking audiences, with gutsy roles for the gutsy actors. Both audience and participants will benefit.

Whichever way you go, whether in one of these stated directions, or a different blending of your own, spell out that direction concretely and fully in your constitution, so that there is no doubt now or later who you are and where you are going.

NONPROFIT OR NONPROFESSIONAL

Before drawing up the constitution, you have another identity question to answer for yourself: Are you a nonprofit organization, or nonprofessional, or both?

You are probably nonprofit; that is, your financial backers and donors receive no return on their money. Salaries for your employees, if any, may be as high as you like (note the income of officials of national nonprofit organizations instituted for charitable purposes), but they must be contracted salaries or wages and not a piece of the action. Legalize your nonprofit status by registering with your state government, attesting to your educational, cultural, and no-dividend qualities.

Nonprofessional means that your participants are not paid, but earn their livings at other jobs. Here, again, you may have salaried leaders—generally a director, often a secretary, sometimes a set designer or technical director or combination of the two, less frequently a business manager. The presence of salaried personnel in these positions does not destroy the nonprofessional status of the theatre; in fact, it may well keep you open and operating.

AMATEUR THEATRE

The term "nonprofessional" is fully equivalent to "amateur," but this latter word has lately fallen into disrepute, as in "amateur theatricals," usually describing cute, well-meaning, but bumbling dilettantes as held up to ridicule in George Kelly's farce *The Torchbearers*. Help restore the dignity to the word "amateur"; follow it back to its Latin beginning and use it as it was meant to be used—to describe someone who does what he does for the love of it, not for the pay—a lover. Amateur theatre is produced by people who do it for love. And that's good.

CIVIC THEATRE

When I was hired by the Rochester (Minnesota) Civic Theatre, I was fresh from Broadway and not too happy with the prosaic name of my new theatre. Why wasn't it called Sock and Buskin, or The Playmakers, or even The Rochester Little Theatre, in honor of the nationwide movement that began the community-theatre boom in this country? It wasn't long, however, before I realized how apt a name the founders had chosen; it was in fact the Theatre of the City, providing good entertainment, producing fine plays, offering artistic leadership to the community and a workshop for anyone from any part of town to try his skills in the theatre arts. If you are still measuring your theatre for a name, do not ignore the statement you will make every time you proudly call yourself the Civic Theatre.

DRAWING UP YOUR CONSTITUTION

Several sample theatre constitutions are included in the Appendix. Look them over. Find the one—or the combination of formats from several—that best suits your group. Insert your special requirements and self-cautions, change the name, and you have a basic constitution.

Now, go carefully over the rough draft, section by section, to be sure you have not said too much. Aim for simplicity, for the barest minimum of do's and don'ts, of rules and caveats. Give yourself a constitution and a set of bylaws that you can use, and that do not use you; that limit without stifling. Be very clear in your wording, so that those who follow in twenty years will know precisely what you meant in constitutionalizing yourself.

Make it easily amendable, as your organization grows and changes and sees its day-to-day reason for being taking a new direction. Do not force yourself, in time, to wink at your guiding document, breaking rules that "everyone knows are foolish." Make it possible to amend the rules. Or stick to them.

INCORPORATION

At this point, you may find it advisable to hire the first—and maybe the only—paid professional you will ever want to engage: a lawyer. Even if your group boasts a friendly (meaning free) lawyer or lawyer's wife or lawyer's child, the next move is going to cost you a little money. But it will be worth it. Incorporate—as the nonprofit cultural organization you have declared yourself to be. Incorporate as a legal body under your state's laws.

Why?

Well, mostly for financial reasons.

To begin with, if you open a theatre without the protection of incorporation, your officers, or directors, or even your members, could be legally liable if anything went wrong, if someone were hurt or something broken—a law or a borrowed lamp, for instance. Under incorporation, the theatre itself is the responsible party, and although each of you who cares about your group will do all possible to see that restitution is made, you will do so without the pain of being personally sued or held responsible.

TAX EXEMPTIONS

Then come the happy reasons for incorporation—tax exemptions. You say you're just a happy band of players, why must you worry about taxes? Because nothing is more certain than taxes (except that the show must go on—and I'm not always sure about that old Thou Shalt). Because taxes are with us, and are going to be, and we might as well find the most pleasant way of living with them, turning them to our advantage if legally possible.

And it *is* legally possible. As an incorporated nonprofit cultural organization, you should be able to have your theatre declared tax-exempt by both state and federal governments. Of course, you'll have to work for it; you'll fill out a lot of forms and have to file special tax returns, reporting all theatre income, expenses, and so forth in

horrendous detail—but you won't have to pay any organizational income tax.

Nor should you be required to pay real-estate tax on any theatre property, nor to add amusement or sales tax to the price of your tickets. Check your state rulings on those last items, however. Some clearly nonprofit groups in various states have had to beg special legislation on such tax matters—and have usually won.

It sometimes takes a roundabout, ludicrous path to winning, as with the midwestern art museum facing a new state sales tax that would have required adding a few pennies to their admission fee, which was a quarter dropped into a turnstile at the entrance. The sheer mechanical adaptations to allow the turnstile to accept pennies, too, would have been terribly expensive, but the plight of the patently cultural/educational museum did not move the lawmakers, so the museum solved its own problem by tying in with a rider to the sales-tax law that absolved companies operating coin-sales machines from retooling their coin slots to allow for the additional state pennies. Touting themselves as businessmen rather than artists, the museum staff circumvented the tax requirement—by having their mammoth storehouse of art treasures legally declared a vending machine!

A long-respected community theatre in the same state found itself, too, unable to convince the legislature that, as a cultural body, it should be free of sales tax, including the tax on the material bought for costumes, scenery, and so on. Finding another rider to the law, designed to ease the load on manufacturers, the theatre declared itself a factory making a product (the play) and swore that everything bought was an integral part of the fabrication of their product. They won—no sales tax.

But how much more a part of the mid-twentieth century that state would have shown itself to be had it not forced these obviously educational groups to, in fact, lie to achieve the same immunity as hundreds of profit-making corporations.

TAX DEDUCTIBILITY

You are not only tax-exempt, but tax-deductible. You are able, at last, to use the existence of taxes to the advantage of your theatre. Gifts, bequests, patron tickets (whose cost is higher than the normal ticket price), donations of merchandise—all are legally deductible from the income tax of the generous soul who needs a certain amount of charitable giving to enter on his annual tax form. He has to give something to someone to ease his outlay to Uncle Sam—the beneficiary might as well be you—but you must tell him, since he is thinking of hospitals, churches, schools, and such and must be reminded of your equally deductible condition.

Incorporate your nonprofitness and go to work encouraging donations of money and needed theatre items for backstage, for a specific play, or for the audience's comfort. When you receive such a gift, write a simple letter on your official stationery (another good investment—it lets people know you're not that band of strolling players but are here to stay and be productive) stating that on this date (the year is important for tax deduction) the theatre has received $X—or merchandise, spelled out very thoroughly, in the value of $X—for use by your incorporated nonprofit organization. Sign it, add your title (again, stability), accompany it with a personal note of thanks, and make a big friend of the man who has given you something.

You're already receiving a fine return on the money you paid the lawyer to help you incorporate; while he's at it, you might as well have him check the wording on your constitution and bylaws, too. It will save you a lot of trouble later on, if something is legally muddy.

Even if you are a school-affiliated theatre, you will probably want to incorporate; check with your adviser and ask him to see what the school attorney thinks about it. Good practice for your members, plus an identity of your own.

CELEBRATING THE CORPORATION

After you have drawn up your constitution, bylaws, and articles of incorporation, tell the community about it. Have them share the christening joys with you (and learn more about you, especially about your ability to govern yourself). Schedule a general meeting of the entire organization, to which the public is invited. Broadcast the invitation in all the media and make it clear that this is not an in-group or a closed shop, but truly an evening for everyone. Serve refreshments, and announce that fact on your invitations; but nothing alcoholic in the theatre building, please, ever. Remember your image. Announce that you will present a play—probably a one-act, to leave time for the other drama of the evening. Put your most talented director in charge of your finest actors.

It's show-off time. Select the play within your stated intent of a theatre philosophy. Keep the style and theme within the artistic limits you describe in your constitution, and forecast the future scheduling by the choice of this type of play.

Invite the town fathers—better still, invite the town mothers, and the fathers will be brought; who determines the spending of the entertainment dollar in America? The women. But this evening will be free, and the promise of a play and refreshments may bring some who would not come for the reading of a constitution. Announce that the play will be first—to get everyone there on time—and then begin your policy-to-be by ringing up the curtain at precisely the stated time.

Have your most articulate and tasteful member serve as master of ceremonies, taking over immediately after the play, introducing the founding board—making sure that any high-powered community figures in your group are in attendance. Read the documents, asking for comments or discussion. Listen, truly, to the voice of the people in this discussion period, incorporating valid suggestions into your constitution. Move that the final papers be approved and have them signed in the presence of every community dignitary you can round up. Have reporters and photographers handy. (Or, if they fail to show up, have one of your membership ready with a camera and distribute photos and your story on the event to all area media first thing next morning.) Then bring on the refreshments.

You're official. You have arrived. You're as deductible as a newborn baby, and, with proper management (sorry to keep bringing in that word), you're on the road to being as lovable and as well loved as that baby. Nothing impresses potential ticket buyers of a community so much as artists who are organized and who work at their art within established structure. And, as I never tire of pointing out, nothing will guarantee you well-produced shows, ready on time, as will that structure. To these ends, you have drawn and offered to your membership and your public your official papers:

Your constitution, defining the concept of your theatre;

Your bylaws, guiding you without shackling you;

Your articles of incorporation, achieving government recognition.

You're not going to flop, because you're managing well.

Chapter III

BOARDS OF DIRECTORS AND COMMITTEES

No one has ever been offended by being asked to serve on a Board of Directors.

A well-known community theatre, in the days when it was not well known, decided that in order to raise enough money for its own building, it ought to weight the Board with community names. A nominating committee agonized through several meetings, compiling a list of the civic leaders they would most like to have on the Board, based on energy, reputation for getting a job done, leadership ability, and the probability of bringing audience and pledges into the theatre on the strength of their names. After settling on a roster of the best of the best, the committee contacted each, asking if his name could be added to the slate (constitutionally, nominations were presented by the committee at the annual meeting, with further nominations possible from the floor; so this blue-ribbon slate were not promised a shoo-in election, but only asked if their names could be put into contention).

Although some came seldom, if ever, to the community theatre, every person asked said yes, and a membership seeking to broaden and widen its activities elected the slate unanimously, adding to the Board such new, diverse, and valuable people as the editor of the town newspaper, the comptroller of the large computer plant, the manager of the largest department store in town, the president of the state's largest hotel chain, the chairman of the theatre department of the local college, a respected surgeon, a battling attorney, and several whirlwind women known for their organization work.

Not only did these active community leaders stabilize the theatre, increase the membership, and oversee the building of a well-equipped, handsome, and paid-for new home, but most of them eventually took roles in the plays, and most are still active on stage, backstage, and in committee work, ten years later.

By swallowing any fears of rejection, by starting at the top and asking the best people to stand for election, the best possible Board can be achieved.

* * *

Whether or not you ever decide to incorporate, you must—*must*—work with a Board of Directors and with committees approved or appointed by the Board.

Many theatres—probably most theatres—receive their initial spark or their continuing stimulus, and produce worthwhile shows, because of the charisma or the stubbornness or the talent, or all three, of one person who believes theatre to be necessary to his community, or who simply wants a place where he can work in the theatre. Worthy reasons both, one more than a little selfish but still generative; but neither will organize your theatre or manage it well.

A Board, however, will take the zeal of the initiating few, shape it, channel it, distill it, and maintain a theatre in which the charismatic, the stubborn, and the talented, all three, can work on their artistic creations. It just cannot be done without a Board. It cannot. Don't try.

Boards of Directors fall into two basic categories:

- The Production Board, consisting of department heads as on the director's production staff (Sets, Costumes, House Management, etc.). This Board, like all Boards, sets the policy for the theatre; it then sets about carrying out the policy and mounting the plays itself.

- The Governing Board is like the Board of Directors of any nonprofit organization, made up of active doers whose skills at running organizations with any goal are numerous.

THE PRODUCTION BOARD

New theatres, small theatres, school theatres, and participant-oriented theatres are often found to have Production Boards. On such a Board, every member except possibly the officers has a firm and term-long duty in the production of the plays, in addition to his normal Board duties of perpetuating the organization. (See Figure 4.)

The Board member in charge of sets, for instance, is responsible for securing a set designer for each play of the season, and for lining up crews to build those sets. Generally, this Board

tion of authority, and the leader need only lead if he has organized his crews and assistants properly. However, most members of this sort of Board usually *want* to be part of their crews' work. That department store manager I mentioned always seems happiest at his daily work

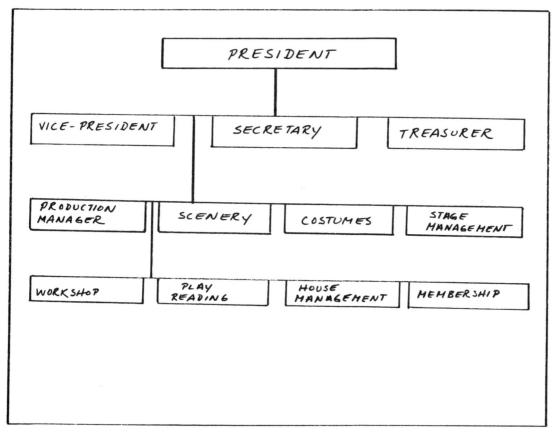

FIG. 4. The Production Board
Compare this Board setup with that in Figure 1. The difference is usually brought about by size of operation. The Governing Board of a large theatre sets policy; the Production Board, with its members also serving as department heads on the shows, sets the policy and then puts on separate hats and implements the policy, usually in a smaller theatre.

member is himself an experienced stage carpenter who knows what he's looking for and how to get it; but the true mark of a leader is in how well he delegates authority, so this post need be filled merely by a very good organizer. The House Management Board member is, similarly, in charge of naming a house manager for each play, of lining up ushers, getting the theatre cleaned, ordering tickets, etc. And so on, in each department. Please be aware that none of these Production Board members need actually hammer a nail or swing a mop himself. Here begins the delega-

when he notices a busy counter, steps into the melee, and sells alongside the clerks. Jule Styne, famous Broadway and Hollywood composer *(Gypsy, Bells Are Ringing),* produced the first New York play I worked on. At auditions, he would frequently give the pianist a break and play accompaniment himself for a dozen or so singers, whose normal nervousness would have increased had they realized who their nameless pianist was.

This desire to work, rather than merely to manage, is typical of most leaders, most places. And of a Production Board. Yes, they are policy

elect. He won't waste his vice-presidency, as is so often done, but will spend that year not as a shadow to the President or an absentee member, but as a trainee president, learning his job when the instant decisions are not his to make.

The seniority system in committees of the U.S. Congress doesn't work because it is open-ended, because the top man achieves his pinnacle and then stays there for years and years, allowing no new minds even to consider chairmanship. But in a theatre, as I have seen again and again, rewarding two years of committee apprenticeship and learning with chairmanship in the third year—for that year only—makes very good sense.

THE DIRECTOR ON THE BOARD?

If the theatre has a paid director, I recommend that he be an ex officio nonvoting member of the Board, the Executive Committee, and of *all* committees, to bring his training, his supreme interest, and his guidance—with no vote—to all areas of the theatre. Also, he is the one with the most daylight hours to devote to accomplishing some of the decisions made at Board meetings, and he should know all the background of each new policy, so that he can best execute it.

If your professional staff extends beyond the director, each member should be present at all meetings. When their contracts or salaries are discussed, the staff may be excused from a meeting, but at no other time should there be star-chamber proceedings with meetings called with the staff uninformed or asked to leave before a meeting is over. I have been in on some of those death walks, and, believe me, it's no way to build confidence in your leaders or respect between the levels of an organization.

The Board knows the community; one of its prime functions is to represent the community in policy decisions. This liaison with the community served by the theatre is alone almost enough reason for working with a Board. But—the staff, the director, know the theatre and must lead the Board, rationally and unemotionally, please, on artistic matters. And must be verbal attenders at all meetings. And must be present when all votes are taken.

AGENDA AND MINUTES

If you want to see an efficient Board member cry, bring him to a meeting without reminding

him what happened at the last session or what is supposed to happen at this one. The busy person has other things in his life than this theatre, and without decent minutes and agenda he cannot function well, but will spend the entire meeting clarifying for himself past discussions and decisions. That, or just retire into himself and wish he were somewhere else. (At a very bad performance of a very bad play, done by reputable professionals at an educational theatre conference, the man in front of me said to his wife on final cur-

PRESENT: M
         Hu
         Mr.

ABSENT: Dr. C

Minutes: The mi
         correction (
         were approve

Treasure's report:
         Arts
         receive the fi
         now available,
         Already we're 14
         shown as 1000 in
         Since this loss hu
         suggested a

Roscoe: Mrs. Warren
Costume: The new racks a
SEMEA: There has been no p
         Thursday of Caesar and
         is 9-1-67.
Building: The four items brou
         separate sheet, were dis
         item being approved for t
         the Finance and Budget cou
CHILDREN's: Mr. suggest
         the summer children's show,
         city recreation department f
Tax: The deadline for the purchase
         3% sales tax is July 31. We ca
         it will therefore, be added to
Roscoe: Read the new set of definit
         The 1968 banquet chairman is Win
         held around the last two weeks in
Membership. A letter of recommendation
         was read from   . It was
         in the paper regarding the purchase
         before July 31.
Director: would like to bid on
         needs rehearsal space
         dancers for West Side Story. Mr.
         Conductor, wants to know a
         some players who would lose income due
         Ask how much he needs, and no to t.
         As of 9-1-67, will be the ne
         Check on delinquent program ads.
Board Meetings: August 15, September 19, Octob
         sure.
Books: Mr. will check on the auditing of
         Co.

FIG. 5. Minutes of a Board Meeting
This actual copy of a set of Minutes has been cut down to give the idea but not the exact content of the proceedings at an existing community theatre. The format is clear, concise and gives everything a Board member needs without burdening him with unnecessary verbiage.

tain: "You know the worst place I ever was in my life? *Right here!!*") Your well-organized Board member, confronted with a haphazard meeting, will echo that poor man.

Have the Board Secretary take careful minutes of each meeting, in outline form if she likes, then type them within a day, before her memory and her notes grow cold and cloudy. This speedy transcript should then be sent to all Board members and to all staff, whether or not they were at the meeting. It's a good idea, by the way, to list who *was* there, so that future meetings will have access to the names of those who participated in a given discussion or decision.

The minutes should include: matters discussed, and their disposition; motions made, and by whom, and their status: passed, lost, or tabled; assignments given, and expected completion dates; future plans, and so on. And the date and location of the next Board meeting, so that everyone can mark his calendar *now* and be prepared. (See Figure 5.)

Then, a week before the next meeting, the Secretary sends out another mailing to everyone on the Board and the staff, with a reminder of the date and location of the meeting, this time including the agenda of the new meeting.

The president draws up the agenda, touching

```
                AGENDA
         BOARD OF DIRECTORS, Rochester Civic Theatre
Next Meeting:  Wednesday, March 12.  8 p.m.  At the Theatre.

         1.  Minutes of Previous Meeting (read your copy now.)

         2.  Treasurer's Report (to include Building Fund report)

         3.  Old Business:
                 a)  Participation in Art Festival?
                 b)  Date to vacate old Theatre.

         4.  Committee Reports:

                 a)  Building Committee
                 b)  Finance Committee
                 c)  Children's Theatre Committee
                 d)  Awards Committee
                 e)  Group Sales Committee
                 f)  Membership Committee
                 g)  Play Reading Committee

         5.  New Business:
                 a)  Elections
                 b)  Donations of costumes
                 c)  Letters from members

         6.  Director's Report

         7.  AOCB

         8.  Adjournment


    It is vital that every Board member attend this meeting.  If you
    find you cannot, or will be late, please call the Theatre now and
    tell them.  But try to come, please.
```

FIG. 6. Agenda for a Board Meeting

This reminder of what's to be covered at the upcoming meeting is sent, together with the Minutes of the previous meeting, to each Board member and to any committee heads, etc., who will be present. It helps them to gather their thoughts on items to be discussed, and gather their notes if they are to lead some of the discussions or make reports.

on items deferred from the previous meeting, called Old Business, and inserting anything that has not come up before, under New Business. Committee reports are listed, as much to remind each committee head to gather his notes as anything. (See Figure 6.)

The AOCB closing the agenda was the addition of that particular president, a twinkly and thoughtful Scot, who was always careful to remind us that our contributions to the meeting were welcome. AOCB means Any Other Competent Business, and is one final opportunity before adjournment for anyone to offer ideas, suggestions, or well-mulled disagreement. Important.

COMMITTEES

The theatre—the Board—the shows—are only as good as the committees who service them, support them, guide them. I cannot think of a nonprofessional theatre that has failed with a solid committee structure. An organization with committees involves the community, which is always necessary; committees are the logical and most useful places for those two dozen hard-working people with whom some theatres load the Board; and, most importantly, a strong theatre is built on strong, constantly regenerating committees, each with a responsibility to an area of the theatre's creative, educational, administrative, or social continuance. As the committees work and succeed, so does the theatre.

The Board-*cum*-committee structure I like best is that in which several vice-presidents are elected, each to manage four, five, or six committees of a common nature. One vice-president would be in charge of all educational activities of the theatre, for instance, and would sit with each of those committees, representing the Board. Another v-p might supervise all promotional committees, etc. The meat of the committee work is then brought to the Board meetings, presented in digestible form by the responsible vice-president.

One of the best variations of this method is that currently in use at a successful community theatre (see Appendix).

CASTING COMMITTEE

A committee that does not appear on this list is a Casting Committee, found in many theatres. I disagree with the entire idea of such a committee, but feel I must mention its existence.

To protect the director from those constant cries of "precasting!," "favoritism!," "stupidity!," etc., the worried Board appoints a *committee* that will attend all tryout sessions and cast all the plays, in committee. Sometimes the director is a voting member of this committee, sometimes he makes suggestions, sometimes he sits by and watches the next five weeks of his life determined by other people, who will walk away after casting, leaving him to try and pull a show together, using their actors within his concept. This practice then leaves the *committee* open to cries of "precasting!," "favoritism!," etc.

Some directors in this situation truly feel protected from the rock-throwing of the noncast; perhaps they are. So, if the point of your theatre is to make everyone happy at any cost, perhaps you will want a casting committee. But, if the constitutionally-described reason for your being is to put on fine plays well, I offer this simple suggestion:

Choose a director whose artistic integrity you can trust, and then leave him alone. If you can't trust him, don't engage him. If you find no one you can trust, then close the theatre.

THE BOARD AND THE DIRECTOR

A Board and a director need each other; they check and balance each other. The director makes artistic *suggestions* to the Board; then, when preparing or rehearsing the plays agreed upon with the Board, artistic *decisions* must be his alone to make. The Board makes administrative *suggestions* to its committees and to the director; and, when working on a project such as fundraising, ticket-selling, and such, the Board of course makes administrative *decisions*. But major policy must be discussed and determined in the company of both Board and director. They need each other. The theatre moves forward only on the successful balance of administration and art, of the mutual need of Board and director.

Chapter IV

SUPPORTIVE OR AUXILIARY GROUPS

Some of the most productive fun I've ever had in the theatre was with the ladies' auxiliary of a large community theatre. The members were asked to bring work clothes and a sack lunch to their regular monthly (morning) meeting and to indicate in advance an area of the offstage theatre that interested them. After a shortened meeting, each woman put on her work clothes and spent several hours helping prepare for the next play. Each department head had been told how many of the women had chosen to put in time in each department, and work was made ready for them. Some built and painted scenery, some sewed or pressed costumes, some prepared a box-office mailing. Each contributed to the chief purpose of theatre—the play—and each had a good time, gave the staff a good time in meeting them in a nonformal situation in the shop or sitting over sandwiches at lunchtime, and theatre was out of the discussion stage and productively taken into the doing stage for able and interested women.

* * *

The Board backs up the staff, the Production Board supports the play—and everyone supports the playwright, the original creative artist of the theatre. Support is mandatory, department to department, to keep any organization alive. And some of the broadest and most important support comes from the auxiliary group—usually a women's organization (or one composed largely of women) within the framework of the theatre. (See Playhouse Guild under Committees of a Community Theatre, Appendix.)

Set up your ladies' auxiliary the same way you set up your Board, with rules, officers, committee heads, and so on. Begin with a core group of interested theatre women, and wives of interested theatre men, encourage them to add to their number, give them their challenge and be prepared for marvelous results.

Such groups are variously called Women's Associations, Guilds, Angels, and so on. The Tyrone Guthrie (professional repertory) Theatre in Minneapolis has a magnificently hard-working group of women called The Stagehands. What-ever their names, the work that is done by such auxiliary groups can mean the difference between a successful ticket drive and a flop, a successful season and a flop, a going theatre and a flop. If we may assume that all citizens of a community are concerned with the betterment of that community, especially its artistic promise, the women are in the vanguard of concern and, properly organized, can accomplish its betterment and artistic fulfillment. Investigate the possibility of their use and use them.

Use them primarily to spread the word. At their other club meetings, at parties, at their jobs, anywhere they will see other women who may not be as familiar with your theatre as you would like. Word of mouth, as we shall see in Chapter V, is your best advertisement, and your women's group is a marvelous proselytizing agent. Those house-bound with children can contribute mightily in their at-home use of the telephone: calling crews, potential patrons, program ad buyers, and such.

From this body can come your Chairman of Season Ticket Sales, and many ticket salesmen. Some theatres offer prizes for numbers of tickets sold—I prefer to think that if prizes are needed, the theatre can't mean much to the salesmen. Enthusiasm is needed, and that enthusiasm can come beautifully from these gals. Captains, majors, generals (if you will) in a well-organized ticket campaign, can put your campaign over the top. Men are needed, too, of course, mostly to sell to their peers in the business world, but—and I cannot state this too often—the women have a large say in the spending of entertainment money, and they can best be sold by other women—by your angels, for instance.

I shall also talk about speakers for clubs and schools in Chapter V. Have your director or your Board outline the areas you want covered in these talks, then trust to the native theatre excitement of these women to make their speeches successful. Whether they are discussing makeup or the history of your group, what will come across is: Isn't Theatre great?!!

Displays, readings, or discussion groups at the local schools or public library, centering on your current production, especially if you are doing a classic or a children's play, are marvelous free advertising, and your Guild can supply the work force. A handful of photos or sketches, a half-hour conversation with the director, attendance at a few rehearsals, and your supportive ladies are armed to support where you need it most: with the young people who are not attending the theatre as much as we would like. Films, TV, music—not live theatre—are where it's happening for so many of our youngsters. With patience, some exciting data, and that standby, enthusiasm, some converts may come over to our side.

Special projects are often the meat of these groups—editing the theatre newsletter, planning a massive opening-night dinner party or an annual costume party (everyone coming as his favorite character from a play, or as a play title, with appropriate prizes) can be beautifully handled by the ladies. Actors can be relieved of the details of a cast party by party-organizing Guild members. Benefit performances for the building fund, special shows for underprivileged children or the elderly will find them eager chauffeurs or bus mothers. And if you move wholeheartedly into the world of children's theatre, which I urge, here are women with at least a little time free during the day to get to the schools, sell your shows, arrange buses, chase down lost lambs, and help make it an extra-special day for the kids. In addition to all else, the ladies can prepare the kids for what live theatre is, in case they have never seen any performances except on TV.

Perhaps your auxiliary can be the keeper of the scrapbook, can take charge of manning the box office on an organized basis (see Chapter VII[a]), can conduct tours of your theatre, if you decide to build one.

MEETINGS OF THE GUILD

The base activity of such clubs, guilds, arms, however, is their monthly meeting, at which reports from their various activities are made, encouragement is given to join the continuing or newly-established committees, refreshments are served, and a program is presented.

This program helps bring along the ladies who are there only for the entertainment, and is an admitted come-on. But, once there, the woman content to pay her $2 dues, drink her coffee, and enjoy-enjoy often finds herself caught up in the obvious fun the rest of the Guild is finding in its supportive theatre work. And another convert joins the active ranks.

So the entertainment at the meeting had better be attractive and well publicized, to get the less-than-committed away from other meetings or from the bridge table or the television set and into your midst. A scene from your upcoming play (sneak previews are American dreams), songs from your next musical—all well rehearsed. Don't sell these ladies short—they're sharp. A knowledgeable review of the current plays in New York (or Chicago, or Los Angeles, or wherever some of your membership is likely to go in the next few months). A talk on some phase of theatre history, especially that which we're living through.

One of the best-received programs for a Guild I ever attended was a discussion of color—my set designer discussed color as produced by stage lighting, and the director of the local art museum took the same subject from the standpoint of pigment. With a very few preliminary discussions to be sure they weren't overlapping and were in fact moving toward the same goal, these men held their audience rapt with a complex, interesting, and seldom-elaborated-on aspect of the arts. Tapping your membership and your staff for knowledge and talent will garner you several years' worth of programs with theatre as their common denominator.

The one negative thing I have found in most auxiliary groups is the narrowness of the base membership. Age, background, section of the city they come from—all too much alike. Any theatre without a broad demographic base is destined for a history of inbreeding and eventual atrophy. This is reflected, woman for woman, in your supportive organization. For here are your word-of-mouth saleswomen, your season ticket workers, your school contacts. But each one must reproduce, for posterity more than for herself, and bring in members and workers and ticket buyers of different ages and from various neighborhoods.

Part 2

FRONT-OF-HOUSE ORGANIZATION

Axiom: To maintain a good theatre you must put on good plays, well produced.
But—
It is not enough to put on a good play well; you must also:

- *bring in an audience to see it;*
- *inform that audience of what and whom they are seeing;*
- *serve that audience from the moment they arrive on your grounds until they leave; and*
- *pay the bills for the whole creative and administrative operation.*

* * *

A fine young director I know gave up directing recently; he could not stand the idea that the Play was not the only thing. He believed to the bottom of his soul that if he did a first-rate job of directing, all else would fall into place of its own accord, and audiences would hear of the play, and come and enjoy as a natural fact. When his shows—uniformly well directed and well acted—failed to draw an audience, or when the audience that came left in midplay or wrote him about the discomfort they felt on folding chairs in a stuffy auditorium after waiting until nearly curtain time in a stuffy and too-small lobby, he couldn't understand it.

Many theatre people can't, and I must admit that the Off-Off-Broadway movement is giving many the chance to spend their energies on the play and ignore the audience. Patrons walk long distances from public transportation through dark, garbage-littered streets, then sit on the floor or high on spindly platforms in too-cold or too-hot makeshift auditoriums to see (some very good examples of) what's happening in the new world of theatre. But until the audiences of Off-Off-Broadway become the audiences of your theatre, remember one of the saddest yet truest statements about our art:

Theatre is not a necessity of life for most people. So it must be accompanied by service.

Theatre may fast be becoming a necessity of your life, but how many of your friends or your family's friends really care if they ever see another live play? In a carefully researched, easy-to-read, but very depressing book called *Performing Arts—The Economic Dilemma,* William J. Baumol and William G. Bowen, economists at Princeton University, point out that during a one-year period, less than 5 percent of all Americans attend even one live performance—not just of theatre—but of any of the performing arts. And the largest part of that tiny number lives in metropolitan areas. To woo them to your theatre, and, more importantly, to try to enlarge that number in your community, you must create in your community the need for live theatre. Certainly this is partially accomplished by high-quality productions of good scripts, but even more by high-quality service. And that means good organization and management of your front-of-the-house departments—Publicity and Promotion, Programs, House Management, and Finances. If any one of these areas is weak, the strength of your play or of the rest of the Front-of-House can't compensate for the laggard. An attractively printed program won't send the audience singing out of the theatre if the publicity folk have fallen behind and brought no audience in. Or if publicity is splendid but the public is fighting for seats in a dirty auditorium manned by inept ushers, you're in trouble.

Finding the volunteers for these nonacting posts isn't easy. People with just the skills you need don't think of volunteering, since they don't know that their skills are needed. "I don't act," they say, "and I don't design scenery; I can't sew or build anything, so the theatre can't use me." It's up to you, through every available means, to get the word out that your theatre does indeed need business people, advertising people, and just plain good organizers and good workers who can be taught these necessary jobs. Because without a solid Front-of-House, you have no theatre.

Chapter V

PUBLICITY AND PROMOTION

I attended a convention of network affiliate radio station managers and program directors several years ago and was astonished to hear the Director of Advertising of a worldwide soft-drink company say to us: "We know how much we depend on advertising. We believe that if we were to stop buying advertising today, we'd be out of business in three years. We'd leave the signs that are up, leave the distinctive coolers in place, leave in effect the contracts for programs now running, but not spend another penny. And we'd be out of business."

An internationally famous name. Out of business. In three years.

* * *

As a household word must work to keep itself known, so does *The New York Sunday Times* Arts and Leisure Section show, in page after page of advertising for current plays, how the professional theatre depends on constant exposure to stay in business, even for smash hits. The non-professional theatre, therefore, must recognize, too, its overwhelming and constant need to promote and publicize itself, to get and keep its name before its public, and to expand its public beyond the friends and family who already know all about it. This is especially true, of course, during season ticket campaigns and during the days the box office is open for the next specific play. But really, always. By any legitimate means.

Publicity refers to the immediate selling of a specific product. (For us, that is generally the current play.)

Promotion takes in the whole philosophy of the organization and the people involved. This is often accomplished by institutional advertising, which is usually low-key, nonspecific mention of the parent organization and what it tries in the broadest sense to accomplish. Interviews with bank employees to show how happy the banking "family" is, for instance, or a simple statement of the name of the firm in a tasteful ad or TV commercial. (For the nonprofessional theatre, this will take the form of free interviews and articles, as opposed to paid ads, showing that the idea

behind theatre, and especially your theatre, is a noble and exciting one, and the community should be pleased that the theatre is there.)

Publicity and promotion are each necessary, each can accomplish its stated purpose, and each must be used in its own specific way.

PROMOTION

For our purposes, promotion will include advertising that is:

● free, incurring no advertising costs to you, and

● tending toward the year-round legitimization of your theatre. Hard as we work, a large segment of the American public still considers the theatre as a home of less-than-respectable members of our society, much as the Elizabethan public considered its theatre folk. Too often, theatre people have brought this on themselves, with all-night raucous parties in the theatre building, deliberately provocative actions in public when representing the theatre as a group, and juicy gossip too readily spread when the treasurer runs off with the cashbox or the president's wife or both. It has always been my opinion that more naughty doings can be found among the members of a church choir, but that showfolk broadcast or invent peccadilloes rather than assume a more circumspect attitude toward them, as most other areas of our society will do. One tabloid-pleasing divorce of a Hollywood star can set back a community theatre more quickly than a defrocked New York priest can hurt a local choir. One bad apple in your midst can do more lasting harm to your theatre than that same unnecessary character turned loose in the choir loft.

So your first promotional job is to make very sure that your group is free from any elements that could keep the public (especially its children) away from your box office and your tryouts: move the cast parties to a private home, tone down your exuberance when traveling as a theatre group, and get the facts—the full facts—to the media as soon as a potential scandal arises, making sure that the true story is known early from you rather than from hearsay. Once sure that what you have to promote, both artistically and morally, is worth promoting, go to work using the following areas of promotion.

Newspaper Articles

Especially of a human-interest nature.

Has a young couple recently become engaged after playing lovers in one of your shows? Write it up.

Have you received a grant from the Arts Council (the university, the city, a foundation) to play shows or teach classes for underprivileged children? Get off an article.

Has your theatre been chosen to represent the state in a theatre festival? Get some mileage out of it.

Has a community leader been elected to your Board? Have him write an up-to-date biography, take a good studio portrait of him, and ship them off to the paper(s).

Has your set designer taken a trip to a large museum to research the backdrop for your next show? Send in an article, with pictures.

Always send pictures, when possible; clear photos with light backgrounds are best, artistically composed, with the emphasis where you want it. If specific photos are not possible at the time, include a photo of your theatre, of an audience, of the playwright, of the director poring over the script—something to equal those thousand words a picture is supposed to do. . . .

A newspaper can make errors, even in good faith, after a hurried telephone interview. Avoid these by sending out a fully-written, newspaper-worthy article of your own, featuring the news you wish to get across, the way you want it said. (If there are several papers in your area, one will not be happy printing the exact words of its competitors, so write a differently-worded story for each, pointing the same focus.) Even if the re-write reporter wants to reword the story his own way, he will know precisely what you're trying to say, and chances are he'll aim his story in the same direction yours was going. And many small, understaffed papers delight in groups that send in well-written stories requiring only minor stylistic changes to fit the paper's format. Familiarize yourself with each paper's spelling and punctuation idiosyncrasies, its paragraph and syntactical style—then write accordingly. They will appreciate it.

If a paper is strong on interviews rather than straight articles, arrange frequent interviews—with your newly-elected president, the visiting theatre professional, the award-winner. Be sure the reporter and the subject have a quiet place to talk, and that all your people arrive ahead of time, thoroughly briefed as to what areas the theatre wants to emphasize in the printed story. Stand by, ready to be of any help you can to the newsmen, with coffee, photos of the play, recent programs, proper spelling of names likely to be included—anything pertinent to the interview. Anticipate and be ready. The reporter will remember that your cooperation has saved him time and trouble and will help you by writing a longer story or by coming back for a follow-up story sooner than if you were the usual disorganized bunch of well-meaning amateurs. A newspaper photographer once confided to me that he actually helps determine the size, shape, and quality of the pictures presented in his paper by presenting his editor with large, well-composed, easily printable photos of subjects who make his job easier, and small, dark, not-so-interesting shots of subjects who complicated his picture call. Determine in advance: how can you help the photographer to help you? Know before he comes just who is to be in the picture. This is especially important if it is to be a scene from a play; a dozen actors cannot all get into one shot, so choose which will make the play most appealing to a casual reader. Have the actors in costume and in light makeup before the appointed time. Select several possible backgrounds from which the photographer may choose. Be sure there is plenty of light—if onstage, have stage lighting plugged in and ready to go; more time is consumed in the setting and striking of photofloods than ever seems worth it. Have your set (whether onstage or in an office) uncluttered and pre-planned to feature the object or person you wish to see as the focal point of the picture. Decide on several possible angles or groupings, interesting, with action (remember, and have the subjects remember, it's theatre they're representing, not a wax museum) and, again, to feature the prime person. Let the photographer choose which setup he likes, and while he is mounting his camera and checking his light meter, write legibly on a clean and full-sized piece of paper the information to accompany the photo—the name of your organization, the properly-spelled names of the people in the picture, listed from left to right (force yourself to forget for the moment stage left and right). List your people as the paper likes them listed: Will they accept an actor's favorite nickname, or first names of married women, or do they insist on Mrs. William Smith and Dr. Charles Jones? With minors, do they want parents' names? If the subject is from another town, do they want that information?

As the photographer finishes his shots, present him with this neatly-written paper and help him get on to his next assignment. You will have earned a friend.

RADIO AND TELEVISION

As a nonprofit organization, you have promotional access to time on radio and television so expensive that few professional theatres can afford it. And it's yours free. The Federal Communications Commission requires that each licensed station make so-called public service time available to just such groups as yours. Use it.

You are a theatre-producing group, so think about doing a play or a scene from a play on radio or TV. If it is not a play you're doing this season, you will more easily sell it as entertainment or education rather than as blatant publicity. Select an original play, if you can find one of quality by one of your members, or a play in the public domain, which means a play whose copyright began at least fifty-six years ago. Most plays from publishers' current catalogs are *not* available for broadcasting, as the radio and TV rights were probably sold to Hollywood with the motion picture rights, and you could be prosecuted for playing even a one-minute scene on the air. Most of Shaw is available, as of course are Chekhov, Shakespeare, etc., though you might think carefully before tackling anything so weighty without a long rehearsal period and plenty of studio time at the station. If you find a play that is clear and that is agreeable to your Board and to the station, cast your best actors, since you will be playing to more people in that one program than in several seasons' full houses at your home base. If well done, you will impress the strangers and possibly bring some to your live productions; if badly done, you have lost them forever.

If you're not ready to produce a full play or scene on radio or TV, see the manager about an interview concerning your new building, or new season, or the new style of play you are about to produce. Or have a round-table discussion with a cross-section of your membership—cross-sec-

tion in their nontheatre occupations as well as their volunteer jobs with you. Help make the public aware by this means that your theatre is not a rich man's plaything or a hippie hangout or a wife-swapping club, but a serious, dedicated group of people of all ages from all walks of life, each finding something different and valuable in his theatre work.

If your stations broadcast editorials or any sort of subjective messages about local events, ask if they could include an evaluation of the region's theatre. Certainly do not tell them what to say; any editorialist is only effective (or affective) insofar as he is true to himself, and will resent, rightly, your saying: "How about a piece on how important the theatre is to our community?"

No, try this: "We're taking a good look at ourselves and think we know what we must do to fulfill more properly our role as an asset to the community's cultural life. Here are some of our plans for improving ourselves. Could you look them over and possibly consider a piece on the state of the arts in the community?" The same approach is equally usable with editors of newspapers or local magazines. You are, after all, a cultural asset to the town; news commentators and editorial writers will be serving their public as they examine you and comment on you, frequently.

SPEAKERS' BUREAU

Nearly every club of every size requires a frequent program for its membership, and more often than not the program will consist of a free speaker who is an expert, real or imagined, in his field. And there you are with an organization full of experts, theatrical and sincere in their delivery, and, most important, free. Drop a note to each club in your community—from the large service clubs such as Rotary and Kiwanis to the garden clubs, church guilds, and small specialty clubs. You will find most of them listed with the Chamber of Commerce, or appearing frequently in the social pages of your newspaper. Tell them simply that your theatre would be willing at any time to make available a program for one of their meetings.

Do not say: "We want to publicize our production of *South Pacific,* opening on December fifth"; make it clear that you're not pushing anything specific but are merely anxious to let their members know what the theatre is doing as a responsible part of the community.

You will get many takers.

Your program can take many forms, such as a one-act play, a good reader of monologues, a review of current Broadway plays, or a speaker on the philosophy and activities of your theatre. The play could be a scene from an upcoming major play or a short play especially rehearsed and kept in readiness for such programs. The monologist can gear his presentation to the group or to the time of year. One of my theatres used to provide the annual Christmas program for a large service club, to which wives were always invited. It usually consisted merely of a good reading of a Christmas story or group of seasonal poems.

If a speaker seems best to the host group and to you, choose from among your best and most personable speakers, equip your choice with a slide projector and a few dozen (no more) clear and attractive slides of recent shows and a barrel of facts showing as subtly as possible how important your theatre is to the community. Include such data as: membership figures, broken down demographically by age, section of town, etc.; children's activities (even people who care nothing about the arts themselves start to pay attention at the mention of children); detailed reports on inquiries by prospective new families or new businesses thinking of settling in town. I have used these true stories to advantage in such talks:

● A major computer firm, in electing to establish a high-level plant in our small town, listed ten reasons for choosing that locale. Their seventh reason was the existence of the community theatre.
● Another computer firm in another town listed the community theatre as its first reason for locating there.
● A large midwestern city took frequent ads in a national weekly literary magazine, frankly stating that they were hoping to attract businesses and educated families, and to this end listed their cultural advantages as their only statement of excellence.
● Another city bought ads in a major airline's free magazine, left in each passenger seat. The ads' messages were all on the same theme: We are not a prairie town, but a city with a symphony, a theatre, and so on.
● A large utility runs a full-page ad four times a year in a national newsmagazine featuring a color sketch of an artistic community enterprise in one of the cities it services.

● Three industries in a dying river town combined forces to finance the construction of a building for the community theatre.

Why?

Because the businessmen in these towns knew that good schools, good water, and good roads are no longer enough to attract industry to a new area or to attract educated men and their educated wives to move to that new industry. To get and keep new business and new employees, there must also be something for the inner man. And theatre is high on the list of food for the inner man.

Add a national anecdote to your talk:

A large federal agency passed the word that any town wishing to apply for consideration in the choosing of a new site must furnish proof of three things:

X amount of water pressure;
X amount of square footage;
existence of a ballet school in town.

The government reasoned that, since dance is still regrettably the least attended of the performing arts in America, a town with a commitment to dance must *already* have evidence of live theatre, a symphony, an art gallery, and the like.

Talk to your state Arts Council—every state now has one—and your Chamber of Commerce; you can find a dozen such stories of your own, with names and places that will mean more to your audience and help prove your point. Document your facts and add a detailing of what your theatre is doing to help sell your town as a cultural haven, such as providing the Chamber with brochures that they can send to inquiring firms, sending letters to all newcomers through the Welcome Wagon, and so on. Conclude by asking your audience what *they* would recommend to help you follow through on serving the community that you share with them. They will be impressed that you're not just trying to keep the theatre open for you to perform in, but really do want to support your town. They will even forgive an offhand reference to your upcoming opening night. By merely stating its name, the Rochester Civic Theatre proclaims its involvement as a civic organization and instructs its speakers visiting club meetings in the town to point proudly to the inclusion of the key word "Civic" in the name of the group.

Write each local club each year, including newly-established groups, re-offering your services and detailing new subjects, new plays you can bring, and new speakers of note. Include children's groups, Brownie and Cub Scout troops, libraries and schools, especially if you also offer children's plays or if an upcoming musical or classic would be of special interest to youngsters. Your Guild members would be excellent members of your speakers' roster.

BROCHURES

The Chamber of Commerce of your community, as mentioned, will happily display and disseminate almost anything that represents the community well and is attractively printed, whether you're a school group, a neighborhood club, or a community theatre. A well-edited brochure, in two colors, with several photographs of recent hits or of your building, a short history of your theatre, and a place to print in each season's schedule, is a wise investment for you and a continuing source of good promotion for the Chamber and for you in mailings, distribution to hotels and motels, membership campaigns, and a dozen other promotional uses you can devise in your community.

When drawing up your brochure, include your logo prominently. A logo (short for logotype) is the symbol of your theatre. Generally designed by a graphic artist, it should be an easily identifiable mark of YOU—list it with the name of your theatre during the early days of its introduction, and later you need only head a newspaper ad with the logo, and your community will immediately identify it as yours, and the ad as news of your theatre. Use it on your stationery, your posters, your programs, TV spots, anywhere your name or message might appear.

Our summer theatre logo, an orange-and-yellow summer sun shaped into an attractive version of the overused comedy/tragedy masks, is shown here in Figure 7. This was designed by one of our students, Jane Goodman, who is responsible for most of the graphic art in this book. In your organization, you too may have someone with the talents to develop a logo just right for you, or an advertising agency in your community might be pleased to take on, free, the assignment of developing a symbol for your theatre, in consultation with your Board. Do not hold a communitywide contest to find a logo; one theatre tried this, despite a beautiful submission from their professional set designer, received and judged over fifty entries from nontheatre-family members, and se-

the mount holyoke college summer theatre

FIG. 7. Logo for a Nonprofessional Theatre
After a show or two, the lettering accompanying a logo may be eliminated if the logo is distinctive enough. Include your logo on every sign, every piece of advertising, every mailing, every program put out by your theatre. Use it proudly, or select a new design that you can be proud of. This summer theatre logo makes the statement of both theatre (the traditional masks) and summer (the sun, and the colors—the darker shades are vivid orange, the lighter a warm yellow.)
Design by Jane Goodman

lected from a mixed bag an inappropriate design —and they're stuck with it.

METERED MAIL MESSAGE

For a small cost you may order a metal plate made to fit the various franking machines (or postage meters) that stamp postage on mail sent by businesses, banks, and utilities in your community. Many of these groups would be happy to insert into their postage meter your metal slug proclaiming on all their envelopes ATTEND YOUR COMMUNITY THEATRE or whatever short message you and they agree on to promote (and implicitly endorse) the theatre. Your message will get into many homes where the theatre may not be well known. The plate is reusable and may be passed from firm to firm, with a new group of recipients hearing about you each month.

CONTEST JUDGING

Make it known that your theatre will supply judges for play contests in the schools, beauty contests, parade floats, and such, and you will have committees calling on you frequently, as volunteers with theatrical background are not easily found. Ask in payment only that the judge provided by you be introduced to the audience as a representative of the theatre, and that all publicity include the same information. Do an honest and considered job of judging, and you will win another group of friends for the theatre. Once established as colorful, articulate, and incorruptible, the theatre will be approached annually, and many of your members can take part, causing no one to give up too much time. Do not be afraid to volunteer for anything you feel you can do—it is an easy, and often fun, chance for promotion. But do not commit yourself or your theatre to anything you cannot complete well and pleasantly. Better to do nothing than to do something badly in the theatre's name. That's bad promotion.

PARADE FLOATS

Speaking of parades, do not miss the chance to use your artistic abilities to show off in a local or regional parade. Depending on the timing of the parade within your season, you might want to enter one float containing set pieces and costumes, or just an artistic concept of the play now running, or a reprise of some of the most handsome costumes from the year just closing, or a preview of the season now soliciting season members. If you can enter several floats, moving in succession, fine; if not, you can cover several shows on one float by having some costumed characters walk next to the float or ride in the car that pulls it. Have your sound man rig loudspeakers so the tape of your last musical can play as you move. If this is all too commercial for the institutional promotion you wish to convey, don't mention any shows specifically, but put your prettiest actress, alone, in a set piece that anyone who saw your most popular play will recognize, and the crowds will speak your copy for you— "Oh, there's King Arthur's throne"; or "There's Bloody Mary's souvenir stand"—while your actress smiles and smiles.

If you have the time and the money, think about your *own* parade. Celebrating your first anniversary or fifth or twenty-fifth? Have a parade! Starting a fund-raising drive? Or season ticket drive? Call it the Community Theatre Parade and get related artistic organizations to enter.

SCHOLARSHIPS

Send a potential theatre professional to school and then make a report on the scholarship grant to the press. Casting bread upon the waters is supposed to bring uncountable returns—but even if it doesn't, think of the use that can be made of that bread by a serious theatre student. You need not endow a college—even $500 is munificent to a young man or woman who has worked with you on a few shows and now is off to complete his training and go into the professional theatre. It may not be polite to broadcast your good deeds, but when you are promoting something that needs constant promotion such as the theatre, it's all right, if tastefully done. The local media will cover the banquet or the show or the event at which the scholarship is presented; they will print news from his college when he gets into shows, identifying him as "Community Theatre Scholarship Winner" each time they do. When he comes and speaks to service clubs or at your annual meeting next year, telling of his experiences, the media will again call attention to your having provided the scholarship. And even if they don't, you know what you are doing to help that young person. And that's all that really matters.

DINNER-AND-A-PLAY

The restaurant business is as eager for good will and promotional activities as is your theatre, and, starting with the best-known restaurant in town, you would do well to tie in a show with a dinner—either for a couple or for an entire organization. Work out whatever deal you can with the restaurateur, whether he makes anything from the theatre ticket or you make anything from the dinner, or neither of you makes anything extra but are happy for the patronage. A customer may order his theatre tickets through the restaurant when he makes a dinner reservation; the restaurant then orders his tickets direct from the box office, presents him with a voucher (the carbon of which the restaurant retains) indicating his seat numbers, and arranges to have him served and out of the place in time to get to the theatre by show time. The patron pays the restaurant and receives a slight discount on dinner or theatre or both. At the end of the play's run, the restaurant presents you with its carbon copy vouchers, you match them with the originals given you by the patrons, and you pay the restaurant the agreed-upon price. Feature this promotional idea in your advertising, as will the restaurant. It may take a few plays to get any real business, especially from groups, because most organizations or even dining groups make plans well in advance, and the restaurant may have a banquet chairman who contacts clubs or similar organizations a year or more in advance for dinner parties. It may never bring in more than twenty-five tickets per play, but it is constant promotion—remember the soft-drink company. Your name is continuing before the public, so when they finally think about dinner and a show, they may in fact think about you and that restaurant.

BUMPER STICKERS

Mobile promotion in the form of bumper stickers will carry your name all over town. Your name and your logo may be copy enough, or you may advertise: *Support Your Theatre,* or *Attend Your Theatre,* or even list the next play. If you have some wits on the board, they may come up with a catchy, humorous slogan as well. For heaven's sake, don't gratuitously slap stickers on cars without asking permission; that's a sure route to negative promotion, or demotion. Make them available in your lobby and give them to Board members and cast members with a strong request that they display them on their cars.

WELCOME WAGON OR NEWCOMERS' CLUB

As mentioned, the professional welcoming ladies can carry your message into new homes, making yours one of the first entertainment organizations to say hello. Send your brochure and a letter. In addition to your history, be sure to include all tryout information, season ticket and single ticket data, and an invitation to come around and watch a rehearsal or see how the scenery or costumes are put together, with the location and usual working hours listed.

An inexpensive promotional device might be a coupon for a pair of free tickets for any play that season. Make it clear that the coupon is not valid if the play is already sold out, and not good for your biggest selling nights—Friday and Saturday—but make it as wide open an invitation as you can, with as few restrictions. Unless your theatre consistently sells every seat, this is in ev-

ery way an investment, and if you are doing good work onstage (since no promotional campaign will work if the new patron brought into the theatre sees a bad production), you have possibly won a new member for life. You might even include a postcard, asking for comments after the newcomer sees the play. This way, you will get his name and address, glean some idea of how well the campaign is working, and also get an unbiased opinion of how the show really went over. Never disregard the possibility of questionnaires, however short or simple.

Be sure your theatre address and phone number are listed clearly in the phone directory, so newcomers will have no trouble finding you. List yourself several times, if there is any chance of your being missed. For instance, if the group is called the Smith County Playmakers, list it under its official title and also under the P's as Playmakers.

BILLBOARDS

Highway advertising is not as expensive as you might think, nor are bus or streetcar or subway ads. And you may not have to pay at all. In some towns, many of the ads in buses are giveaways to just such nonprofit groups as yours. You would need only to pay for the printing. Check with your friendly outdoor advertising agency to see if there is a billboard they haven't filled for some time that they might donate for a year. Remember, you're a nonprofit organization, and the advertising firm can declare this donation for its full value on its income tax.

The big cost on billboards and carcards is in changing the copy frequently as a new show comes up; circumvent this by including the entire season, with the dates of each play, and full ticket information, then leave it up all year. And be sure not to switch plays. If you are presently in the position of not choosing your entire season as a unit, this might be an incentive. (See Play-Reading Committee, Chapter III.)

Get one of your best commercial artists to work on the billboard and come up with a format that the advertising company, your theatre, and your town will be content to have staring at them for that time.

STATE OR REGIONAL CALENDARS

Most state Arts Councils and/or Recreation Boards and/or Chambers of Commerce issue frequent calendars of attractions to be found in their states. There is no reason why you should not be on that listing, and every reason why you should. The more they can promote your artistic worth, the better business and tourist climate they will generate. Find out which offices are responsible for printing such a calendar—it may even be through a Fine Arts Council at the State University—and get your plays listed, with accurate dates and ticket information.

Most large newspapers periodically list statewide artistic events—especially at the beginning of summer and the beginning of the school year.

Learn the deadlines for all these listings, especially those compiled in distant cities, mark them down in the folder your publicity chairman is keeping to pass to his successor, and meet the deadlines faithfully. Keep in mind: You are not a necessity of life to anyone but yourselves. The public does not need you, and those calendar printers and newspaper reporters surely do not need you. But they can learn to love you, if you make their job easier. They want a full listing, but they want it legible and complete and on time. Make it so.

WORD OF MOUTH

Get your auxiliary ladies out into their neighborhoods and clubs and schools between shows, talking up what a good thing the theatre is for the community. Give them specific data, including anecdotes and human-interest stories (easier to work into conversation) and turn them loose with the challenge: Make new friends for the theatre. Done tastefully and with tact, these stories showing you off as civic leaders will cover the town in less than a week. Have them promise that they won't attend any party or meeting or meal outside their families without relaying at least one theatre anecdote. They are not selling tickets—just making good conversation about one of our most important civic agencies.

You will find that unsolicited word of mouth, from happy and satisfied theatregoers, will give you excellent promotion. The people of the town not associated with your group will be your best spokesmen, if you give them consistently good productions of good plays—certainly always your best promotion.

PUBLICITY

Publicity includes advertising that is:

- generally paid for by you, and
- tending toward the hard sell of a specific play or ticket drive. Many areas of publicity overlap

or duplicate the broader field of promotion, so the same do's and don'ts generally apply here. You can often cut publicity costs by trading on your educational nonprofit status to get free listings, articles, or interviews. The first areas mentioned below fall into this free category.

NEWSPAPER ARTICLES

It is not easy to convince some city editors that every article about your theatre is newsworthy; they feel community theatre news belongs on the women's page or lumped into the small-type social notes. Use the civic-pride data mentioned earlier, and start at the top of the newspaper staff. If your president knows the publisher, start there. A word from on high will usually convince an editor that if his boss, a civic leader, feels the theatre's activities are news, then indeed they might be. (However, if you have already been turned down by a city editor, don't go over his head; he will resent it, rightfully, and you'll never get anything printed. Stay with him and wear him down with ever more stories focusing on your contribution to the community.) Once won over, an editor should print all or most of the articles you send him generated by a specific play, such as:

- Tryout notices—in which you call for actors to audition for the next play. List, in an interesting fashion, types of actors needed, dates (including the day of the week—do most people really know when October 13 is? Better to say, Wednesday, October 13.) times, exact location, and a strong statement that those trying out need not be members of your group nor highly experienced actors. This has the double value of truly encouraging new people to join you and convincing the editor that he is not giving space to club notices of interest only to the inner circle.
- Casting stories, telling who was cast at the recent tryouts, with photos of the leads, if possible. Point up any human-interest angle to avoid the dull listing of names and roles. If a married couple is cast as a married couple, or a retired naval officer prepares to play a naval officer (or is cast as an army officer, gritting his teeth), or if you are using a girl straight from France to play the French maid, mention it.
- Feature stories during the rehearsal period: a photo of the designer reproducing an authentic mummy case at the museum; a first-person story by Peter Pan on her first attempts to fly onstage; graphic detail on the special designs allowing the scenery to travel in two station wagons on its

grammar-school tour; the old vaudevillian dancing for the first time in forty years, and loving it . . .

●Tickets-on-sale stories, giving, again, accurate, full details: price, time, location, and a strong mention of student rates. (If you haven't yet instituted student rates, this is a good time to start. It will help fill your houses and begin encouraging your audience of the future to attend the theatre regularly.)

●Opening-night stories, listing any festivities planned, mentioning that tickets are still available, anecdotes from dress rehearsal, with a photo of the leads in costume on the set.

The above stories should all have been prewritten by you and sent to the newspaper for printing intact, as discussed under Promotion. Now comes the printed review; now the paper and the public have a chance to see you through their own eyes, not through your backpatting publicity. After writing and rereading all those stories about how wonderful you are, you are open to honest dramatic criticism, benefiting the reading public and benefiting you. Maybe you need polishing in some areas—maybe your sets are too derivative of the Broadway production; maybe your ingenue is getting too old for those roles; maybe your director has used the same gimmick in three plays running. Criticism, by-lined, from outside the group is to be welcomed. Also, it's more free newspaper space. Even if you should be slaughtered by the reviewer, it's column inches; your name will survive a few bad reviews as long as it's spelled properly, and a few good reviews soon show up to counterbalance the bad. If they are all bad, perhaps you shouldn't be producing plays at all.

If the newspaper has not yet reviewed your plays, give the editor some more civic-service arguments, with the assurance that you *want* an honest review, not a whitewash or an outline of the plot. Convince the editor that you're willing to take a well-founded knock, if that's what the reviewer feels. Tell him it's a service to his readers to let them know what one staff member thinks of this artistic product offered to the public.

Once the critic has been selected, contact him, and ask him if there is anything you can provide him with—a copy of the script, photos of the show, an advance copy of the program? See if you can spend a few minutes with him, convincing *him* that you'll welcome an honest review, not just a bouquet. Say, however, that you hope he will review *the production*. The script has long since been reviewed elsewhere; those reviews are available in books and magazines (unless this is

an original production; then use *that* as a selling point). Tell him you hope he will tell his readers—not the story—but how well he thinks you have brought it to life.

Be sure that he gets the best opening-night seats in the theatre, free, for himself and a guest, that the tickets are available when and where he needs them, and that someone from the staff or the Board is handy during intermission in case he has questions about who the leading lady's husband is, or where you got those drapes. (A critic once called me at 6 A.M. to ask the color of the leading lady's eyes. He used it in his review, too.)

Then, once the review is printed, be sure to thank the critic, especially if he bombs you. Thank him for his honesty, tell him you disagree but you see his point, and you hope he will enjoy the next production more. In addition to giving complimentary tickets to the critic, check with his bosses—the editor, the amusement editor, and so on. If they would like to attend the show, marvelous. Provide them with comps, too. It's a good investment for future publicity.

RADIO AND TV PROGRAMS

Most stations are conscious of their need for more local coverage, and are being made more aware all the time by FCC regulations. Contact the news directors and then supply them with the same sort of news articles you send the papers, but written with the human voice in mind—short, easily understood sentences. Words that might be mispronounced should be followed by an easy-to-read phonetic spelling in parentheses, e.g., *John Gielgud (GEEL-good).* I once heard this famous name pronounced "Google" on a very respectable radio station. It can happen to the best announcers. Anticipate the problem and solve it.

Make an event of your opening night—have it covered live or on tape by a local station, asking the audience what they thought of the play, and so on. . . . It convinces the station, their listeners, your audience, and you that you have quite a fine operation, worthy of news coverage.

Interview shows devour guests by the dozens every week and find that most of them freeze in front of the mike or the camera and aren't worth inviting back. If you can get your most attractive and most articulate people on the air to publicize a specific play (with lots of visuals if you're on TV—set models, interesting props, costume sketches, several pretty girls in costume), you'll find the station will want you back. They're in show business, too, don't forget, and they lose listeners with dull guests.

The dangers of doing scenes from plays whose broadcast rights have been sold to the movies were discussed under Promotion. But you may still show off the actors in their costumes on television, and if broadcast rights should be available to you, or the play is a new one or in the public domain, by all means try to get a short scene on the air. Pick the best scene with the best people, always being careful not to give away the climax of the play or any surprise twists of plot or character that would spoil the theatrical event on your stage.

If you are doing a musical, check with the music librarian of the station to see if they are licensed to broadcast some of the songs from your show. They probably are, so you can put on your best soloists in full costume against a few set pieces and really impress that new audience and bring them into your box office.

If your play or your songs are not cleared for broadcast, content yourself with a lively on-the-air discussion of the fun you're having doing the play, showing off the visuals, and encouraging the listeners to come join the fun. Talk about tryouts for the next play, and make it clear that newcomers are always welcome.

Watch the program several times before you're scheduled to appear to see what holds *your* interest and what sort of format and questions and guests the host leans toward. Then prepare yourself and your troupe accordingly. When your broadcast is over, ask the host and his director what suggestions they would make in case you are ever asked to appear again. They want quality shows, will be pleased that you don't think you are automatically perfect, and will probably give you those suggestions and also ask you back.

As with newspapers, provide everyone connected with your radio and TV appearances comp tickets for the play. Perhaps they would even consider a one-minute opening-night review on their late news programs, as is done in New York, or a longer postopening discussion on a personality show the next day.

Again, be sure everyone involved, from the manager to the unseen director, from the talk-show host to the announcer who reads your copy, gets free tickets.

NEWSLETTERS

Your loyal following comes to most of your plays, but even the most loyal skip a few, so that season ticketholders must be sold anew on each play just as you sell the general public. "I've already seen *The Odd Couple* four times" is a standard evasion. So is "I'd like to come, but my husband only likes musicals." These arguments can be met and beaten by a handsome newsletter, sent before each play, carrying news of the show into the dissenter's living room—and the living rooms of potential theatregoers all over the community. As effective as you will find posters, newspaper stories, and the like, you have more space and more control over that space in your own printed newsletter.

Two-color, two-fold newsletters or brochures printed for each play are not expensive. On a tight budget, even one-color, one-sided printed fliers can be creatively edited and laid out to catch attention and entice an audience to attend the play. Edit the copy carefully to praise your work (but not too much), describe the innovative set, point out the appearance in the cast of popular actors, and appeal to experienced theatregoers with a short discussion of the new approach to Act III. Invite them via the newsletter to the party after the show, and remind them of tryouts for the next play.

Chapter VII(a) describes the compilation of the mailing list. Be sure you add to it continually from newcomers' lists, single-ticket buyers, new actors' audition cards, and names submitted by members. Typing or handwriting the addresses for the mailing is time-consuming and may produce errors in copying. Automatic or manually operated addressing machines are not expensive to buy or rent, or perhaps you can buy only the paper or metal address plates and use them in a machine owned by a local business and used by them only a few times a month. It won't hurt to ask.

Feature your logo prominently in the newsletter, establishing it more firmly as the symbol of your attractions; include photos or sketches if time and budget allow; mention names wherever possible—a community theatre is composed of members of the community and should proclaim that fact, with specifics. Many attend the plays solely because of whom they know in the cast.

As a nonprofit organization, you have the right to mail your newsletters under a bulk mailing permit at a very low cost—less than 2¢ apiece at current post-office rates. Take your nonprofit corporation papers to the bulk-rate window at your post office, pay the low annual fee for the privilege, and get your bulk rate number and a copy of the rules for such mailings. Then stick to those rules.

Generally, you will be required to send at least two hundred per mailing and guarantee that each mailing piece includes the identical matter as two samples you will provide the post office. You will need to fill out a special post-office form with each mailing, including a lot of tedious and bothersome information: In addition to the number of pieces, you must determine the total weight of the mailing, the number of pieces per pound, the weight of one piece, and the like.

A zip code must appear on each address, and you must stack the mailers in numerical order by zip. A zip code master book at the post office will give you numbers for any addresses lacking them. A lot of trouble, but it will garner you the very low rate and expedite the delivery, and some volunteers who do not act or design may be pleased to contribute their service to the theatre by doing busywork such as this. (Be sure to include their names on the program . . . as always.)

Follow all rules of the post office and fill in all blanks on the form. Omitting something may delay your newsletters for many days. In any case, mail early. Even if all the bureaucratic details are correct, the post office may be overloaded, and the lowest-priced mail moves last.

A time-saving practice is that of printing on one side of your newsletter your return address and the bulk mail permit box, as shown you by the post office. Leave space for the recipient's address, using the mailing piece as a unit: message and address on the same sheet, removing the necessity and cost of envelopes, sidestepping the need for envelope stuffers and for the addressee to remove your newsletter from an envelope. Some people automatically throw away all bulk mailings rather than take the trouble to open envelopes. If there is no envelope, your message will jump out of the stack of mail, and possibly save itself from the wastebasket.

This same newsletter or a smaller publicity flier of envelope size can be inserted into bank statements, florists' bills, or the monthly mailing of any large business or utility. Ask your Board members and ask around town for permission to include the message of your nonprofit community organization in one of their mailings. Its weight will add no cost to their postage bills and will identify them as community boosters. Most places will turn you down, but if only five or six agree, you have a mailing for each play assured, and once you have done it, you can probably take advantage of their help each year. (This once-in, always-in system is true of most of the publicity requests you will ever make. It's equally true of selling a business on buying season tickets for its employees, borrowing props and furniture, and so on. The first sell is the hard one; but once sold, if the theatre delivers what it promises and proves to be sincere, decent, and hardworking, you can usually repeat your request often—though not too often. We once borrowed fur jackets worth thousands of dollars for the "Take Back Your Mink" number in *Guys and Dolls,* wholly on previous good relationships with the store manager, who knew we would bring them back safely or pay for damage.)

You may not even need to stuff such envelopes yourself. The staff of the firm doing the basic mailing—or a machine—may insert your newsletter or advertising broadside along with their usual bills, as long as you have delivered them on time and to the size specifications they have set down for you.

Store Windows

Tapping the same Board members and local businessmen, you can probably tie in with window decorations in a well-located store for each play. Most department stores design their displays in advance, so be sure to ask well ahead of the time you wish to be included in their windows. You may even be given an entire window to yourself; certainly if you find an unrented, empty store, the owner may let you set up a tasteful display there to plug season tickets or the next play.

Have definite ideas on possible setups before you approach the managers, to show them how you could be included. But be flexible, too, to mesh your plans with their concepts and long-range plans. Interesting, attractive formats can be created for any play you are doing. *My Fair Lady* or *Camelot,* with their costume emphases, would fit well in a high-fashion window, including your costume sketches, fabrics, or even a completed costume on a mannequin (or, at certain hours, on your actresses); posters, color photos from the movie, shots of your seamstresses at work—the possibilities are limited only by space and imagination. Children's stores are likely targets for children's plays. And *Barefoot in the Park,* with its Act II interior-decorating metamorphosis could inspire a home furnishings window, and so on. Even if you have only a small poster in one corner, the inspiration of the display came from the play and will be so identified in the minds of the beholders.

Everything mentioned so far in this chapter has been free or at very small cost. Now we get into the sometimes-great expenses of publicity. Most theatre economists say that 40 percent of your budget should go to publicity, and in a new group this is not an outrageous figure. Once you have been in business for a while, this percentage can be lowered, but it can never drop too low, or you will surely perish for lack of interest or knowledge by the public.

POSTERS

There is an old argument about the effectiveness of posters. Do people really see them or look at them? On college campuses, especially, routine-looking posters are ignored, and handsome posters are stolen right after being posted. Is that money better spent on newspaper ads or on the air? Each market is individual on this problem, and your best bet is to try several plays with and several without, to see which works for you.

As with everything else that comes from your theatre, make posters attractive and neat. Hand-done or silk-screened posters, except in the hands of an artist, will be sloppy and will prejudice the discriminating audience against the play. As stated, it will cost money, but savings are possible by careful selection of colors, of size of poster, of typestyle. Also, who says you have to use the same printer for all your work? Shop around and get rates. If you have to cover a wide area with your posters, perhaps they should be on paper instead of cardboard, foldable to manila envelope size, and mailed to outlying areas for posting. Colored paper or cardboard with interesting colored type can give a fine design at low cost. Almost anything that can be drawn can be reproduced on a poster. But the more intricate, the more expensive.

As with any printing you have done: Make the copy legible and get it to the printer early; then be sure to see and approve a proof before he does the final printing. Don't be afraid to ask him to correct his errors—that's what you're paying him for. However, any corrections of *your* errors, or changes on the proof, will cost you more.

Be selective about where you hang the posters. True, you're looking for a demographically balanced audience, but don't hang 70 percent of your posters for an antiwar play in the Conservative Club, nor the better part of your posters for the nineteenth-century operetta in the motorcycle gang clubhouses. Bars are hardly ideal for kid-show posters, nor nursery schools for existentialist plays. You get the point—plan your route carefully to cover every part of town, with a little extra stress on those areas from which you know you are not drawing an audience, or in which this sort of play would go over big if it were known about. Supply your posterhangers with transparent tape and thumbtacks both (don't hang them on living trees) and give them a specified district, overlapping with no one. If they must take a car, reimburse them for gasoline or provide them with comps for the play in proportion to the amount spent on gas. Don't send too many people in one group—it would be more fun for them, yes, but would also decrease the territory they could cover.

If the posters are for an entire season, count on their being taken down after a while—or fading or falling. Have your hangers make an accurate list of the places that let them hang posters; then, midseason, send another crew out to replace those that have disappeared. The sight of new, clean, unbent posters will give a shot in the arm to your campaign, at little extra cost; once the printing press is running with one color, one setup, another hundred or two hundred cost little more. Paper stock isn't that expensive, if you have planned carefully. To make the second hanging more effective, the lecture committee of our college began with black ink on green paper, then had the printer simply shove in a stack of orange paper as the green was getting low. The second hanging then showed precisely the same information, the same black lettering, but on a vividly different colored paper, designed to catch the eye as if for a new poster. And for little extra cost. Be sure the logo for the theatre and for the show are both worked into the poster. Identification of the play and the organization becomes more and more important as your reputation and word of the play get around. Changing your logo or the official name of your organization is as bad as changing location of meetings or of performances. After a while people get tired of looking for you and just stop.

NEWSPAPER ADS

Many theatres think this is the most intelligent area in which to put a small publicity budget. Even in this age of TV, people do read the papers, especially to find out what's happening in the entertainment or sports field. Movies do advertise on TV, but to find out what time the feature starts the moviegoer usually picks up the paper to find out details. And that's where your ad should be, too.

Visit your local advertising editor and beg for the cheapest rate you can get. Most papers have a church rate or something similar that you too should be able to get. Show him your nonprofit corporation articles and cry a lot. Make a list of all prices in all papers, remembering that Sunday and daily carry different rates, and sometimes the number of times inserted will change the rate. Be sure you include shopping-center newspapers, weeklies, school papers, and nearby large city newspapers. Then sit down, examine your budget, and decide where you want to spend it.

Here again, decide on your demographic needs. Yes, you want to draw from that wealthy suburb; yes, you want to draw from the working-class section of town; yes, you want the college students . . . and yes, you want the rank-and-file membership of your theatre.

Try to get at least one ad in each paper, to earn you more free articles—most papers will work this way, once they realize that you have even a small advertising dollar to spend, and will not be happy if you stop advertising with them but continue with other papers in the area. And you can't blame them. So give everyone something, the day or so before the box office opens. Include a statement that "The Box Office Will Open Tomorrow" or list the hours it will be open, the location, and complete information about the play. Most contracts with play publishers specify what data you must include on posters and in ads. Follow it unless it is too patently ridiculous for the space you have. They'll understand. A very effective size for a theatre ad is 2 columns by 2 inches. (See Figure 8.) Remember that all editions have closing dates after which you cannot insert an ad. Note in the folder you are making on newspaper ads the closing days for all papers, and then get your ads in at least a full day earlier, specifying that you want them to run on the Amusement, or Entertainment, or, heaven help us, the TV page, however your paper designates that section.

After the first box-office-open ad, several more, depending on your budget, should be placed in the newspapers covering the largest area of potentially interested theatregoers for this specific play. Each should list the days and dates of the show and stress the single most attractive aspect of the play—its Pulitzer Prize, its timeliness, its comedy, its music, its classic characters, for instance.

If the play sells out before the run is over, cancel the remaining newspaper ads quickly. No point in spending money needlessly. Also, there is a negative reaction caused by advertising what doesn't exist, as a seat for a sold-out play. If there's an ad in *tonight's* paper, it can be a point in your favor for your box office to say "Sorry, we've just sold out," but it's detrimental to say, "Sorry, we sold out yesterday." If the newspaper won't let you cancel the space but will allow a change in the copy, insert something like "Our thanks to the good people of this community who have given us a total sellout on *Go Down Moses.* Reserve seats early for our next big production, *Mary Had a Little Lamb,* running Wednesday–Saturday, March 6–7–8–9."

FIG. 8. A Newspaper Ad

This 2-column by 2-inch size is about the best; it's large enough to be noticed but not so large as to run up the expense. Note the inclusion of the logo to catch the eye as quickly as the large-typed title of the play. Days as well as dates are listed, to add specificity to the timing of the play in the lives of potential theatregoers. Box-Office phone number and hours are always listed, as are prices, including student rates. A statement of what kind of play it is will make the advertising more honest, and, as with a musical or comedy, attract a larger segment of the population whose chief interest in going out is to find amusement, rather than art.

RADIO OR TV SPOT ANNOUNCEMENTS

Continue looking for free publicity, even on commercial media; many radio and television stations, to justify themselves to the FCC, will make available to nonprofit groups a weekly free thirty-second (chainbreak) or one-minute spot announcement. Or perhaps they will give you a free spot for each so-many that you buy—by all means, find out. Radio advertising is expensive, and TV is probably out of your reach altogether, so beg for free time, but be realistic, too, and get the rate-card (church rates?) prices from all local stations and compare them with one another— based on their stated listening audience—and with other paid sources of publicity open to you. You may want to try one play with a heavy commitment to the airwaves, to see the results, or settle on buying one or two spots for each play, to catch that audience.

After you have tried radio or TV for several shows, include a questionnaire in your program, listing the various means of publicity used and asking where the audience first heard of this play. You'll learn which method of advertising is doing you the most good and where you're wasting your time and money.

When writing copy (here again you will do best to give the station the specifics of what you want to get across in your short time on the air), never begin with a question to which the listener can (and may) answer No! "Looking for a good time tonight?" or "Seen any good plays lately?" will turn off the listener before he turns you off. Make a positive and appealing statement on the order of "Start your weekend off with a delightful evening of live theatre as the Smithville Civic Theatre presents *My Mama Done Told Me,* opening tonight at 8:30 in the Smithville High School Auditorium, Main Street and Cross Road. Bring the entire family [a good selling point in this age of dubious family entertainment] to Michael Morrisey's hilarious comedy about mutiny on the high seas. Phone ANchorage 3-3456 daily between 9 A.M. and 9 P.M. for tickets; just $3 for adults and $1 for students through college. See *My Mama Done Told Me,* opening TONIGHT."

Always begin and end with a positive statement, including the title of the play. The listener who is caught up by the message in the middle will be waiting for specifics as you go on. Give them to him.

On TV, of course, what the viewer sees is even more important than what he hears. Even if the station gives you a free one-minute spot, it's still going to cost you something for the slides or the tape or both, unless one of your members can get out to the TV station every time your spot is scheduled, but it's doubtful that a live camera would always be available. So slides must be made—you can have several institutional slides, used in each spot, consisting of the theatre's logo, a photo of the theatre building, and so on, plus a specific slide with the logo of this specific show and/or a photo of an enticing scene. Write the copy from the same standpoint as the radio copy, indicating places for the insertion of your slides, and specifying which slide goes where. If your play is a musical, call for some of the best-known music from the show (on records) to back up or open the audio part of the spot.

If your theatre is difficult to find, be sure to include directions in all advertising. If you take your curtain up on time—and it's to be hoped that you do—you don't want latecomers swearing their way to their seats because they couldn't find the theatre.

STREET BANNERS

You may not want to stretch a banner across the street for every play, especially if you have hard winters, but occasionally it's a theatrical and attention-getting bit of publicity to present to all passing the streetwide news that your theatre is presenting *Such and Such* next Tuesday through Saturday at 8:30 P.M. Here again, some money must be spent, for heavy-duty canvas must be used, with air-flaps cut professionally into the billowing sign. There may be a fee for hanging banners in your town, and there is certainly the prerequisite city permission. See about all this early, so you won't order the banner unnecessarily if you can't get the permission. It is possible to reuse such a banner with a new paint job. Again, be sure it is professionally done, so the new play doesn't have half the old play's copy bleeding through, posting a sloppy job for all to see.

TABLE TENTS

A small printing job, but money nonetheless, accompanies the table tent publicity idea. Cocktail lounges, restaurants, dormitory tables, and the like usually will allow a nonprofit theatre to set small, attractive, one-fold, free-standing advertisements on their tables. Include all pertinent information (including your logo) and put them in place only a day or so before opening. Check back occasionally, as small objects often are taken or are shredded in the course of an evening. Make replacements.

JOHN NOTICES

This may be peculiar to the women's college where I teach, but some of the most effective advertising through its history have been what are and must be called, I guess, john notices—simple, informative mimeographed memos about 3" x 4" taped onto the wall or inside the doors of all the toilet stalls of the campus. Yes, include the logo.

BUTTONS, PINS, AND SWEATSHIRTS

New techniques make it possible to print anything onto anything, it seems, and for a price you can publicize your show throughout the town on the persons of your cast, your board, your friends, or anyone who will wear your pin, button, sweatshirt, or what have you. We gave summer theatre pins to our opening-night patrons one year, and they fought for the chance to wear them and ballyhoo us. The logo (Figure 9) was eyecatching, and we in the company wore them, not just as advertisement but because they made an attractive and artistic statement. But there is a cost involved. Inexpensive buttons can be made from the tops of coffee-to-go containers (unused, bought direct from a supply house) hung onto your clothing by safety pins or paper clips. It is preferable to have your message printed onto the cardboard; however, for a low-budget show, artistic and fastworking handicraft is possible.

Whether you spend a full 40 percent of your budget on publicity or get away without spending a penny, put as much care into your advertising campaign as into the production of the play itself. Make it tasteful, make it indicative of the show (formal for a classic, humorous for a comedy, bouncy for a musical), and, above all, make it truthful. Do not mislead your audience just to get them into the theatre—better an empty house than a group of unhappy people lured under false pretenses. I once heard spot announcements for *Philadelphia, Here I Come* that have worried me whenever I've thought of them. The play is a very delicate Irish piece about a boy's last night at home before emigrating to the States. He desperately wants his father to ask him to stay; the old man will not. The boy sees his old girl friend, now

married; he drinks a bit with his pals; none of them shows any sorrow at his leaving, though patently everyone would *like* to say the magic word—Stay. The radio spot for this lovely play was: "Enjoy an evening of wild Irish laughter . . ."

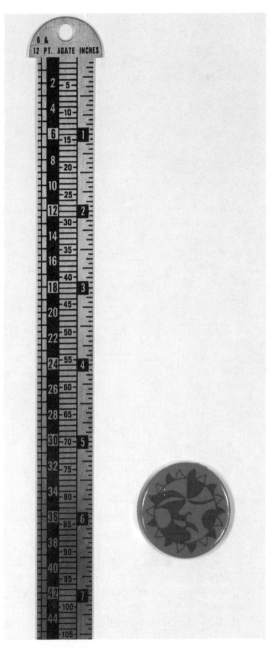

FIG. 9. Logo Printed on a Button
Using your distinctive colors, print your theatre logo on a thousand buttons and pass them out to be worn shortly before a show opens, or during season ticket drives. Since anything can now be printed on buttons, set the title of the show, or its logo, on other buttons, if the budget will allow.

Chapter VI

PROGRAMS, CREATIVE AND INCOME-PRODUCING

On the opening night of a 1946 production of Philip Barry's The Animal Kingdom *by the Augusta (Georgia) Players, a teen-aged crewman who had given many hours to the building and running of the show found that his name was not included on the program. Before he had time to be disappointed, he was called onstage with the entire company for preshow words by the stage manager. There, because his name had been omitted by a hurried typographer and missed by a more-hurried program editor, he was presented with an identification bracelet bearing his name and the name of the theatre. So important did that theatre consider proper program listing.*

The boy was thrilled, of course, and swore he would keep the ID bracelet forever.

And I still have it.

* * *

Whether it's a simple, mimeographed sheet or a forty-page, multicolor, professionally printed souvenir book, or something in between, an accurate program must accompany each play, to be handed to each member of the audience as he arrives at the theatre and kept as a memento by everyone in the cast and crew.

The program tells the audience the necessary facts about the play (some of them *required* by the publisher who grants you the rights to the play): the playwright, the creative and administrative staffs responsible for the production, and the specifics the audience really cares about—the names of the actors and the characters they play, in the order in which they appear or speak, and the locale and time of each scene.

That is the minimum information your program should include, and it can easily fit on one side of one page, if need be. But, however simple, the design and layout should reflect this production of this play and be neatly and attractively presented. (See Figure 10.)

A program is also a permanent record for the theatre itself of this production and all who participated in it. And even though you cannot pay your cast and crews what they are truly worth, the proper listing of each participant, properly spelled, is more important than cash to most theatre amateurs. If any of them should go on to professional theatre work, moreover, the program is tangible proof of their experience and background.

With these three important considerations —information for the audience, souvenir for the company, and archives for the theatre—your budget, your creativity, and the production itself are the only limits as to how elaborate your program should be.

It can be creative, or it can be income-producing, or it can be both.

CREATIVE PROGRAMS

The program is more than a factual listing of names and data. Even more than photographs and tape recordings, the program should keep alive the style and feeling of your production, jogging the memory where the ephemeral theatre arts remain alive even after the close of a play.

An institutional program, in the same style and format a theatre has used for years, is a permanent accurate reminder of the concept of the theatre itself, but hardly representative of this specific production. This play has a life, an identity, a style, that is unlike any other play you have ever produced, and unlike any other production of this play anywhere else in the world. Even if your director deliberately sets out—God forbid—to duplicate another production, he can't and you can't. Wherever it was conceived, your play will be born as itself, and the permanent program should so reflect.

The creative people on the program staff should meet very early with the director (the producer?) and the set and costume designers to determine just what the style of the production will be. Realistic? Impressionistic? Constructivist? Fairyland? The Lower Depths? Heaven on earth? Learn all you can of the director's concept and how the designers are bringing it to life; study the sketches, the colors, the lines, the emotional feel-

ABBEY MEMORIAL CHAPEL

Sunday, February 28, 1971

11:00 A.M.

"A Sleep of Prisoners"

by

Christopher Fry

A Laboratory Theatre Production
by the Department of Theatre Arts and Speech

Directed by Jim Cavanaugh

THE CAST
(in the order in which they speak)

Pvt. David King	STEVEN MacINTYRE
Pvt. Peter Able	. CHIP TUCKER
Cpl. Joseph Adams	. JOHN GRASSILLI
Pvt. Tim Meadows	. HORACE CORBIN

The setting is a church in a foreign country, occupied by the "Towzers," pressed into service as a temporary wartime prison camp.

(*There will be no intermission.*)

Scene	1	The Imprisonment
Scene	2	Meadows' Dream
Scene	3	David's Dream
Scene	4	Peter's Dream
Scene	5	The Corporal's Dream
Scene	6	The Prisoners' Dream
Scene	7	Awakening and Re-sleep

Stage Manager - Ann Brown Grassilli	Assistant Stage Manager - Laurice Firenze
Sound Recordings by Linda Macklin	Props Gathered by Lois Dowd
Costumes Coordinated by Tamara Jacobs	House Manager - Susan Harvuot

* * * * * * *

This production is being offered free to all area churches for presentation in their sanctuaries. Please call Mr. Cavanaugh for information.

* * * * * * *

The offering will be used to defray the expenses of the chapel program. Collection plates will be found in the vestibule.

Everyone is cordially invited to a social hour in Eliot House immediately following the service to meet the cast.

FIG. 10. A Simple One-Page Program

There's no disgrace in passing out a well set-up, one-page program printed on only one side of the page. Even if your budget can afford an elaborate, multipage, multicolor book, an inexpensive, tastefully laid-out program of this size may be a better statement of your play. Just be sure all pertinent information is included—the chief purpose of a program is to give the audience the facts it should know.

FIG. 11. Program Cover: *The Caucasian Chalk Circle*
The logo alone. No copy is necessary and would probably detract from the statement to be made by the play, thus by the program.
Design by Jane Goodman

ing you get from the work of the stylistic arbiters of the play. Based on these meetings and impressions, draw up the first creative concept of the program and get back to them.

Defend your ideas, add their suggestions, subtract their objections, and go back to the drawing board to draft the finished program concept, of size, color, style, typefaces, and content. (The general style of the program and the logo for the show, which will probably come out of these discussions, will also be helpful to the publicity crew in drawing up posters and such. They should be part of these meetings, and the graphic artist should probably serve on both crews.)

There are no rules as to how a program must look, but we can invent a few:

● The medium it's printed on should not make a distracting noise when flipped through during the performance.
● The program should not be so large nor the printing so small as to give the audience trouble in handling or reading it.
● Whatever else it contains, the pertinent information (cast list, etc.) should be easily found within the program.

After that, size, color, method of opening, content, and the rest are up to you and your creative juices.

I have included here three separate types of programs from one season in the college theatre department where I work. The creative artist in each case was Jane Goodman, the theatre plus art major who designed our summer theatre logo (Figure 7). She was not the editor of any of the programs; in fact, a different editor put out each.

The first is Bertolt Brecht's great epic theatre piece, *The Caucasian Chalk Circle,* as translated by Eric Bentley. Simply stated, the play deals with ownership, as parable-ized in the Chinese legend of the child claimed by two mothers, who decide true motherhood by attempting to pull the child from a circle. Our production leaned heavily on the oriental aspects of the play, and on Brecht's stark this-is-theatre-not-life approach, and the program was to reflect both feelings. (See Figure 11.)

The rather large shirred-edge paper handed a patron as he entered the theatre showed Jane's magnificently simple logo (also used on all posters) of the two women and the child bound forever in the circle of chalk, giving a statement of the East, of the sort of theatre ahead, and of

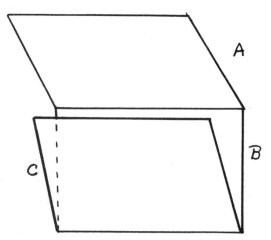

FIG. 12. Sketch Showing the Folding of the *Chalk Circle* Program
The logo (Figure 11) is printed on the back of A, which unfolds first. C unfolds down, revealing the body of the program (Figure 13) B, running down the entire length of the paper from A through C.

our feeling about the show. Brown ink on white paper echoed the earthy atmosphere (and design colors) of the production.

The program did not open like most programs—like a book—and why should it? It opened with the feeling of a Chinese scroll, into a simply produced program, printed on both sides of one sheet of paper and folded twice. (See Figure 12.)

And there, unfolded, was all the information, and more, that the audience needed. (See Figure 13.)

I think now that it was perhaps too long a sheet to be easily handled or referred to, but we could not justify at the time reducing the size of the type or of moving some of the information to the back page. (The back, by the way, listed the entire production staff, the acknowledgments, rules of the theatre—No Smoking, etc.—and blurbs on the coming productions.) It was a unique program, designed with this specific production in mind, and one that will always bring to mind those performances. And yet its one-color ink on white paper, its two-fold design, cost no more than many less excitingly conceived programs.

The second play of that season was a folk/rock version of *Sleeping Beauty,* replete with light-show, slides, movies, vivid modern colors in sets and costumes, and in every way a bright, happy, today feeling. Jane designed a psychedelic poster showing the Beauty surrounded by mod lettering of the necessary information. She took a detail from the poster for the program cover, which was simply black ink on fluorescent pink paper. There were two additional sheets, one a vibrating cerise, the other a neon orange. The fluorescent paper was white on the back, so we had six pages, three of them in the colors of the show, three a calmer white. Black ink throughout. The editor had wanted four sheets (eight pages) and a metal ring in the upper left corner holding the pages together. Budget defeated her, though, and we settled for three sheets and a staple. The stapling was done by her volunteer staff, to save still more money. The type style inside the program (see Figure 14) was simple but effective, the layout distinctive. No extra cost.

For the final play of the year, *Mourning Becomes Electra,* Eugene O'Neill's restatement of the Orestia in Civil War New England, Jane drew a simple Greek design in white on black (called *reverse printing* and used a great deal in graphics today) representing the Greek origin of the myth and the neo-Greek architecture of the New England mansion in which most of the play is set. (See Figure 15.) The heavy blackness of the re-

verse printing echoes the mourning of the title.

The program unfolded traditionally. Inside, simple and dignified type was selected from the printer's catalog and laid out in the standard fashion of most programs. The only innovations were a genealogical chart of the house of Mannon, around which the play centers, and a black border around the entire program, as on funeral cards.

Other innovative program formats I have seen in recent years include long vaudeville-like bills on newsprint, origami, a rolled-up scroll tied with a ribbon, and a round program for *Stop the World, I Want to Get Off.*

Sometimes it is financially necessary to maintain the same program format for an entire season. This may seem to negate what has been said, but distinctiveness can still be salvaged.

In our college summer theatre, in addition to a tight budget, the time required for a printer to turn out a weekly twelve-page program was not at our disposal, so we followed the leads of many professional stock companies and printed the outside eight pages at the beginning of the season. Then each week we printed only the one-fold, one-sheet (four-page) insert containing the information about that week's play.

The summer logo in warm yellow and orange dominated the permanent cover (and posters, buildings, buttons, etc.) set above a listing of the entire season with its dates (free take-home publicity); the outside eight permanently printed pages included ads, a welcome to the theatre and a statement of its philosophy, a listing of our patrons and contributors, and photographs and biographies of the entire company. The center four (weekly changed) pages included the cast and production staff lists, synopsis of scenes, acknowledgments, a reminder of what other roles tonight's leading actors played during the summer, a preview of next week's play and, most importantly, leading into these four pages of specific information, the logo and title of this week's show.

For *The Knack,* designer Noonie Shear took the brass bed around which the action mostly revolves and put the letters of the title into the bars. (See Figure 16.)

If paper used for the weekly insert is of a different color from that used for the outside eight pages, this differentiation adds more punch to the special section featuring this week's play.

So even though the weekly patron is handling the same old program *exterior* week after week, he finds what he needs in the interior, including a visual graphic statement about this particular

LABORATORY THEATRE   MOUNT HOLYOKE COLLEGE
NOVEMBER 6, 7, 8, 9, 1969

the caucasian chalk circle

by Bertolt Brecht

English version by Eric Bentley

Original music from Brecht's Berliner Ensemble production composed by Paul Dessau

Setting Designed by OLIVER ALLYN   Directed by JIM CAVANAUGH   Lighting Design and
Musical Direction by TAMARA KNELL and ANN BROWN   Technical Direction by CARMINE PICARELLO
Costumes Designed by JOAN GLEADALL   Assistant Director — FONTAINE SYER
Preparation of the Musical Score — TAMARA KNELL and KATHRYN HOBBE

THE CAST
PROLOGUE

MEMBERS OF THE COLLECTIVE FARM "ROSA LUXEMBURG"
Surab, the leader	RICHARD T. SOLLENBERGER
The woman who tells of the orchard	PAMELA THIELE
The tractorist who burnt the barn	VICKI CASARETT
The wounded soldier	JAMES CABOT
The tractorist who speaks of rationing	LINDA McELHENY
The soldier who scoffs at eternity	CHIP TUCKER
Kato Wachtang, the agriculturist	CATHERINE HAUSWEDELL
The peasant woman who looks to a productive land	LUCY McMICHAEL
Young boy	MARGARET WARDEN
The old woman who remembers Prince Kazbeki	BETSY RUDELICH

Farmers, their wives, their sons and daughters:
BRUCE ALLEN, F. X. ALMEIDA, CLIFFORD BULLOCK, P. MARTIN CONWAY, ROGER FOOTE, BILL HENNESSEY, DEIRDRE Mac-CALLAN, CLAUDIA REID, MICHAEL G. VENET, JOHN ZACHARY.

MEMBERS OF THE COLLECTIVE FARM "GALINSK"
Aleko Bereshwili, the leader	ROBERT KEMBLE
Makina Abakidze, his assistant	CONSTANCE METCALF
A very young worker	WILLIAM ROBERTS
An elder	FREDERICK HAMPSON
His wife	CAROL PETITMAIRE
Little girl	TAUBEY SHEDDEN

REPRESENTATIVES OF THE STATE RECONSTRUCTION COMMISSION
The Delegate	GALEN R. KLINE
His assistant	SUSAN COX

THE ENTERTAINERS
Arcadia Tscheidse, the storyteller	COURTNEY FLANAGAN
Jura, the actor	JOHN GRASSILLI

The Musicians   CHRIS DIETRICH, Flute; KATHY SHELTON, Piano; SHARON RICE, Clarinet; MARGERY HEINS, Percussion

The action of the play takes place in a ruined collective farm in the Caucasus at the end of World War II.

ACT I — SCENE 2, The Flight Into The Northern Mountains
The grandfather with the milk	RICHARD T. SOLLENBERGER
Corporal Shotta, who pursues Grusha	CHIP TUCKER
Private Blockhead	BRUCE ALLEN
A possible adopter	PAMELA THIELE
Her husband	FREDERICK HAMPSON
The merchant at the bridge	ROBERT KEMBLE
The merchant woman	CATHERINE HAUSWEDELL
The merchant with a stick	BILL HENNESSEY

ACT I — SCENE 3, In The Northern Mountains
Lavrenti Vashnadze, Grusha's brother	FREDERICK HAMPSON
Aniko, his wife	DEIRDRE MacCALLAN
Their servant	LUCY McMICHAEL
Yussup, a dying man	MICHAEL G. VENET
His mother	CONSTANCE METCALF
Brother Anastasius, a monk	BRUCE ALLEN
Wedding musicians	WILLIAM ROBERTS, CHIP TUCKER
A drunken peasant	GALEN R. KLINE
Puppeteer for Michael	BETSY RUDELICH
Puppeteer for big boy	CONSTANCE METCALF
Puppeteer for little girl	LUCY McMICHAEL
Puppeteer for fat boy	CATHERINE HAUSWEDELL

And make
My curtain half high, don't seal off the stage!
Leaning back in his chair, let the spectator
Be aware of busy preparations made for him
Cunningly; Let him see a tin foil moon
Float down on a tiled roof
Being carried in;
Do not show him too much,
But show him something!
And let him notice
That you are not wizards,
My friends, but workers . . . . *Brecht.*

THE CIRCLE OF CHALK
ACT I — SCENE 1, The Noble Child
Georgi Abashwili, Governor of Grusinia	P. MARTIN CONWAY
Natella Abashwili, the governor's wife	CAROL PETITMAIRE
Maro, the child's nurse	CONSTANCE METCALF
Mika Loladze } DOCTORS	FREDERICK HAMPSON
Niko Mikadze }	ROBERT KEMBLE
The leader of the Ironshirts	CLIFFORD BULLOCK
Ironshirts	BRUCE ALLEN, ROGER FOOTE, MICHAEL G. VENET
Shalva Tzereteli, the Governor's adjutant	BILL HENNESSEY
Arsen Kazbeki, the fat prince	F. X. ALMEIDA
The messenger from the capital	JOHN ZACHARY
Simon Shashava, a palace guard	JAMES CABOT
Grusha Vashnadze, a kitchen maid	VICKI CASARETT
The palace cook	SUSAN COX
Royal architects	CLIFFORD BULLOCK, ROGER FOOTE
Asja, lady-in-waiting to the Governor's wife	LUCY McMICHAEL
The palace groom	GALEN R. KLINE
Nina, a servant with hysterics	PAMELA THIELE
A young servant	LINDA McELHENY
An old servant	BETSY RUDELICH

DIRECTOR'S NOTE

As a violent reaction to the schmaltz of the German classical stage, Brecht conceived his Epic Theatre, vowing to erase overblown emotionalism with rigorous chastity. His Epic techniques (slides — or narration — to introduce scenes, music to neutralize rather than intensify emotion, compression or elongation of time/space) manifested his credo of *Verfremdungseffekt* (variously translated as Alienation or "Make Strange" Effect) with which he hoped to move the audience to social thought at the total expense of emotional involvement. In this he did not fully succeed; Kenneth Tynan has said: "Brecht was a man whose feelings were so violent that he needed a theory to curb them. But human sympathy, again and again, smashes his self-imposed dike." It is this modified and recognizedly human Epic Theatre that we have used as our guide in preparing this production.

--- 10 MINUTE INTERMISSION ---

I require no tombstone, but
If you require one for me
I wish it to be inscribed:
He made suggestions.
We accepted them . . . . *Brecht.*

ACT II, SCENE 1, The Story of the Judge
Azdak, the village recorder	JOHN GRASSILLI
The fugitive grand duke	F. X. ALMEIDA
Shauwa, a policeman	P. MARTIN CONWAY
Bizergan Kazbeki, fat prince's nephew	WILLIAM ROBERTS
The invalid	RICHARD T. SOLLENBERGER
The limping man	ROBERT KEMBLE
The doctor	ROGER FOOTE
The blackmailer	FREDERICK HAMPSON
The innkeeper	GALEN R. KLINE
Ludovica, his daughter-in-law	CLAUDIA REID
The stableman	BRUCE ALLEN
Wealthy farmers	GALEN R. KLINE, F. X. ALMEIDA, WILLIAM ROBERTS
Granny	BETSY RUDELICH
Irakli, her son-in-law (a bandit)	JOHN ZACHARY

Who owns a child? And who says so?
We find such questions à propos.
Like: Who owns Natchez and Birmingham?
Santo Domingo? Or Vietnam?
Or to be very impolite:
Who owns America, and by what right?
. . . . *Eric Bentley, A Prologue To "The Caucasian Chalk Circle", 1966*

ACT II, SCENE 2, The Circle of Chalk
Illo Shuboladze } PALACE LAWYERS	FREDERICK HAMPSON
Sandro Oboladze }	ROBERT KEMBLE
The old married woman	PAMELA THIELE
The old married man	RICHARD T. SOLLENBERGER

Villagers, Servants, Beggars, Petitioners, Horses, Ladies-in-Waiting, Wedding Guests: P. MARTIN CONWAY, SUSAN COX, JOHN GRASSILLI, FREDERICK HAMPSON, CATHERINE HAUSWEDELL, BILL HENNESSEY, ROBERT KEMBLE, DEIRDRE MacCALLAN, LUCY McMICHAEL, CONSTANCE METCALF, CAROL PETITMAIRE, CLAUDIA, REID, BETSY RUDELICH, WILLIAM ROBERTS, TAUBEY SHEDDEN, RICHARD T. SOLLENBERGER, PAMELA THIELE, CHIP TUCKER, MARGARET WARDEN, JOHN ZACHARY.

Singing Chorus: JOHN ZACHARY, BRUCE ALLEN, GALEN KLINE, CAROL PETITMAIRE, DEIRDRE MacCALLAN, SUSAN COX.

Truth is concrete . . . . *Brecht.*

FIG. 13. Body of the *Chalk Circle* Program

Unfolded, this shows the full extent of the paper on which the program is printed (9½" x 17¾"). In addition to the basic information, a larger program such as this allows inclusion of program notes, quotes from the playwright and the translator, etc. The layout picks up the episodic feeling of the play.

f

o

r

stage manager	COURTNEY FLANAGAN
assistant	MARCIA BRESSLOUR
props	MICHELE ROBITAILLE
make-up	CATHERINE HAUSWEDELL
publicity and programs	LUANNE COACHMAN
house manager	SHELBE FREEMAN

t

h

e

set building BEE BEE HOROWITZ, MARGY SIMON, MARY WORD, JAMIE CABOT, BARBARA COHEN, JANE HOWARD

set painting JULIE GIBB, AMY KIMBALL, IBBY LANG, ELLEN McGUIRE, KATHERINE O'BRIEN, CINDY CUMMINGS, KATHY PLOWITZ, CHRISTINE CLUNE, BRIGETTE WALDMAN, MILLES CAVANAUGH

p

r

prop building JAMIE CABOT, SUZANNE BECK, SANDRA GRAY, DIANNE ESCOTT, DEIRDRE MacCALLAN, ANN BARCLAY

prop running ANN BARCLAY, ALICE GUIDO

o

costume building POLLY COOPER, ELOISE FULLER, NANETTE CLINCH, MAMEE CLARK, MRS. WILLIAM DURFEE

d

costume running MAMEE CLARK, LEAH PAGEN, MARY FOOTE

stage CINDY CUMMINGS, DEIRDRE MacCALLAN, ELOISE FULLER

u

media and special effects SHARON CAMPBELL, SANDY SHINNER, BARBARA COHEN, TAUBE SHEDDEN, BRETT DIGNAM

c

lighting MARJORIE JARNSON, SUSAN ROTH, CHRISTINA RINI

t

make-up CONSTANCE METCALF, VICKI CASARETT, PEGGY EGBERT, CAROL PETITMAIRE, LUANNE COACHMAN

i

music KAREN AHLQUIST, KATHRYN PLOWITZ

o

publicity JENNIFER McLAUGHLIN, JANE GOODMAN (Design)

n

graphics DODIE HILLGER

FIG. 14. Production Staff Page in *Sleeping Beauty* Program

The paper is 5" x 5" and is an electric orange color. The unusual layout of the printing costs no more and captures the bright, modern feeling of the show, a rock version of the classic. Each department of the production is listed here, with the names of all who worked in that department. The main creative staff of the show is listed with the title on a previous page, as on the Chalk Circle *program (Figure 13).*

show, making this evening what it must be—an event in itself. And money and time budgets are met.

Other creative program possibilities are the selection and mixing of typefacing, and the use of photos and other art work within the body of the program (photos for the cover are also specific to this play and add a professional touch [see Figure 17], but a photograph has to be ready so early that makeup, costume, background, and such usually cannot be completed to meet the deadline of the photographer and the printer).

Other informational possibilities include biographies of the staff and cast; production history of this play (when it was first produced, famous people associated with it, number of Broadway performances); a critical article on the script by a local scholar or knowledgeable theatre person; announcement of meetings, tryouts, other plays; a calendar of theatre events in the community, including but not restricted to your own; request for items your theatre needs, both general and specific: a rug for the green room and a rug for the next play; men's hats to be made into period hats for the next costume play; photos of past productions for lobby display; and so forth.

And—advertisements.

INCOME-PRODUCING PROGRAMS

Since the program is a necessity to the production why not make it pay for itself, and for other

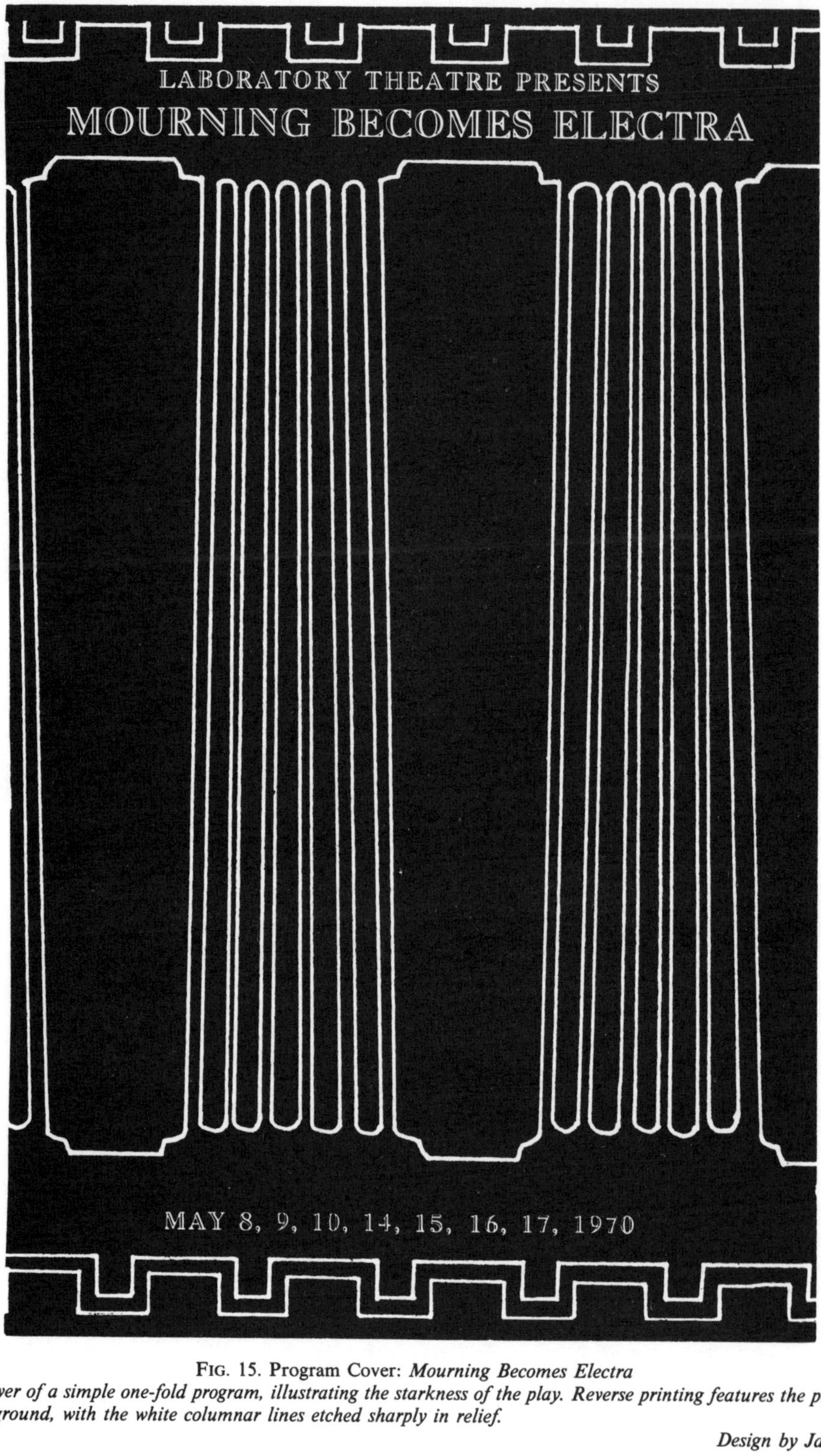

FIG. 15. Program Cover: *Mourning Becomes Electra*

A simple cover of a simple one-fold program, illustrating the starkness of the play. Reverse printing features the predominantly black background, with the white columnar lines etched sharply in relief.

Design by Jane Goodman

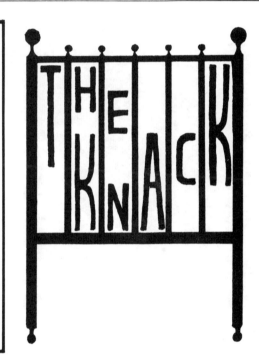
FIG. 16. Weekly Middle-Fold Insert for Permanent Program

With the outside eight pages printed at the beginning of the summer, the middle four pages are made up freshly each week, including new and pertinent material about the play running tonight. The logo and the dates begin these pages, which are printed on a colored paper different from the constant eight outer pages. The ads on these four center pages are unchanging all summer, allowing the printer to have them set permanently, filling in around them with the special weekly material.

Design by Noonie Shear

a full page ad, but *a little more than half.* The same is true with *each* reduction by half—the cost is always a little more than half. This is to pay for the extra time, setup, and so on involved in selling and putting two or four ads in a space where one large one, requiring only one sale, would as easily fit. The broad economic principle in any field is that buying in large quantity (in this case, a full-page ad) costs the buyer less than many small purchases totalled together.

For each ad salesman who will canvass your community's businesses, make a clean mockup of the program, showing clearly where each article will be placed, and the size and cost of adjacent ads. When an ad has been sold, fill in the name of the purchaser, so that two pharmacies will not occupy the same page, or two banks, or any competitive businesses. Gently warn your salesmen to dress neatly and to keep their mockups pressed flat, and send them off.

Before a buyer even thinks about an ad, he must be sold on the idea that he is not being asked for a donation, but that yours is a legitimate medium for advertising his product—that people who have money to spend going to the theatre (a non-necessity of life, remember) will have money to spend with him. Encourage him to place an ad that stresses a specific service or salable item—discourage CONGRATULATIONS FROM JOE'S SODA SHOP; or A FRIEND; or THE FIRST BANK SALUTES THE LITTLE THEATRE PLAYERS. These are demeaning to you as a valid form of advertising and will discourage serious advertisers in the future. If the advertiser doesn't want to ballyhoo his new one-hour cleaning service, or the specific movie he's showing next week, urge him to place a simple, dignified ad featuring merely his name and his logo.

Prime prospects for program ads are truly anyone. Any retail business in your community could profit from exposure to your ticket-buying audience. Make a list for each salesman, beginning with the best-known businesses in town and those represented on your Board and in your membership. Include any businesses dealing in luxury items, in entertainment, in meals before (or cocktails after) a performance. But, really, there is no type of business that should not be approached. Funeral parlors frequently advertise in theatre programs, as do insurance agencies, and I have seen ads in community theatre playbills for well diggers, artificial insemination for animals, oil-refining plants, chiropractors, and beauty parlors for dogs. Sell your nearest competitor an ad, and buy one in his program.

Salesmen should carry a stack of contracts for ads—if a sale is made, sign the customer on the spot. The contract should be as simple as possible (as should all contracts), including just the necessary information in the clearest language possible. Information that both parties can agree to and sign their names to. (See Figure 18). Fill in the necessary information on two copies, sign both, have the advertiser sign both, and each of you keep one. Then live up to every item in the contract.

Collect the ad copy from him in plenty of time to have it set up by the printer; show him a galley proof if he wants it, or if there is any question in your mind about the setup he wants. Then place his ad in the location he has specified. Immediately the program is printed, check his ad to be sure it is as he ordered, then send him a copy of the program, folded open to his ad, with your bill. Be sure the amount you bill him for is the amount he signed for. Most firms pay bills once a month, and if you miss the bill-paying day, your theatre will have to wait another month for that needed income. So get the bills out as soon as you have a program as proof-of-ad to send along.

Generally the advertiser will pay for any special art work in his ad—many will provide you with cardboard or metal mattes containing their logo or a photo or drawing of something to be featured in the ad. The printer will usually include this matte in his layout at no extra cost, depending on his method of printing.

A photo or drawing not in matte form will have to be photographed by the printer and set into printable form and will, therefore, add to the price of the program printing. The usual tactic here is to include in the contract with the advertiser a clause in which he agrees to assume any extra printing fees. Either have the printer bill him directly, or list such fees, by advertisers, separately on the printing bill sent you; then include such charge on the program ad bill to the appropriate advertiser.

It is possible, of course, to make quite a bit of money on program ads. Once again, the cost of ads throughout a program is based on what you can sell them for. If you can convince enough advertisers that the number of people who will be seeing their ads, and the spending power of these people, is great enough, you can ask and get high prices. If you would rather not ask a lot, or if you feel you haven't enough of a selling point yet to ask very much, be sure at least to sell your ads for a rate that will pay for the cost of the program.

If you have a large number of ads to sell, send a small army out selling. Once committed to a

CONTRACT BETWEEN

    The Mount Holyoke College   and   —————————————————
        Summer Theatre
    South Hadley, Mass. 01075   —————————————————

                                  South Hadley Mass 01075
                                  The Advertiser

Mount Holyoke College will officially sponsor a Summer Theatre as an extension of its Department of Theatre Arts and Speech, under the direction and supervision of members of its faculty. The Mount Holyoke College Summer Theatre will present 7 plays between June 29 and August 21, 1971, in a tent on the Woolley Green on the campus of Mount Holyoke College, each play to run for 5 successive nights * playing to a potential capacity of 300 patrons per night. The bill of plays will be well advertised throughout the Connecticut Valley, will be chosen from today's most popular and playable works, will be well-produced, and we have every reason to expect full houses.

A 16-page Program will be presented free to each attending patron each night of the summer. This program will be financed by the sale of ads, for one of which the above parties enter into this contract.

The Summer Theatre agrees to furnish space for an ad of *75.00*

size to be located on Page __*3*__ (any special position on the

page? *bottom*).

The Advertiser agrees to furnish all copy necessary for the ad no later than June 20, 1971, and to provide needed cuts or mats or to pay any engraving costs for art work or photographs not included in cuts or mats.

Copy will be the same for all programs, unchanging.

The Summer Theatre will send a copy of the Program, including the Advertiser's ad, to the Advertiser the day after the opening of the first play (June 29, 1971). The Advertiser will remit, within 10 days of the receipt of the Program, the sum of $ *7500* for the advertisement's appearance in the Program for all 7 plays.

Elizabeth C Gerard   *Joan L. LeBlanc*
For the Summer Theatre   For the Advertiser

DATE: *May 27, 1971*

* The musical, CARNIVAL, will run for 10 nights. The total audience potential for the summer is 12,000.

FIG. 18. Program Ad Contract
The information is specific, and you must keep your part of the contract, or, if you have to adjust the size of the book and move the ads, get an OK from the signer of the contract.

fat program (and its printing costs) you don't want to fill the spaces with nonpaid filler and have a money-losing program. Establish a central checkpoint with whom each salesman will check before signing an ad contract, of whom he can inquire about the availability of an ad location, and with whom he can deposit information on ads sold and prospects solicited. Such a checkpoint can save much time and avoid the embarrassment of trying to sell a prospect who has just turned down another of your salesmen (or, worse, has just signed with another).

THE BASE PROGRAM

To return to the reason for a program—information—let it be repeated that you do not have to sell ads or make any money at all on your program. One side of one piece of paper, neatly printed with the basic data on the play can do the job and fit into the most modest budget.

Some closing hints:

In deciding how many programs to order from the printer, estimate how large the audience will be, then add one for every advertiser, two per cast and crew member for souvenirs, and about twenty-five for the theatre's files.

If you have been in business for a while, you should have a good idea of how large a crowd to expect at each type of play. Is your audience more interested in comedy than drama, or vice versa? Is a musical your guaranteed sellout? Or a classic? Based on past attendance, predict attendance for this play. If it's your first season, you will just have to guess, and you should guess big—assume you will fill every seat in the auditorium, as it's better to order too many rather than too few. It's embarrassing to run short of programs, forcing the ushers to pass out only one per couple. Once the presses are running, it costs very little more to have them print another hundred or so. Throw away extras, if you have to, rather than slight the audience.

Include a program with each program ad bill, make several available to everyone who has worked on or in the play, and have the House Manager pull those twenty-five for your archives. You will use past programs for future lobby displays, for historical observances within the theatre, and for newspaper stories, articles in future programs, and just for reference (Who played Henry Higgins? Is the new Broadway star the same girl who was so good in your children's plays?).

As a nonprofit theatre you pay a salary to few

if any of the hundreds of people who contribute to each production. You cannot afford to, and most would not want it. But you *can* afford to pay the one thing that is usually dearly wanted—program credit. If someone has contributed his time (the most valuable thing he has to give) to a role or a crew or an advisory job, you can pay him handsomely by a program listing. If he has given an inordinate amount of time or a specialty job, perhaps you can list him in capital letters, boldface type or a separate column. But everyone must be listed. Have each crew chief and each department head keep an accurate and up-to-the-minute listing, for the program editor, of everyone who works, gives advice, or lends props, furniture, or an empty store for your use as a scene shop.

List your people in four separate categories:

● The Creative Staff of the play (Director, Set Designer, Musical Director, etc.).
● The Cast and the roles they play.
● The Production Staff (Stage Manager, Set Building Crew, House Manager, etc.).
● The Thank-You or Acknowledgment column.

The Creative Staff is usually quite small, and is usually listed in large type on the same page or in the same part of the page as the title of the play.

The Cast List may be all together on one page or, as in Broadway programs, spread over several pages, in sequence, so that more advertisers have a chance to place their ads adjacent to at least part of the Cast List.

The Production Staff is one of the hardest pages for accuracy but one of the most important; a new volunteer slapping paint onto a window backing at midnight doesn't always feel a part of the group or that he's contributing much to the success of the play. His name in the program under Scenery Painting can convince him that he is wanted and needed, and bring him back. Impress on each crew head the importance of listing every single person who has worked on the play, and of listing them in their proper categories. A member of the audience seeing a long, accurate list of backstage workers will feel that he is watching a communitywide cultural presentation. He may well come around for crew work himself sometime, adjudging you to have arrived, as more and more familiar names appear show after show.

Alert the printer ahead of time that this part of the program will be subject to additions up to press time, as new workers will come to you in that last push before dress rehearsal, and they, too, must be added.

The Acknowledgment Page, too, will often require late additions as that hard-to-find prop is turned up just before dress rehearsal; its lender must be credited. Distinguish between firms and families, and don't be afraid to insert a special line for a very big item. In the *Guys and Dolls* program I put a box around a large-type notation on the loan of the fur stoles. Several thousand dollars worth of costumes from one source merits recognition.

It has been years since theatrical playbills heralded Mrs. Fiske or Mrs. Patrick Campbell in a play, and I applaud the passing of such appendages. In a Thank-You column, I always list Mrs. John Smith who has lent her gateleg table as a private individual, and as such she is recognized. But in the Cast and Production Staff lists I deplore the sight of Dr. and Rev. and Capt. and Mrs. and the like. The good doctor is not healing the sick on our staff tonight, nor is the good Reverend preaching the word of God. They are part of an ensemble company presenting a play, and no more would I list Grocer Sam Smith or Pilot Charles Brown or Nurse Mary Johnson than Dr. Smith or Sgt. Brown. And Mrs. Harold Greene may love her husband, but she's not here as the mistress of a house, but as a seamstress or a prop girl, and we hope she hasn't lost her identity as good old Marian Greene. And as such she should be listed.

Check all spelling for accuracy, both in the copy referring to the play and in the names of people and firms contributing to the show. The stage manager or his assistant can take a carbon copy of the proposed program to each actor and crew worker and ask him to initial his name if it is spelled correctly or change it if it is not. Any errors can then be corrected before they reach the printer. Check for the proper listing of firms in a telephone directory. Everyone in the neighborhood may call a store Harry's, when the official name is H. Jones, Groceries, and Mr. Jones probably wants his program credit (for lending all those apple boxes) to be in his official name. But be safe and *ask* him how he wants to be listed. Other firms not usually thought of as Co. or Inc. will be listed correctly in the phone book, and should be so in the program.

Nearly every printer is busy and has continuing weekly or monthly printing jobs he is contracted to get out, such as church bulletins or reports for city hall. And once-in-a-while print jobs like yours must be sandwiched in. This you must understand, as you do your best to bring legible copy, on time, arranged so that it will fit onto its assigned pages. Photos and such must be brought in early. However, no printer is so busy as to require that your program be printed a week ahead of opening night, and don't let him tell you it must. Thank-You's and Production Staff changes, as noted, are always last-minute insertions; you may decide to put the intermission somewhere else, or a last-minute cast change may be necessary. Many late entries are possible; the printer must be convinced of how important late access to the program is to a play and of your need for equal consideration with his other printing clients. The best way to handle this, so that you are not a nuisance to him and get your program the way and the day you want it, is to ask for delivery of galley proofs a week before the program is to be printed. Then bring them back the day before press day. In those five or six days, read the proof carefully, making changes only when necessary. Read your original copy side by side with the proof; correct any errors the printer's staff has made, but assume that any *changes* you make—apart from a few additions that you warned him about—will cost you money. (Make grammatical, stylistic, and spelling corrections on the original type-written copy before taking it to the printer's in the first place.) If changes must be made, then make them; the quality of the entire evening must be considered, but don't spend money capriciously because you suddenly think an idea should be placed in paragraph one instead of paragraph three. That sort of change is major and will require that the typographer reset both paragraphs entirely. Stick with your original choice of typeface, too; if it's not marvelous, correct it for the next play, but realize that changing anything as basic as type will also cost a great deal.

The program will be a tangible recollection of the play for years to come. Put your best people onto it, both editorially and soliciting ads, and let them give it sufficient time and talent and thought to make it worthy of the play and the organization.

Chapter VII

HOUSE MANAGEMENT

During one of the frequent summer tornado watches in a midwestern town, residents were suddenly alerted by the radio to seek cover from the tornado, which was now reported to be active and headed their way. Those in cars were advised to stop and get into the nearest large building. The audience of the community theatre production of Teahouse of the August Moon *was just breaking for intermission as several dozen frightened people came running into the lobby shouting about the tornado. This onslaught started a near-panic in the audience, many of whom had left their children with babysitters. The house manager, who had been in touch with the airport weather station throughout the first act, tried to calm both crowds with his information that the weather system had not in fact turned into a tornado; but no one would listen, and the pay phones were immediately taken over by terrified parents. A new arrival shouted out that the radio had said that the tornado had just touched ground in Stewartville, a nearby town. One poor couple whose family was in Stewartville ran to the box office to beg use of the theatre's phone. The house manager, still trying to repeat his official weather information, let them in.*

Before they could call, the phone rang. The house manager answered and heard: "Are there any tickets left for tomorrow night? This is Mrs. Smith from Stewartville." "Where are you calling from?," he asked. "Why, from my home." "No tornado there?" "No; it was pretty blowy for a few minutes, but it's a beautiful summer evening now." The house manager said: "Would you repeat that for one of your neighbors here?" and handed the phone to the worried parents.

* * *

It is probable that very few of your audience will be in personal contact with your actors or crewmen, but that the people who will represent your theatre by face-to-face or spoken communication with the audience will be ushers, box-office staff, and parking attendants. Only a tiny percentage of any audience ever comes backstage after the show, invite them though you do, so the strongest memory of your company that anyone will carry away will be of those under the charge of the house manager.

Everything in your theatre (both the tangible theatre building and the intangible theatre organization) from the proscenium arch forward is the responsibility of the house manager. This geographic domain is his whether you occupy your own building, or, like most community theatres, move into the high school three days before opening. The territory of the house manager includes:

- the auditorium with all its seats and aisles and stairways and house lights and aisle lights and exit signs and escape doors and heat and cooling and ushers;
- the lobby with its ashstands and phone booth and art exhibit and photos of past shows and posters for forthcoming shows and ticket takers and drinking fountain and checkroom and soft-drink stand and mat for wiping muddy shoes;
- the rest rooms and their supplies and proper functioning;
- the box office with its treasurer and its workers and accounting system and ticket racks and adding machine and telephone and correct filing of mail orders and speed in serving patrons;
- the exterior of the building, with signs identifying it as your theatre with the play being done this week and its parking lot or parking areas and its steps and sidewalks all free from snow, leaves, and mud.

In each of these areas—in any area directly involved with the audience as opposed to the production of the play itself—comfort, cleanliness, courtesy, safety, and service to the public are the direct responsibilities of the house manager.

A strong and friendly house manager can start the evening off so well for an audience that a weak play may be more fully enjoyed; polite handling of a drunk in the next seat, understanding help when tickets are lost, quick response to a dented fender, gentle assistance to a wheelchair patient—when the house manager and his staff handle any problems efficiently and with a smile, the whole theatre experience before the play even begins has established a pattern of efficiency and humanity. The actors will then profit by the receptivity of a comfortable audience.

On the other hand, the best-produced play cannot survive sloppy house management. A hot, stuffy auditorium; ushers talking too loudly in the lobby; no toilet paper; a shortage of programs; being seated in the wrong seat and then moved just as the curtain is going up; a splinter or a nail on a seat, tearing stockings . . . each of these common examples of bad house management can be avoided, and must be, to give the actors every chance of doing their best work.

The house manager must be conversant with every aspect of the play. What time are intermissions and the final curtain?—is there action in the aisles for which the ushers should be prepared? —are there wild sound effects that might startle a Seeing-Eye dog?—for what age range is the play suitable? (one mother's worldly-wise 12-year-old is another's protected darling—the house manager's best tack is to explain any doubtful moments in the play and let the parents decide). Each peculiarity of this specific play he will explain to each member of his staff who will serve in the affected area.

He will know all of the enforced fire laws of the city (and those assumed by the city from state and national codes) and see that they are followed. How many may safely occupy the lobby at one time; how much aisle space must be maintained—the temptation is great to drag kitchen chairs into the center aisle at the first sold-out performance in a theatre's history; where smoking is permitted—probably not ever in the auditorium itself, and in some school buildings only up or down some stairs or even completely outdoors.

He must have all fire exits unlocked and their escape corridors unblocked, and his ushers must know procedure for speedy evacuation of the audience; he must post fire-reporting techniques by the phones and advise his staff how to follow them.

He must also post and make known phone numbers or directions to the nearest doctor, hospital, and rescue squad. His crew will be trained to spot erratic behavior in the patrons, indicating illness, injury, or drunkenness, so that the continuity of the play and the comfort of everyone in the audience may be maintained through the efficient and quiet handling of problems.

The house manager is the one to give that ancient cry (with steady voice) "Is there a doctor in the house?" if it absolutely cannot be avoided.

He will know emergency first aid, including treating of fainting and making a temporary splint from a folded newspaper, and will have access to a freshly stocked, fully equipped first-aid kit.

Accident reports will be required by your insurance company, and forms should be kept in the box office and filled out by the house manager as soon as possible after an accident. These forms give every pertinent fact concerning the harm to the person or his clothing or property at the time when all memories are likely to jibe. Waiting too long to make a report will cloud or color the recollection of what happened. If it is within the bounds of decency, the house manager should speak with the person involved to get his initial statement on how he believes the accident happened and how he feels. It is betraying no secrets nor inventing no disdain to say that some attorneys are masters of the massive lawsuit on behalf of a slightly damaged piece of clothing or automobile or nicely mending sprained ankle. If the person is truly hurt, you want to do all you can to make amends. But find out—the courts won't take the house manager's statement that "He said he could walk all right" over a qualified physician's report that the ankle was broken in three places; but a malingerer might be less inclined to institute a false lawsuit if he did say on the scene of the accident something to the effect that "It was all my fault" or "I'm all right, it's an old football knee" or "The car had this dent already—it's just this scratch here that's new." An immediate dated and signed release, however simple in layman's terms, can protect you against the few but aggravating opportunists who might be persuaded to turn a small accident into a gold mine. Theatres are fair game and called in many lost precedental cases "Attractive Nuisances." Protect yourself by training alert and concerned house managers who will hold dear the life and limb of the audience and soothe injured patrons or dignities; and who will also shield the organization from wrongly motivated nonfriends of the theatre.

The rest of this chapter will deal with the people directly responsible to the house manager; it will be he who trains them, so he must be in possession of all this information as well.

A. BOX OFFICE

If there is only enough money in the bank to hire one employee, many nonprofessional theatres will hire a box-office treasurer before a director. And perhaps they're right. The delegating of the collection and handling of the prime source of theatre income into several dozen willing but disorganized hands is a frightening and possibly money-losing plan. Unless you can be sure of thoughtful, diligent, and honest volunteers to man your box office, think of *hiring* a mature and organized person for the few weeks tickets are on sale and putting into her hands (it will probably be a woman, with the many daytime hours needed) all the operations described here.

But if you can share the burden and the wealth (of experience) with a number of people, do so, as this is an area for the involvement of dozens of members of your community who may have no theatrical or artistic talent of any kind but who want to contribute themselves. That is not to say that you should not use actors out front, too—it's an exciting moment when a ticket buyer recognizes an actress from the previous play and compliments her. And it helps show the audience that you're not a group of prima donnas intent only on grabbing center stage. To see the last play's leading man hanging lights or selling program ads is to help convince your audience of the sincerity and stability of your theatre. And, though you can't afford salaries, perhaps free tickets for the box-office volunteers and their families is a good way of saying thank you.

So—you have a box-office staff, whether of one or two full-timers or a raft of volunteers working two or three hours at a stretch. Where are they going to set up shop? If you have your own building, there's no problem—put them in a lockable office just off the lobby. But if, as with most nonprofessional theatres, you do not have your own building, find a central location where tickets can be sold the week or so before a play opens—and daytimes during the run of the play—and keep that location show after show. Moving from place to place is the surest way to promote the instability of your theatre and to confuse your audience to the point that they won't even try to find you.

A good location for a box office is any place where the kind of audience you want to attract will pass frequently. A store manager can sometimes be convinced of the promotional tie-in value of giving you office space or a booth in a corner by the main door, if you feature his firm name prominently in your advertising: "Box Office Located in Joe's Music Shop." If he has a phone but doesn't use it much, he may even allow you to take incoming calls. If not, an investment you *must* make is the installation of your own telephone, keeping the same number in that continuing location, show after show. (At about

7 P.M. on show nights, move the box office to the theatre and publicize that time and move.)

In this age of income tax, everyone needs to make several donations to nonprofit organizations. A storekeeper or shopping center manager or the owner of an empty shop can be convinced of the public service (and deductibility) of making available to your nonprofit theatre free space for the box office and then declaring the potential rent of such space as a donation when making out his income tax.

If you have a centrally located workshop or office or rehearsal hall, put your box office there, combining all your functions in one area, even if you haven't a full theatre building yet.

All right; now you have a box-office location. Within that box office, you must have: a lockable cash drawer with change dividers; a phone; serviceable office equipment, such as adding machine and typewriter; ticket racks; a large, clear seating plan showing by number all seat locations in your theatre with their relationships to each other, to the stage, and to aisles, posts, exits, etc.; a supply of stamps and theatre stationery; a listing of your season ticketholders with their phone numbers; accident report forms; emergency phone numbers; accounting forms; bank deposit slips; brochures on the theatre and on this season's plays; ticket envelopes; file boxes for advance reservations; a calendar visible to the public and the staff; a wastebasket; rubber stamps and stamp pad made with whatever designations your system requires: "Complimentary," "Season," and so on; office supplies such as pencils, pens, rubber bands, paper clips, transparent tape, carbon paper; complete rules for running the box office, including emergency procedures and instructions for selling and handling every kind of sale, both individual and group; complimentary ticket list; and, as the final decider on when to cancel reservations, an accurate clock.

And—tickets, both for the season and for this play.

Start each day and each show evening with ample change in the cash box, both in single dollar bills and in the sort of change needed for the price of your tickets: a lot of quarters if your prices are so many dollars plus 25¢ or 50¢ or 75¢; nickels and dimes aplenty if ticket prices include other combinations of change: $2.80, for instance. Many theatres round off all prices to an exact dollar, so that change-making is less of a problem, both in the amount of time a patron must spend at the window and the chance of running out of specific coins for change.

An adding machine will be needed at the end

of each day, to total checks and cash, but need not be *bought* until you are well established and have a decent bank account. It will be needed only once a day for the length of time the box office is open, and can probably be borrowed from any business, or even from an office-supply store. The same is true of a typewriter. Mail orders and letters of inquiry must be answered the day they come in, if you are to garner and maintain good word of mouth. Handwritten letters are not a sign of efficiency.

Ticket racks should be easily transportable, if you have separate daytime and showtime box offices, and must hold the tickets snugly (but not so snugly as to give the box-office personnel trouble in removing them and putting them back). They should be designed and built in your shop, to match the floor plan of the theatre, with rows and sections clearly separated for easy finding and returning of tickets. If possible, the cubbyholes should slant down and into the rack, and should not be quite so long as a ticket, so that the tickets project over the edge for easy grasping. Tickets are prevented from falling out by the slope.

Many theatres print a separate seating chart for each performance and instruct the box-office workers to X out the seats as they are sold. This gives a quick picture of just what seats are left for sale, but so does a well-organized ticket rack, and the chart-X system is a nuisance when tickets are returned and their location restored to un-X'd "for-sale" condition. During a busy time, box-office workers are apt to forget to change the chart, and during the big push just before curtain the chart becomes useless, anyway, so I recommend against it, and urge instead that energies be spent in the design and teaching of the use of the rack.

The tickets themselves may be as plain or as fancy as you like, as long as they carry the necessary information: name of the producing theatre, name and address of the theatre where the play will be given, date of performance (usually the date digits themselves are the largest print on the ticket), time of curtain, price of ticket, and the seat and row numbers. (See Figure 19.) Anything else will probably clutter the ticket, but you may want to print such information as

"Anyone arriving after the curtain has gone up will not be seated until first intermission," or "This play not recommended for anyone under 12," or any specifics to do with this play, this location, or your organization.

Tickets may be ordered from a company specializing in the printing of theatre tickets. Send them your seating chart once, and they'll computerize it for future printings, running off tickets printed with your exact seat and row numbers quickly—for a price. Or any local printer with a rotating numbering device in his presses can also print location numbers, but for local printshops this is a fairly long process and will also cost you money. If your budget is tight, avoid either of these expensive processes and simply have the local printer set in type the words ROW and SEAT. Your house manager will find the best penman on his crew who will ink in the proper numbers from the seating chart onto all the tickets.

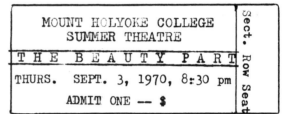

FIG. 19. A Single Ticket
The mock-up of an inexpensive ticket format to be given to the printer. Seat numbers and prices are added in ink by the House Manager's crew to the printed tickets. Different color tickets for different nights and different prices add little to the cost if the basic printed information remains the same.

Whichever method of inserting seat and row numbers you use, run at least one double-check by a different person, comparing every ticket against the chart to make sure no seats are left out and none are duplicated.

One other entry on the ticket is necessary—a method of recording how much that ticket was sold for (student prices, complimentary tickets, group rates, and season tickets will all bring in less money than the face value of the ticket and must so indicate). There are several ways of doing this, which will be shown under ticket sales procedure.

SEASON TICKETS

Before discussing single-ticket sales, types of *season* tickets must be known, as box-office procedures will differ with each.

Many large theatres are finding that the changing world is reflected in the change in attitude toward season tickets. Families who used to know precisely what they would be doing next March 25 don't even know what they'll be doing next Tuesday. And they're not as willing as before to commit a large amount of money to season tickets for plays they may not really want to see or may indeed not even be in town for. Your faithful membership will still buy season tickets, of course, but often only out of loyalty, as they may not use them all.

But season tickets must be sold, with a large well-run campaign, to give you a bank balance to start the season with, and to assure you of at least a token audience with which to begin each play's single-ticket sale. The common denominator of all types of season tickets is the money-saving they carry. How much of a discount you offer is up to you. Some are a straight 10 percent, whereas some offer "five plays for the price of four," and others round off the price so that the cost of the season book is an even dollar figure—anywhere from $5 to $20, depending on the cost of single tickets, number of plays offered, and so on.

Fixed Nights. The most common type of season ticket gives the buyer the same seat for the same relative night for each play (first Friday, second Saturday). He is in fact given all the tickets for all the plays at the time of season ticket purchase. If, as each show approaches, he finds he can't attend the night his tickets specify, he may exchange for another night, if tickets remain.

The strength of this type of ticket, as far as the theatre is concerned, is the presale of a certain number of seats for each night of each show, bringing in that money early and giving the box office fewer actual transactions show by show. The weakness, as stated, is the increasing desire of the ticket-buying public to be free of distant commitments, and possibly, therefore, to pass up a season ticket.

Coupon Tickets. A growing favorite is the coupon form of season tickets (see Figure 20), which allows the holder to see only those plays he wants to see, or is in town for. It's mainly a money-saving device for him, and another opportunity for the theatre to increase its mailing list and bank some money at the outset of the season. Each coupon is good for one admission for one play, as long as tickets remain when the ticket-holder calls. He then exchanges the coupon for actual tickets when he comes to the show.

A danger of coupon tickets lies in the very fact that they are usable at the whim of the holder, who may want to use many of them for the most popular show of the year, and avoid the quality but sometimes less attractive shows that need audiences. If too many coupons come in for the big musical, at the expense, say, of the classic, you are taking in very little money (and playing to few

people) on the show that needs it, and taking in very little immediate box-office money (and playing to full houses of coupon-givers) at the show that might ordinarily be filled with a cash-paying audience. This can be avoided by limiting the use of the coupons—either, as illustrated in Figure 21, by specifying that only two may be used per play, or, if your musical is indeed the biggest seller, by printing on all but two special coupons in the season book: THIS COUPON MAY *not* BE USED FOR THE MUSICAL and on the special coupons: THIS COUPON MAY BE USED FOR *any* PLAY OF THE SEASON INCLUDING THE MUSICAL. This will encourage attendance at the other plays and not pack your musical house with paper.

More Expensive Season Tickets. Additional money may be raised, and extra service (and tax deduction) given to those who will pay for it, by adding several more-expensive classes of season tickets. These have various names in various theatres; the Rochester Civic Theatre uses "Patron Ticket" and "Sustaining Memberships."

Patron tickets cost just a little more than straight season tickets—if the base price is $15, patron tickets might cost $25 and carry with them extra privileges, such as listing of the patrons' names in each program, granting earlier reservation privileges for each play, and the like.

Sustaining memberships might cost $100, and carry all benefits the patron ticket does, plus any extras you can provide, such as your telephoning the members to see when they would like to see each show.

Every dollar over the base price is tax-deductible for the purchasers of these extra-price season tickets. Use this tax benefit as a selling point, coupled with an appeal to "be a patron of the arts." Some theatres put the income from these special season tickets into a building fund.

OTHER FORMS OF TICKETS

Your box office may expect to receive: group rate tickets, comps (complimentary tickets), tickets sold through a large organization or through a restaurant, entertainment books, and student tickets; it will also be asked to handle house seats.

Group Rates. Group rates occasionally fall on your doorstep but generally have to be sought, taking a lot of time and effort. Generally, twenty-five or more tickets in the same price range for the same performance garner a discount—no smaller than 10 percent. This helps fill a large block of seats on one sale, even though at a discount, and brings people into the theatre with

mount holyoke college summer theatre

64

This PATRON TICKET COUPON is good for ONE ADMISSION to any one of the 7 Adult Plays or FOUR ADMISSIONS to any ONE PERFORMANCE of one of the 2 Children's Plays of the 1971 season whose titles and dates appear on the enclosed card.

YOU MAY USE AS MANY COUPONS AS YOU LIKE PER PLAY

PLEASE NOTE: This Coupon is NOT a ticket. You must phone or stop by to reserve tickets for each play, then exchange this Coupon for your ticket by curtain time. This Coupon does NOT guarantee you a seat if all seats have been reserved by the time you phone or stop by.

PLEASE RESERVE EARLY, SO WE MAY BETTER SERVE YOU.

mount holyoke college summer theatre

64

This PATRON TICKET COUPON is good for ONE ADMISSION to any one of the 7 Adult Plays or FOUR ADMISSIONS to any ONE PERFORMANCE of one of the 2 Children's Plays of the 1971 season whose titles and dates appear on the enclosed card.

YOU MAY USE AS MANY COUPONS AS YOU LIKE PER PLAY

PLEASE NOTE: This Coupon is NOT a ticket. You must phone or stop by to reserve tickets for each play, then exchange this Coupon for your ticket by curtain time. This Coupon does NOT guarantee you a seat if all seats have been reserved by the time you phone or stop by.

PLEASE RESERVE EARLY, SO WE MAY BETTER SERVE YOU.

mount holyoke college summer theatre

64

This PATRON TICKET COUPON is good for ONE ADMISSION to any one of the 7 Adult Plays or FOUR ADMISSIONS to any ONE PERFORMANCE of one of the 2 Children's Plays of the 1971 season whose titles and dates appear on the enclosed card.

YOU MAY USE AS MANY COUPONS AS YOU LIKE PER PLAY

PLEASE NOTE: This Coupon is NOT a ticket. You must phone or stop by to reserve tickets for each play, then exchange this Coupon for your ticket by curtain time. This Coupon does NOT guarantee you a seat if all seats have been reserved by the time you phone or stop by.

PLEASE RESERVE EARLY, SO WE MAY BETTER SERVE YOU.

mount holyoke college summer theatre

64

This PATRON TICKET COUPON is good for ONE ADMISSION to any one of the 7 Adult Plays or FOUR ADMISSIONS to any ONE PERFORMANCE of one of the 2 Children's Plays of the 1971 season whose titles and dates appear on the enclosed card.

YOU MAY USE AS MANY COUPONS AS YOU LIKE PER PLAY

PLEASE NOTE: This Coupon is NOT a ticket. You must phone or stop by to reserve tickets for each play, then exchange this Coupon for your ticket by curtain time. This Coupon does NOT guarantee you a seat if all seats have been reserved by the time you phone or stop by.

PLEASE RESERVE EARLY, SO WE MAY BETTER SERVE YOU.

mount holyoke college summer theatre

64

This PATRON TICKET COUPON is good for ONE ADMISSION to any one of the 7 Adult Plays or FOUR ADMISSIONS to any ONE PERFORMANCE of one of the 2 Children's Plays of the 1971 season whose titles and dates appear on the enclosed card.

YOU MAY USE AS MANY COUPONS AS YOU LIKE PER PLAY

PLEASE NOTE: This Coupon is NOT a ticket. You must phone or stop by to reserve tickets for each play, then exchange this Coupon for your ticket by curtain time. This Coupon does NOT guarantee you a seat if all seats have been reserved by the time you phone or stop by.

PLEASE RESERVE EARLY, SO WE MAY BETTER SERVE YOU.

mount holyoke college summer theatre

64

This PATRON TICKET COUPON is good for ONE ADMISSION to any one of the 7 Adult Plays or FOUR ADMISSIONS to any ONE PERFORMANCE of one of the 2 Children's Plays of the 1971 season whose titles and dates appear on the enclosed card.

YOU MAY USE AS MANY COUPONS AS YOU LIKE PER PLAY

PLEASE NOTE: This Coupon is NOT a ticket. You must phone or stop by to reserve tickets for each play, then exchange this Coupon for your ticket by curtain time. This Coupon does NOT guarantee you a seat if all seats have been reserved by the time you phone or stop by.

PLEASE RESERVE EARLY, SO WE MAY BETTER SERVE YOU.

mount holyoke college summer theatre

64

This PATRON TICKET COUPON is good for ONE ADMISSION to any one of the 7 Adult Plays or FOUR ADMISSIONS to any ONE PERFORMANCE of one of the 2 Children's Plays of the 1971 season whose titles and dates appear on the enclosed card.

YOU MAY USE AS MANY COUPONS AS YOU LIKE PER PLAY

PLEASE NOTE: This Coupon is NOT a ticket. You must phone or stop by to reserve tickets for each play, then exchange this Coupon for your ticket by curtain time. This Coupon does NOT guarantee you a seat if all seats have been reserved by the time you phone or stop by.

PLEASE RESERVE EARLY, SO WE MAY BETTER SERVE YOU.

FIG. 20. A Season Ticket Coupon Book

This seven-coupon book was issued for a seven-show season, with no restrictions on the use of the coupons. As long as they lasted, one coupon was good for exchanging for one actual ticket for a play. All seven could be used for the same play, or two or three for a show, or, as was actually intended, one coupon per play. Use a different color paper each season, so that old coupons are not exchanged in error.

their friends, when they might not have come the first time alone. Clubs, schools, and dinner parties are all possible here, as is the buying of a block by a major employer for a group of his employees. They must all be sold in an organized campaign, much like your season ticket campaign. The Chamber of Commerce can provide you with a listing of what conventions are coming to town over the next year, and how many conventioners may be expected. Write to the local arrangements chairman early, offering the group-rate discount on the show that will be playing during their meeting days, and ask if he wouldn't like to include fine community entertainment for

mount holyoke college summer theatre

This SEASON TICKET COUPON is good for ONE ADMISSION to any one of the 7 Adult Plays or FOUR ADMISSIONS to any ONE PERFORMANCE of one of the 2 Children's Plays of the 1971 season whose titles and dates appear on the enclosed card.

YOU MAY USE 1 or 2 COUPONS PER PLAY—NO MORE THAN 2

PLEASE NOTE: This Coupon is NOT a ticket. You must phone or stop by to reserve tickets for each play, then exchange this Coupon for your ticket by ½-hour before curtain. This Coupon does NOT guarantee you a seat if all seats have been reserved by the time you phone or stop by.

PLEASE RESERVE EARLY, SO WE MAY BETTER SERVE YOU.

mount holyoke college summer theatre

This SEASON TICKET COUPON is good for ONE ADMISSION to any one of the 7 Adult Plays or FOUR ADMISSIONS to any ONE PERFORMANCE of one of the 2 Children's Plays of the 1971 season whose titles and dates appear on the enclosed card.

YOU MAY USE 1 or 2 COUPONS PER PLAY—NO MORE THAN 2

PLEASE NOTE: This Coupon is NOT a ticket. You must phone or stop by to reserve tickets for each play, then exchange this Coupon for your ticket by ½-hour before curtain. This Coupon does NOT guarantee you a seat if all seats have been reserved by the time you phone or stop by.

PLEASE RESERVE EARLY, SO WE MAY BETTER SERVE YOU.

mount holyoke college summer theatre

This SEASON TICKET COUPON is good for ONE ADMISSION to any one of the 7 Adult Plays or FOUR ADMISSIONS to any ONE PERFORMANCE of one of the 2 Children's Plays of the 1971 season whose titles and dates appear on the enclosed card.

YOU MAY USE 1 or 2 COUPONS PER PLAY—NO MORE THAN 2

PLEASE NOTE: This Coupon is NOT a ticket. You must phone or stop by to reserve tickets for each play, then exchange this Coupon for your ticket by ½-hour before curtain. This Coupon does NOT guarantee you a seat if all seats have been reserved by the time you phone or stop by.

PLEASE RESERVE EARLY, SO WE MAY BETTER SERVE YOU.

mount holyoke college summer theatre

This SEASON TICKET COUPON is good for ONE ADMISSION to any one of the 7 Adult Plays or FOUR ADMISSIONS to any ONE PERFORMANCE of one of the 2 Children's Plays of the 1971 season whose titles and dates appear on the enclosed card.

YOU MAY USE 1 or 2 COUPONS PER PLAY—NO MORE THAN 2

PLEASE NOTE: This Coupon is NOT a ticket. You must phone or stop by to reserve tickets for each play, then exchange this Coupon for your ticket by ½-hour before curtain. This Coupon does NOT guarantee you a seat if all seats have been reserved by the time you phone or stop by.

PLEASE RESERVE EARLY, SO WE MAY BETTER SERVE YOU.

mount holyoke college summer theatre

This SEASON TICKET COUPON is good for ONE ADMISSION to any one of the 7 Adult Plays or FOUR ADMISSIONS to any ONE PERFORMANCE of one of the 2 Children's Plays of the 1971 season whose titles and dates appear on the enclosed card.

YOU MAY USE 1 or 2 COUPONS PER PLAY—NO MORE THAN 2

PLEASE NOTE: This Coupon is NOT a ticket. You must phone or stop by to reserve tickets for each play, then exchange this Coupon for your ticket by ½-hour before curtain. This Coupon does NOT guarantee you a seat if all seats have been reserved by the time you phone or stop by.

PLEASE RESERVE EARLY, SO WE MAY BETTER SERVE YOU.

mount holyoke college summer theatre

This SEASON TICKET COUPON is good for ONE ADMISSION to any one of the 7 Adult Plays or FOUR ADMISSIONS to any ONE PERFORMANCE of one of the 2 Children's Plays of the 1971 season whose titles and dates appear on the enclosed card.

YOU MAY USE 1 or 2 COUPONS PER PLAY—NO MORE THAN 2

PLEASE NOTE: This Coupon is NOT a ticket. You must phone or stop by to reserve tickets for each play, then exchange this Coupon for your ticket by ½-hour before curtain. This Coupon does NOT guarantee you a seat if all seats have been reserved by the time you phone or stop by.

PLEASE RESERVE EARLY, SO WE MAY BETTER SERVE YOU.

mount holyoke college summer theatre

This SEASON TICKET COUPON is good for ONE ADMISSION to any one of the 7 Adult Plays or FOUR ADMISSIONS to any ONE PERFORMANCE of one of the 2 Children's Plays of the 1971 season whose titles and dates appear on the enclosed card.

YOU MAY USE 1 or 2 COUPONS PER PLAY—NO MORE THAN 2

PLEASE NOTE: This Coupon is NOT a ticket. You must phone or stop by to reserve tickets for each play, then exchange this Coupon for your ticket by ½-hour before curtain. This Coupon does NOT guarantee you a seat if all seats have been reserved by the time you phone or stop by.

PLEASE RESERVE EARLY, SO WE MAY BETTER SERVE YOU.

FIG. 21. Season Ticket Coupons with Limited Use

To prevent a member from buying a book of coupons and saving them all for the biggest show of the season, limit their use as indicated here: no more than two coupons allowed to be exchanged per play. Include in the copy the year(s) of the season for which these coupons are valid, or they will be turning up for years to come. Note the continuing use of the logo.

his visitors. Be very sure not to offer the wrong show to the wrong group—ask yourself if this convention would really enjoy this show. If not, forget it. If so, sell.

Complimentary Tickets. We spoke of comps in the chapter on Publicity, but their use can go well beyond the media. Anyone who lends you any-thing substantial for the play should be offered comps, and it's a good idea to pass out a few to the Mayor (Principal, Dean) and anyone else whose presence will be a tacit seal of his approval, and whose continuing support of your operation can open many doors for you. Unless you have a large house to fill and seldom fill it, don't be capricious in handing out free tickets, or you will be knocking out too many income-producing seats. But, when possible, bring in on comps anyone who has helped you in a major way, or who might decide to help if he is courteously treated and appreciates this play.

Provide the box office with a neat and up-to-date list of those people eligible for comps (and have only one or two people—the director and the publicity chairman, probably—approve the list; if the entire company throws in names, the comp list will soon fill the house. If anyone else has suggestions, have them filter through the leaders named above) so they can quickly fill comp orders, with no delay or embarrassment to a friend of the theatre.

Complimentary tickets are generally referred to as "paper," and an auditorium largely filled with comps as a "papered house."

Organizational Tickets. Many large corporations gain and keep employees with fringe benefits ranging from underwriting moving expenses to sponsoring Christmas parties to paying part of the cost of tickets to sporting and cultural events. Here again—if you can get your theatre on their list—is money saved for the ticket buyers and possible new converts for you. Talk to any large employers in your community to see if they are willing and able to tie in with your theatre. If they are currently subsidizing only baseball and football games, give them your spiel on the importance of this theatre to community life.

Theatre and Dinner. Buying tickets along with dinner was discussed in Chapter V. Send your best-spoken board member to sell the restaurants on the mutual benefits of such a program. As they plan organization dinners or dinner parties for the future, have them suggest dinner plus theatre; and for their slow days and weeks, have them push heavily this "evening-on-the-town" package.

Entertainment Books. A fast-growing money-raising activity that also boosts community businesses is the selling of books of "twofers" by service clubs throughout the country. ("Twofer" is the standard theatre term meaning two for the price of one.) The sponsoring club assembles a book full of coupons solicited from beauty parlors, restaurants, movie theatres, bowling alleys, and the like and sells the book communitywide for a very low price. The purchaser may then patronize any or all of the organizations represented—they all center around a night out—and gain one free admission (or dinner, or hairwash-and-set, etc.) if he pays for one at full price. Two for the price of one. Of course, if your theatre is selling out nightly, avoid this plan. But if you can

stand more patrons and want to win future friends who will eventually pay a full price, participate in such a venture, specifying any limits you may have (not good on Friday or Saturday; good only for certain plays). Chalk up the free tickets to promotion, and bank the one paid admission, recognizing it as a ticket you probably would not have sold without the entertainment coupon book.

Student Tickets. If you intend building an audience for the future, you must begin with the students and children of today. If you don't have a children's theatre program, begin one. And certainly for the adult plays, offer special rates to all students. Cut off the availability of these tickets where you like, but I would suggest carrying it all the way through college. College students haven't a lot of money to spend, are theatre-knowledgeable, and will make up the majority of your audience and Board members in a very few years.

The price you set will depend on the basic ticket prices for adults. If your prices are already very low, you can't knock off too much, but make an effort. Our college theatre, virtually a self-supporting organization, charges $2 for adults and $1 for all students and children. Our summer theatre has base prices (on various nights) ranging from $2.50 through $3.50; students are $1 off any seat, any night. We haven't found this cut to be too little to do the students any good nor too great to hurt the budget; and we have masses of students at the summer plays, even though the local colleges are not in session. Whether you make them produce a student ID card or not is up to you. I tend to trust them.

House Seats. The director (producer) should pull from four to ten (depending on your seating capacity) of the best tickets from the racks before they ever go on sale, to keep on his desk as house seats. These will serve as a cushion, should one of your Sustaining Members try to reserve seats on a sold-out night, of if there is a mixup at the box office and an irate patron threatens unpleasant consequences. They are released only by the man who holds them, though the house manager —or anyone—may ask for first call on them for friends or family if they are not needed to give preferential treatment to a community VIP or to soothe unhappy nerves.

Generally house seats sell at their full face value, but they may be adjusted all the way down to comp status if the circumstances call for it. I have often pressed house tickets, free, into the hands of nasty, yelling patrons whose order was fouled up at the box office. For the few dollars you don't take in, you have made them happy and also built good public relations for the theatre. If not called for by emergency or company members, most house seats should be released for general sale several hours before showtime, avoiding a gap in the best sections where unsold house seats would stand empty.

BOX-OFFICE OPERATION

As with everything else under house management, the box office must *serve* the community. The personnel working in this area must be more intelligent, neater, and more courteous than most anyone else in the theatre, as they will meet and talk with the public more than anyone else. (Here's a perfect spot for your willing, intelligent auxiliary members.) Train them well, for unusual circumstances as well as the normal routine of filling ticket orders.

Give them each play's script well ahead of time, so they have an idea what the playwright is getting at. Possibly bring the staff to a dress rehearsal, so they can better describe the show to anyone in doubt. Give them office equipment that works, information that is accurate, and plenty of change.

Telephone Orders. The major part of your pre-show sale will most likely be by phone. Provide your staff with ticket envelopes printed with the data they *must* get from each phone order (see Figure 22):

NAME _____

NUMBER & TIX _____

DATE _____

PHONE _____

FIG. 22. A Ticket Envelope

A little larger than the tickets, these envelopes may be bought inexpensively from any stationery supply house. Your printer, equally inexpensively, can print the necessary information on the face of the envelope, or make a rubber stamp containing the same lettering (Name, etc.) so you can stamp your own over the years. Instruct your box-office workers to fill out EVERY BLANK on each envelope and to actually pull the tickets from the racks while the ticket buyers are still on the phone, to prevent any mixups and to forestall having to phone them back. The blanks marked NAME and PHONE are self-explanatory; DATE means the date of the performance for which the tickets are bought; NUMBER & TIX call for the number of tickets wanted and the price of those tickets.

There is no shame in asking a caller how to spell his last name, and it saves errors later; the same is true of jotting down his first name. Even the most unusual surname may crop up twice at the same show—and common last names are a real problem unless the first name accompanies them on the ticket envelopes. The phone number is for possible confirmation, and the date must also include the day of the week as a double check.

All the information put onto the envelope must be *printed* clearly, especially if another person is likely to be covering the box office when the tickets are picked up.

A good way to tie up the phone and prevent other callers from getting through is to ask the purchaser where he would like to sit. This will always lead to a five-minute discussion of the advantages of various sections, and memories of past shows and long moments of deliberation. Unless the caller is determined to discuss available seats, tell him he will be given the best seats available in the price range he has asked for, repeat to him *all the information you have written down,* and get off the phone quickly and politely. This repetition will correct errors before tickets are pulled and trouble is in the works. One further statement to the caller before hanging up is the time of performance and the time by when these tickets must be picked up. Make this pickup time no later than fifteen minutes before curtain, and if you are in a small community where distances are not great, have them picked up by 5 P.M., or the day before. That long line at the box office as the curtain is due to go up will get the show off to a rocky start night after night. And you probably will also be left with a stack of unclaimed, unpaid-for tickets, because someone was too thoughtless to call and cancel when he learned he wasn't coming. Say: "Tickets must be picked up by — o'clock *or they will be cancelled.*" Use the word "cancelled" every time, and no one can complain that he wasn't warned. Then, when cancellation time comes, go ahead and release those tickets as promised, and make them available to the waiting list or to the next ticket buyer who comes. Treat the audience with all deference, but ask that they respect your operation, too, and follow the simple rules of getting the tickets at such a time as not to hold curtain, or to call you and cancel in time to have them used by someone else. If only one box-office worker fails to use the word "cancelled" just once the whole system is dead, as that will be to the person who comes at showtime and yells when his seats aren't there.

Before you even hang up, the actual tickets must be pulled from the racks and in your hands. Then, after the call, put the tickets into the envelope and file it alphabetically in the little file box for that performance. Waiting any time at all to fill orders may result in giving the early caller worse seats than you promised, or doing him out of seats altogether, necessitating an embarrassing phone call by you.

Mail Orders. Encourage out-of-town patrons, especially, to write for tickets well in advance of box-office opening. (It works well for Broadway and for many community theatres as well.) This gives you a chance to fill a batch of orders in the quiet days before the box office officially opens, and to get a head start on filling the house. But demand of all mail orders: at least one alternate date when they could see the show; payment in full by check, money order, or season-ticket coupon; a stamped, self-addressed envelope in which you will send back the tickets or a note stating that his chosen performances have already sold out. This saves you stamps and stationery and prevents any error in addressing the envelope, possibly causing loss of tickets, or delay in the mails.

Then do fill them early, and send them out as soon as they're filled. Keep a mail-order notebook indicating who was sent what on what mailing date, for use when someone calls to say his tickets haven't arrived.

Mail orders arriving after the box office opens can also be filled during quiet times, but be sure they get priority, as they actually placed their orders ahead of any phone or in-person purchaser.

If a mail order comes in too close to the performance date, don't take a chance on sending out the tickets lest they arrive too late. Call the person, if he's not too far away, and advise him that his tickets will be held at the box office marked PAID, as you're afraid to mail them now. If he lives too far away to call economically, don't make the call; file them marked PAID, and he either will call you to check on them or will show up at curtain time expecting rightly that you have held them.

In-Person Ticket Buying. If someone takes the trouble to show up in person to buy tickets, give him priority over people phoning while he's there. Don't constantly interrupt your transaction with a patron right in front of you to fill orders for people who have merely picked up a phone. Ask the caller to hold the line for a minute, or, if your office is filled with people, ask him to please call back in five minutes.

Here, again, don't spend undue time pointing out the merits of one seat over another—give him the best you have and tell him, if he asks, that that's what you're giving him. Make correct change quickly, mark the tickets properly for the ticket report records (described later in this section), and as you hand him the tickets with the printing facing him, confirm the whole affair right there by saying: "Thank you, sir; these are your tickets for *My Fair Lady* for Tuesday, October 29. Curtain time is promptly at 8:30. The location of the theatre is marked on the tickets." He or you will catch any error in date right there.

If the buyer is not a season ticket-holder, ask if he wouldn't like to be on the mailing list for future productions and indicate the sign-up book. If he came once, he is likely to come again and should have a chance to be a season ticket-holder, or at least to receive your frequent newsletters on upcoming shows.

MAILING LIST

This mailing list must be maintained, if the theatre is to expand, and must be increased constantly. In addition to the sign-up book, you can find useful names on the rosters of the service clubs in town, the country club, lists borrowed from other arts organizations, the slate of the City Council, faculty lists of schools and colleges, Yellow Pages listings for lawyers and doctors (and any other likely prospects), and by two obvious but seldom-used methods your box-office people can implement during their spare time, if any.

At night, when totaling the checks that have come in, simply copy the name and address from each check onto the mailing list. Also, though this requires a little more work, go through the ticket boxes and, from a local telephone book, extract addresses to go with the names and phone numbers you have on the ticket envelopes and add them to the mailing list. Names and addresses of patrons sending mail orders should also be added.

If any of these people want to be removed from the mailing list, they will soon tell you; but most will be pleased to receive information about future shows. You're not selling judo courses by mail—you're promoting a civic cultural organization; they'll realize that, and probably come more often with mailing pieces reaching them at home.

We are more than ever now a mobile society, and your mailing list will reflect the American family's frequent moves as it gets more and more out-of-date. Bulk-rate mail is not forwarded if the addressee has moved; it is thrown out unless you print on all bulk mailing pieces: ADDRESS CORRECTION REQUESTED. It will cost you about a dime for each piece of undeliverable mail returned to you, but there's little point in wasting postage mailing after mailing on newsletters that are sent only to the post-office wastebasket. The new address will be written onto the returned piece; if they have simply moved across town, you can change the address on your mailing list and still reach them. If they've moved away from your community, strike them from the list.

KEEPING TICKET-SALE RECORDS

It is vital to your bookkeeping to know how much money you take in under each category of income, and the overwhelming bulk of that income will be from ticket sales. So, each box-office worker must clearly mark on each ticket how much it went for. Then, after each performance, as the ticket takers are counting their stubs, they'll make a separate stack for each price category and enter on their daily reports how many admissions were by season ticket, how many by straight price, and so on. This gives your bookkeeper a basic figure to begin with, and your publicity people another indication of where heavy publicity is needed. If the basic sale price of the ticket is printed right on the ticket, that's one step forward. Then, if nothing further is printed on the ticket by the box office, that ticket represents a cash transaction at full face value.

But there must also be a way to mark the tickets as comps, group sales, student rate, etc. The most common way of indicating these other prices is by means of rubber stamps. Order LARGE stamps reading COMPLIMENTARY, STUDENT, etc. for each of the categories other than straight cash. Then, as the ticket is paid for (*not* when it's reserved by phone, as these tickets may be released and re-reserved three times or never picked up at all), simply stamp on the back of each how it was paid for. These stamps should be large enough so that the lettering covers most of the surface of the ticket; thus, when the stubs are counted, enough of the lettering remains to immediately identify its source, whichever end of the ticket the ticket taker has retained.

Another, newer method is to circle with a pen appropriate small code letters at one end of each ticket: S for season; ST for student, and so on. The ticket taker must then be very sure he keeps the proper end of each ticket; this may be assured by printing the seat numbers at one end and the code letters at the other, so that the patron receives the operative half to find his seats, and the theatre the other half to account for the evening's attendance.

The trouble with both these methods is that they are not totally accurate since they reflect only the accounting of those buyers who actually *come* to the performance. There is always a small percentage who take their tickets and then never show up, leaving the bookkeeper with an inbalance each night. This may be corrected by one small additional step to the second method described above.

Onto the code-number end of the ticket, have the printer leave a small stub, separated by dotted lines from the basic ticket. (See Figure 23.) Repeat on that stub the date of the performance and the code letters, exactly opposite where they appear on the ticket itself. The box-office worker then, instead of circling just the single code letter on the ticket, makes a larger circle to include both the letter on the ticket and the same letter on the adjacent stub. She then tears off the stub and drops it into a box marked with that performance's date, giving the bookkeeper a clear record not only of what sort of paid attendance actually paid and attended, but, more to his point, what sort of payment was received, attend or not.

The only problems with this method arise when someone exchanges tickets; appropriate stubs must be found in the box and clipped to the

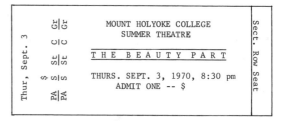

FIG. 23. A Ticket with Auditor's Stub
The printer can make the dotted line on the left side of the ticket deep enough to make the stub simple to tear off by the box office at the time of sale, after one set of letters has been marked. One quick circle of a pen will include the letters on both sides of the dotted line, indicating what payment was made for this ticket:

    PA indicates Paid Admission, or the full face value of the ticket as shown above the letters.
    S indicates a Season Ticket coupon was exchanged for this ticket.
    St indicates Student Rate.
    C means Complimentary, or no money given.
    Gr is the catch-all category for any form of Group Rate; specifics may be spelled out on the back, or by changing the dollar value above.

At the end of the day, a separation and count of these auditor's stubs will help the box office fill out the Daily Box-Office Cash Report (Figure 24) and each night of the show they will help fill out the Ticket Report (Figure 25).

base tickets (though, since the stubs don't include seat numbers, any stub of that date and that marking will do).

WAITING LISTS

The happiest time for the theatre—but one of the most hectic for the box office—follows a total sellout of a night or of a show. A great deal of time is taken explaining that there are no seats available, placating angry members, making a waiting list, and then contacting that waiting list to dispose of returned tickets. Make a separate waiting list for each performance that is sold out, and enter legibly onto it the name and phone number and the number of tickets needed for the person to be contacted.

Do not call someone who wants four seats if you have only one returned; go down the list and call the first person who has indicated he wants one. Don't leave messages if you can't reach the person on the list; you'll wait for him to return your call, and you'll hold those seats forever. Don't even leave the theatre's name—just say "Thank you" and hang up and go on to the next name. When the next set of tickets is returned, recall that first person and see if you can reach him then.

If you make a sale to someone on the waiting list, conduct the procedure just as if it were a straight ticket sale—ticket envelope information, time for cancellation, etc. And be sure to strike his name from the list, so he isn't called again.

At the time you add each name to the waiting list, advise the caller that, even though no tickets may be returned this afternoon, you often have last-minute cancellations or no-shows fifteen minutes before showtime; invite him to come to the theatre at that time and take a chance. You will find you can satisfy upwards of a dozen people a night.

Keep the waiting list current right up to showtime, but don't bother calling anyone after about 7 P.M. (for an 8:30 curtain), as they will never be able to make arrangements in time to make curtain. Keep any tickets that come back after that to sell at the door.

When people arrive in the evening without tickets for a sold-out show, add them to the *bottom* of the waiting list. Then, as tickets are returned, or you cancel those not picked up, start calling names through the lobby—starting at the top of the afternoon's waiting list. Chances are that not many of them will be there, but you owe it to them to call their names each time tickets

are released, and keep calling down the list until you reach those who *are* there. Then sell them as you would any straight tickets.

CONFIRMING RESERVATIONS

You can avoid a large percentage of no-shows by calling everyone who has reserved tickets the day before his performance to make sure that he is coming, and that he knows his tickets will be canceled at X o'clock. The most efficient method is a flat and courteous statement: "This is the —— Community Theatre. I'd like to confirm your order for four tickets at $4 for tomorrow night's performance of *The Lion in Winter*. Do you still intend to use them? All right, please remember that they must be picked up by 8:15 tomorrow night, or we will have to cancel them."

Surprisingly, you will find that about 10 percent of your calls will result in some such answer as "Oh, I'm so sorry; we'll need only three." Or, "I'm so glad you called; we won't be able to come." You will have saved yourself a lot of last-minute waiting-list trouble and released better seats earlier. It's time-consuming, and might better be done by an extra box-office person on a phone other than the box-office open line, so as not to tie up personnel and telephone with the show getting close.

And it is another thoughtful service rendered your patrons.

CLOSING THE BOX OFFICE

When the curtain goes up on performance nights, and at the end of each nonperformance ticket-selling day, the box office must—if you are not to perish—make an accounting of what transactions (involving actual exchange of tickets for coupon, cash, or check, or from the complimentary list) took place that day. (See Figure 24.)

With a number of volunteers relieving one another constantly, it's a miracle if these reports balance every day, but you must try, and emphasize the need for accuracy to your whole crew.

The person who opens the box office enters immediately the amount of *cash on hand* he is given. The rest of the report is filled out by the person who closes up, probably working with the house manager.

The first part of the closing report is simple—total all the checks (by adding machine, clipping the adding machine tape to the bundle of checks) and enter that figure; then count each denomina-

DAILY BOX OFFICE CASH REPORT

DATE _____

I. On hand at close of Box-Office day:

    A. CHECKS (Total): $_____

    B. CURRENCY:

        $20s $_____

        $10s $_____

        $5s $_____

        $1s $_____

                       Total Currency $_____

    C. COINS:

        Halves $_____

        Quarters $_____

        Dimes $_____

        Nickels $_____

        Pennies $_____

                    Total Coins $_____

    D. TOTAL OF A, B, C: $_____

    E. CASH ON HAND AT OPENING
        OF BOX OFFICE TODAY: $_____

Subtracting E from D:
    F. TODAY'S SALES: $_____

DAILY BOX OFFICE CASH REPORT

II. Breakdown of today's sales:

    1. _____ Paid Tickets
       (How many?)   @$3.00 = $_____

    2. _____ Paid Tickets
                      @ $2.00 = $_____

    3. _____ Season Coupons
                      exchanged for
                      $3.00 Tickets = $_____00.00

4. _____ Season Coupons
exchanged for
$2.00 Tickets = $_____00.00_____

5. _____ Student Tickets @
$1.00 = $_____

6. _____ Group Rate Tickets
@ $2.70 = $_____

7. _____ Complimentary
Tickets = $_____00.00_____

8. _____ Entertainment
Package Coupons
exchanged (1
coupon + $3.00
= 2 Tickets) = $_____

9. _____ Dinner Theatre
vouchers
exchanged = $_____00.00_____   (Check
from res-
taurant
will go
directly to
Business
Mgr. at
end of
run.)

10. TOTAL OF 1 thru 9 = Today's
Gross Sales — $_____

MINUS:

11. _____ tickets (@ $_____)
(How many?)   returned for cash
refund = $_____

Subtracting #11 from #10:

12. TODAY'S NET SALES = $_____

#12 should equal F on page 1.
If it doesn't, please write on the back of this page a note of explanation or speculation
as to why you feel you have an overage or a deficit.

III. Today's Season Ticket Sales:

_____ Season Tickets @ $15 = $_____.

Season Ticket Income should be kept separate from regular Box Office Income, in spe-
cially marked cash box, and given to Business Manager in separate, specially-marked
envelope.

FIG. 24. Daily Box-Office Cash Report
To be filled out and given the Business Manager each night, with all the day's receipts.

tion of currency separately and enter these totals, and the grand total, including checks. Deduct the *cash on hand* the day started with, and you should have the day's income. Some or all of this money may have to be deposited by the house manager in a bank's night-deposit drop, or locked in the theatre safe, rather than in the vulnerable box-office cash drawer.

The second part of the report will take more figuring, and will tell you not only how you are doing financially, but how accurate your box office really is. Using your stub count—if you use that extra stub; otherwise, by your own method—determine the number of tickets sold (or given away). Enter the totals on their proper lines, do the necessary multiplication and addition, and line F should equal line 13. If they don't mesh, check your figures, and if you're still in trouble, state at the bottom of the page the overage or shortage, and any opinions you have as to why this has happened.

On show nights a PERFORMANCE TICKET REPORT must be made in addition to the eternal CASH REPORT. (See Figure 25.) This report is derived from the stubs counted by the ticket takers and gives the best possible statement of how much money should be attributed to tonight's performance (though, as stated, the no-shows will throw it off a bit). As counting stubs can be tedious, allowing errors to creep in, it is wise to have two separate people count the stubs, checking their totals with each other upon completion.

A PRODUCTION TICKET REPORT and PRODUCTION CASH REPORT must be made at the end of the run, probably by the bookkeeper and the house manager, combining the nightly reports into one overall show report of CASH SALES and TICKETS ACTUALLY USED. (These are not pictured here, as they are merely show-long versions of daily forms.) Such overall reports can help weed out small errors and give a clear picture of how the publicity is working and how well the box office is functioning.

DRESSING THE HOUSE

Into this world of commerce, let me make one artistic comment.

For the best reception of the play by the audience at large, the box office must know how to dress the house. (See Figure 26.) I use the word artistic purposely, because house dressing must be done with control and an eye to making a better performance. Unless a ticket buyer adamantly wants to sit in the first row, or off in a

corner, the box office must sell tickets that will balance the house, making the spectators a tightly-knit, unified, responding group, not scattered souls who react only individually and never become that single reacting mass, an audience.

Begin selling seats in the center of the center of the auditorium, gradually adding seats a row ahead of center, then a row behind center; then adding seats left and right of center, then ahead, then behind, then left again, always keeping a modified diamond formation, with the core at house center, and extended points of patrons front and back and left and right.

Allowing no empty seats to separate people ties everyone into the whole, erasing any nervousness and encouraging spontaneous laughter or applause, and making them feel part of something. Avoiding the long straight equal rows of filled seats allows a laugh to build and to grow through the spectators, who, not feeling like students lined up in a classroom, can respond freely.

Practically, too, these are the best seats in the house, sold to the first buyers, with the least good far-front, far-back, and far-side seats sold to the latecomers.

It's an important art, and not easy to fall into. Instruct your box office carefully.

B. USHERS AND TICKET TAKERS

Now in possession of his ticket for the play, the patron passes into the theatre proper and into the hands of the ticket taker and the ushers who have reported to the house manager for duty about an hour and a quarter before curtain time to receive their assignments for the evening and double-check the entire front-of-house for cleanliness and safety.

The ticket taker's job would seem to be described in its title—just taking the tickets as handed to him. And it can be that simple, especially in a theatre with no reserved seats, in which the only checking he must do is for the proper date on the ticket. But he must also be familiar with emergency procedures, times of intermission and ringdown (end of play), location of phones, rest rooms and concession stand, and must part with this information willingly and courteously.

In a way, the ticket taker is the audience's host, standing at the door of the inner lobby, or somewhere between the box office and the actual entrance to the auditorium, with a smile and a "Good evening" for everyone who comes to the theatre. A perfunctory or sour moment here may

TICKET REPORT

DAY _____ DATE _____ (MATINEE) (EVENING).   PRODUCTION _____

SOLD FOR THIS PERFORMANCE (Based on Box-Office Count of Audit Stubs):				ACTUALLY USED AT THIS PERFORMANCE (Based on House Management Count of Ticket Taker Stubs):		
Type of Ticket	Number of Tickets	Rate	Total	Type of Ticket	Number of Tickets	Rate
Single		$3.00	$	Single		$3.00
Single		2.00	$	Single		2.00
Season Coupons exchanged		3.00	$00.00	Season Coupon		3.00
Season Coupons exchanged		2.00	$00.00	Season Coupon		2.00
Student		1.00	$	Student		1.00
Group Rate		2.70	$	Group Rate		2.70
Complimentary		0.00	$00.00	Complimentary		0.00
Entertainment Package		3.00 for 2	$	Entertainment Package		3.00 for 2
Dinner Theatre vouchers		$	$	Dinner Theatre vouchers		$
TOTALS (A)	_____		$_____	TOTAL (B)	_____	

Unsold for this performance:				Number of Tickets sold for this performance (from A):		
Single		$3.00		Deadwood (Subtract B from A)		
Single		2.00				
TOTAL (C)	_____					

Total of entire column should equal the number of seats in the house.

FIG. 25. Ticket Report, Filled Out by Both Box Office and House Manager for Each Performance
The show-long total of these reports should equal the show-long total of daily Box-Office Cash Reports, or a careful check of box-office procedure is in order. If there is too much Deadwood (tickets bought but not used for the show) night by night, your house cannot be properly dressed. If patrons are buying tickets as simple donations, never intending to use them, try to encourage them to just make a donation, in any amount, without leaving empty seats on possible sold-out nights, and throwing off-kilter your dressing of the house.

BOX OFFICE RULES—LAB THEATRE   **DRESSING A HOUSE:**

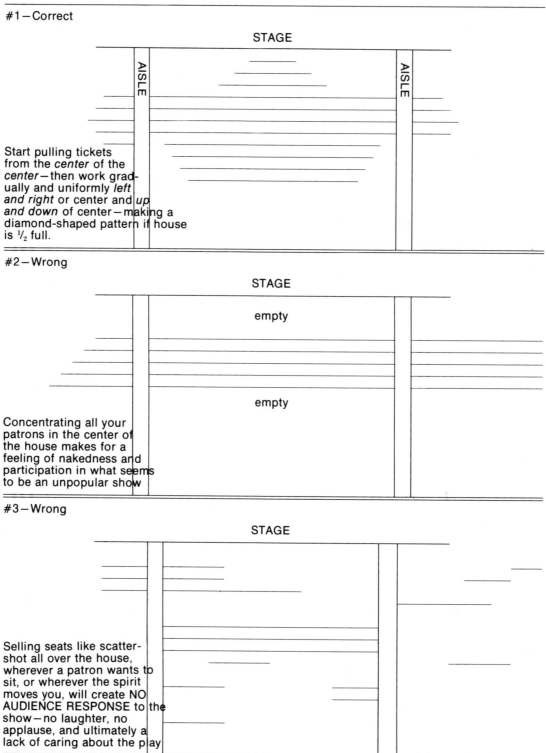

#1—Correct

STAGE

AISLE   AISLE

Start pulling tickets
from the *center* of the
center—then work grad-
ually and uniformly *left
and right* or center and *up
and down* of center—making a
diamond-shaped pattern if house
is ½ full.

#2—Wrong

STAGE

empty

empty

Concentrating all your
patrons in the center of
the house makes for a
feeling of nakedness and
participation in what seems
to be an unpopular show

#3—Wrong

STAGE

Selling seats like scatter-
shot all over the house,
wherever a patron wants to
sit, or wherever the spirit
moves you, will create NO
AUDIENCE RESPONSE to the
show—no laughter, no
applause, and ultimately a
lack of caring about the play

FIG. 26. Dressing the House
This chart should be posted in your box office if you have reserved seats, or given to each usher if they in fact determine the seating arrangements of a nonreserved house by leading ticket holders to seats. A badly dressed house can damage a good production and totally kill an iffy one.

cloud the whole first act, whereas a sincere welcome will start things off well.

If your seats are nonreserved, the ticket taker need not tear the tickets, but just collect them intact from each patron. If they are reserved, he has a more complicated job, sending each person to the closest auditorium door to his seat location.

A simple chart fastened to the top of his ticket box should show the relative position of all seats to all doors, helping him to determine immediately where to send the ticketholders, until he can memorize the routes. Or, most theatres are set up regularly enough to allow a short written outline, which is provided the ticket taker to key all doors to all seats; e.g.:

ROWS A-through-M:

Seat numbers 1–10 _ _ _ _ _ Door 1
Seat numbers 11–20 _ _ _ _ Door 2

_ _ _ _ _ _ _ _ _ _ _ _ _ _ _ _ _ _ _

ROWS N-through-W:

Seat numbers 1–13 _ _ _ _ _ Door 1
Seat numbers 14–26 _ _ _ _ Door 2

With reserved seats, the ticket taker will tear the tickets, giving the patron the half with the seat numbers and holding for record-keeping the other half, which shows what price was paid for the ticket. (See A. Box Office).

As soon as the play begins, the ticket taker gathers all the ticket stubs from his box, sorts them into stacks by price paid, and tallies the numbers in each stack, asking the house manager to double-check his count.

He should stay on duty in the lobby by the doors to the auditorium throughout the performance, or until relieved, to greet latecomers and get them into the theatre quietly, to handle troublesome visitors, to check the lobby for cleanliness before the first intermission, and generally to be a responsible representative of the theatre, on duty at the gates. This guardlike job during performance may be performed by the house manager himself or by a box-office person, but it's ordinarily the post of the ticket taker, unless he is a one-night volunteer really here to see the show free in exchange for an hour's work beforehand. In that case, of course, send him into the auditorium as soon as the play begins and put the lobby under the charge of a permanent house crew member.

Theatregoers will frequently show up with tickets for the wrong night. The ticket taker does not try to straighten out the error, but sends the patrons directly and politely to the box office, hoping they have house seats or unsold seats they can provide. A fast-moving flow of ticketholders through his wicket is the goal of the ticket taker. Quick, smiling answers to any inquiries, keeping the line moving; immediate admission of the fact that he doesn't know the answer to something and sending the questioner to whoever does; speedy solution to problems that may arise; quick dispatch of all patrons to proper auditorium doors; in every way a desire to keep the ticketholders from standing forever in the queue— these are the ticket taker's aims.

Once inside the auditorium, the ushers take over the comfort and well-being of the audience. Well-supplied with programs and a flashlight, each usher is neatly dressed (including a smile) and has studied the sections she serves so that she can quickly seat each ticketholder in the proper seat, if seats are reserved.

Taking the reserved seat ticket stub, she moves immediately down the aisle, saying: "Follow me, please," and stops at the row indicated; directions to the seats within that row must be clearly given, for here is where so many mixups occur. Even if the seats bear metal numbers, it's not enough to say "Seats 24 and 25." Be more specific: "Seats 24 and 25; those are the eighth and ninth seats in this row." Or: "The last two empty seats."

She then returns the stubs to the last person entering the row, along with one program for each one in the party. And then back to the head of the aisle to greet new arrivals. Once the play begins, this routine must be accomplished in the semidarkness with as little fuss as possible. Shining the flashlight right onto the tickets, keeping it away from anyone's eyes and always shielding the light from the stage with her body, the usher whispers her directions to the latecomers and seats them with minimal bother to those who came on time.

Many theatres have a rule that latecomers must stay in the back of the theatre until first intermission. If you can do this, fine; it trains audiences to respect the actors by coming on time. But it is another responsibility for the usher, as most patrons become more offensive when they know they are at fault, and their guilt at being late manifests itself in a pompous demand for immediate seating. Stick to your rules, and seat them in empty seats in the back if there are any, but don't disturb the thoughtful early-arriving patrons already engrossed in your show. And *under no circumstances* ask people to move to different seats once the play has begun. If someone is in the wrong seat, whether through his fault or the usher's, you cannot ruin the show and the attention of those in the vicinity by trying to effect a neat substitution after the curtain is up. Let them stay where they are, and place the newcomers somewhere until intermission; then immediately set things right when the lights come up. If the proper (but late) seatholder demands his seats, explain as nicely as you can that you can't move people now; if he persists, offer him his money back and get rid of him. You don't need those extra dollars badly enough to destroy the whole reason for the evening—the play.

In a theatre with no reserved seats, ushers should know the techniques of dressing the house and not let a small audience scatter itself all over a large house, never unifying itself and thus enjoying the play less (and causing the actors to work uphill with never the give-and-take they find with a well-dressed house). If someone demands to sit off in the corner, let him, but point out the better sight lines in the center, and try to avoid any empty seats between patrons. Tell them where the cloakroom is, if they have commandeered a seat for their coats. Seat people at all times adjacent to other people, not empty air. Empty air cannot create group (or audience) responses, especially to a comedy. If the box office has advised that the house will be full, keep an eye out for single empty seats, and try to put single patrons into them as soon as they arrive, and not find yourself at curtain with thirty-six single seats empty and eighteen couples at the door. Curtain will be delayed, split parties will be unhappy, and the show will suffer.

As soon as house lights go to half, ushers should move immediately to the auditorium doors and shut them, to cut off the possibility of lobby lights ruining opening light cues on stage. It will also be a sign to latecomers that the play has begun, to quiet them as they enter. As the play begins, the ushers settle at assigned posts from which they will watch the play, and watch for trouble in the house. Smoking, picture-taking, and running children must be stopped; illness and drunkenness must be handled; late arrivals must be met immediately; patrons leaving to find the phone or rest room must be helped courteously but quietly.

At intermission, ushers throw open lobby doors as soon as house lights start up (but *not before*); they then stay on duty at new posts, watching for smoking, gatecrashers, soft drinks being brought into the house, and so on. As the intermission ends, they follow the same routine as at the beginning of the play.

After the play (and the curtain calls) are over, ushers again open the doors and stand by to be of help and to see that everyone does in fact leave the auditorium. The ushers should then go through each row, looking for lost objects (which they turn in to the box office) and picking up large, clean trash, such as programs, to give the auditorium a semblance of neatness as you close up for the night.

Ushers, too, must know locations of all the features of the building and be ready to answer questions by the public; they should know about actors in the aisle and keep the way clear for stage business, these days ever more and more spilling out into the house. They should be instructed in fire escape measures, and whom to call for each possible emergency (usually, the house manager).

Many theatres use the same team of ushers every night, gaining the efficiency of a well-experienced crew. But this is hard to maintain, as the ushers do not feel the same dedication to showing up every night that the cast and crew do. But if you can manage it, it's a plus.

Otherwise, recruit ushers on the basis of their seeing the show free in exchange for their ushering duties. But make it clear to one-time volunteers that, even if the show is holding their attention magnificently, they must keep one eye out for trouble and for patrons in need of assistance, and jump to it. If you do bring in a different crew each night, allow plenty of time before the house opens for instructions and answering questions. (The house usually opens a half hour before the play begins.) In no case, however, should the house manager or any usher allow even one audience member into the auditorium until the stage manager has given his OK, meaning that all light cues have been checked, the sound system works, any onstage warmups or rehearsals have been completed, and the grand curtain (if there is one on this play) has been closed.

After you have run out of wives, daughters, and such for ushering, a marvelous source is the local student-nurse dormitory. These busy, not-too-wealthy girls are used to working with people, know at least rudimentary first aid, and enjoy an evening away from the dorm. Most such schools have entertainment directors who will be glad to work with you on every show in exchange for a pair of comps, and will do some of your training for you. This recruiter of ushers should be advised by the house manager of the nature of dress requested of the ushers. Heels and hose? Sweater and skirt? Blue jeans and bare feet? The director and the costume designer should make known to the house manager several weeks before opening what they would like to see on the ushers to help further unify the entire evening into one line, color, fabric, and style.

Ushers and ticket takers too often feel left out of the show and unappreciated in the face of all the excitement and artistry around them. A good house manager will check with his staff throughout the evening to be sure they aren't beset with problems, and at the end of the show will personally thank them all for their help. He may even arrange transportation home for them and see them to the cars with a thank you and a good night. They will be likely to come back, bringing to your next show training and experience of more value than a whole staff of new girls.

Treat your front-of-house staff well—they may be your chief contact with the greatest part of your audience.

C. CLOAKROOM AND REFRESHMENT STAND

Further service by the house manager and his staff is provided in the lobby area by the coat-check facility and a stand providing refreshments.

Cloakroom

A member of the audience hemmed in by a heavy coat, a hat in his lap, snowy boots on or at his feet, and an important package wedged under his seat isn't going to give much attention to even the finest show. Provide a safe, convenient place to check these items, and devise a fast, foolproof method of returning them when the performance is over—or even during the performance, should someone need glasses, tickets, or other necessaries left in a pocket—and you will be helping to assure audience involvement in the dramatic event.

If the house manager or an attendant can absolutely guarantee to be on duty within sight of the cloakroom throughout the performance and all intermissions, there is no need to wall it off and lock it. But chances are this can't be guaranteed, and the possibility exists for someone to walk in from the street or auditorium and walk out with an expensive coat or parcel. So a small room or lockable grill must be provided for the safekeeping of all items under your charge. Even so, a prominent sign: NOT RESPONSIBLE FOR THEFT OR DAMAGE, is a good idea and will protect you from real or imagined loss.

The size of the coat-check area is determined by the simple equation—number of seats in the auditorium equals number of coat hooks or hangers in the cloakroom. In the winter, sold-out nights will result in a full cloakroom, but the rest of the time the hooks will remain largely empty. In the case of a rainstorm, however, even in midsummer, everyone attending must have the opportunity to be relieved of all impediments.

You may design your cloakroom attractively or for utility, but the simplest setup consists merely of a hanging bar, or a series of bars, with a plain board shelf overhead, looking very much like an overlarge clothes closet. Sturdy wooden hangers on the bar hold coats; hats, packages, and such are placed on the shelf. For identification, neatly number each hanger, beginning with #1 and going up through the number of seats in the house. Hang them in sequence on the bar, leaving ample space between hangers to accommodate a bulky coat on each with no cramming or wrinkling. At a stationery store, buy a supply of cardboard disks about 1 1/2" in diameter, each prepunched with a single hole, and number two complete sets. Slip onto the hook of each hanger the two disks bearing the same number as the parent hanger.

One disk will be given to the patron leaving checked items; the second disk is inserted into a hat band, onto an umbrella prong, or under the ties of a package as it is put on the shelf directly above its same-numbered hanger, or, as with boots, set on the floor beneath. So the disk carried away by the patron identifies his numbered hanger and any extras stored nearby and bearing the same check number.

The best and fastest procedure for checking coats is based on the checkroom attendant's saving the patron time by laying several empty hangers on the counter before anyone arrives. As a person approaches with a coat, the attendant whips one disk off a hanger and holds it out with one hand as he receives the coat with the other. The patron has spent one second at your counter and is able to proceed directly to the play, preventing the forming of a long, tedious line. The checkroom attendant then immediately hangs the coat on the hanger as he is walking quickly to the proper space at the hanging bar; he snaps the hanger into place and returns to the counter with the next numbered hanger, removing the disk and holding it out as he approaches the next patron.

If two people approach the counter at the same time, *each* is handed a disk, the coats go quickly onto the properly numbered hangers and are carried to the bar at the same time. Hats or packages add a little time to the procedure, but not much.

If your theatre capacity, or tonight's advance sale, is fairly large, staff the cloakroom with *two* workers, to keep the service swift and efficient.

One attendant starts filling the coat bars from the left, the other from the extreme right, to give each a separate traffic pattern to and from the racks, avoiding collisions or the wrong hanging of a coat.

After the show, be sure the same staff is in the cloakroom for returning coats. Each attendant takes disks from two patrons at a time and actually *runs* to the racks to retrieve coats and back to the counter to deliver the proper articles to the proper people. As a disk is slipped back onto a now-empty hanger, he checks to be sure the second disk is already there; if not, an extra item exists and should be sought on the shelf or the floor before returning to the counter.

If your theatre encourages the audience to come backstage after the performance—and I hope it does—someone must stay on duty at the cloakroom until all audience belongings have been claimed. If it gets late and the attendants want to close up and go home, they may carry the leftovers backstage on the numbered hangers and find the owners. A lovely evening can be ruined for a patron if its last moments are spent stumbling through a dark cloakroom trying to find a coat. Be thoughtful, even if the audience isn't always.

You cannot make a lot of money with a checkroom, but some theatres make upwards of $500 a season, depending on the length and number of plays and the severity of the weather. Try it. You may charge a fixed amount for each item checked (price prominently displayed at the counter) or place an attractive dish within easy reach of each patron, salted with a quarter before the end of the show to encourage tips for service.

If this seems too commercial, make it a free service, but be sure it's *known* to be free by a tasteful sign. Those afraid it will cost something may otherwise needlessly encumber themselves with coats in their seats. Or you are liable to find yourself with a handful of embarrassing quarters when closing up.

Something is to be said for both approaches. I lean toward the idea that people are accustomed to paying for service, and a quarter is a small cost. And $500 per season is nothing to ignore.

Additional community reciprocity might be achieved by allowing a different nonprofit organization, such as a high-school fraternity, to run your cloakroom each play, taking the responsibility of handling it well and keeping all tips for their treasury. The cloakroom staff would be invited to see the show free, of course, and might develop the habit of coming to the theatre, to see a show or to try out, even when not on duty.

Refreshment Stand

Money *can* be made, and another service provided, through the sale of refreshments before the show and/or during intermission. The variety and type of refreshment and the profit possible will depend on your audience. Research it; put questionnaires in programs, ask frequent patrons, and determine what will sell and how much it can sell for.

Movie theatres sometimes equal or exceed box-office income with refreshment-stand income; you can't and probably won't want to attempt that kind of merchandising feat, which often makes money at the expense of the show. But it's nice to enjoy a before-theatre soft drink or cup of coffee, and intermissions are more pleasant for some people with drinks in their hands.

So plan a refreshment stand. But organize it well.

Because you may have different ushers or house personnel staffing the refreshment stand each night or each production, make the setup and the prices easy to learn and to remember. Too many items, each with a different price, will slow down the line as a patron tries to decide what to buy and the attendant tries to remember the price of the item. Keep it simple. If it's soft drinks, decide on one brand, and don't complicate the transactions by offering diet soft drinks alongside nondiet and then a few grape drinks and orange drinks for those that might want them. One type, period. If it's coffee, provide a nearby table with cream and sugar, and sell nothing but black to expedite sales. If you choose to offer candy or other edibles, again, be selective in the styles offered—one type only.

To further speed things, hang a price list from the ceiling or on the wall high over the table, so that the buyer isn't suddenly confronted with the selection as he reaches the head of the line and only then begins the process of choice.

Provide the attendants with ample change of a type they will be likely to need. If all items for sale are a quarter, they don't need lots of nickels and dimes, for instance; but if you have 10¢ or 15¢ refreshments, give them plenty of nickels, dimes, *and* quarters. Also about $10 in one-dollar bills for easy change when a big spender offers a ten-dollar bill for a 10¢ drink.

If you are renting an auditorium for the show, be very sure that you are allowed to bring in such a concession stand. Perhaps the nonprofit status of the building you are using will be violated by the sale of merchandise other than an amateur play; perhaps they don't want sticky cups or wrappers on their ledges and stairwells. Before you implement a decision to offer refreshments, check with the host and find out the law and the feelings of the home organization. As always, be a good guest.

Whether it is your theatre or a rented hall, you probably don't want food in the auditorium itself. Apart from the mess for the janitor, there are likely to be more messes as a patron spills a cola on the expensive coat in the row ahead; or a dropped chocolate bar becomes a slippery hazard capable of landing an elderly person in the aisle. At the refreshment stand, post a clear and unmistakable sign: No FOOD OR DRINK ALLOWED IN THE AUDITORIUM, and alert your ushers to watch for smuggled goodies, as well as smoking and cameras.

If your town, your code, and your host permit, you might want to consider alcoholic refreshments. I must say, however, that I'm against it from every standpoint, as it adds a cocktail-party atmosphere to what I hope is a serious piece of work. Even (or especially) an easygoing comedy requires solid rapport between stage and house for proper setup and delivery of laugh lines, and the gay, squishy, nonunified response to the third act of a comedy from an audience with several intermissions' worth of booze is impossible to gauge and to play against with any degree of control. And the intermissions are likely to get out of hand, too, especially if the bar is run by your financial committee whose eyes, by virtue of their theatre interest, are largely on the income column. I've known an intermission to stretch to forty-five minutes as the house manager refused to close the bar as long as one more patron wanted to buy one more drink, and many of the less theatre-oriented audience refused to come back for Act III as long as drinks were on sale. But it is done, and, with proper control on the closing time, several Broadway and summer theatres make a handsome profit and don't give anyone time for more than one. But it must be absolutely controlled.

How much can you make at a refreshment stand? It depends on the deal you can make with the supplier (remember your nonprofit status—he can write off low-profit sales to a group such as yours as tax deductions) and the top price you feel you can really ask. A 100 percent markup isn't unreasonable for a group that is admittedly selling the stuff so that it can provide continuing and well-budgeted entertainment for the patrons. A small cup of cola from a premix machine costs you about 3½¢; add a penny for the cup, and the product has cost you a little less than a nickel. You can surely sell it for a dime or even more. Like the price of anything, it's based on what the public will pay. There's bound to be spillage, waste, and even a few drinks snitched by the ushers, so don't scale your prices so low as to assure *losing* money, and consider the possibility of a good profit. (One community theatre receives its entire supply for one full show a year free from a large cola distributor. A note in the program proclaims: "All refreshments for this play donated by the Blank Cola Company; all proceeds will go to our Building Fund." The distributor gets a tax deduction and a lot of promotional goodwill; you up your sales and boost your Building Fund.)

Even a modest profit grows with the volume of sales; our summer theatre sells soft drinks (one brand) at its outdoor children's theatre. We have estimated that we sell fifty-seven *gallons* per performance. Even at a small markup, it mounts up.

If you feel the profit margin isn't worth bothering about but still want to provide something besides the tepid water in the drinking fountain, consider free refreshments. Make these *really* simple, and provide the service without too much expense to you in money or personnel hours. Coffee and homemade cookies (from the auxiliary) are a good bet in winter, and a cheap, cold lemonade in summer. It's a nice gift to the audience, who will remember your thoughtfulness.

Whatever the refreshment, whatever the price, make the operation simple to teach and simple to run. If your attendants are seeing the show free in exchange for their work, you don't want to haul them out of the first act before it's over, and yet you must have the refreshment stand open when the first audience hits the lobby. You don't want the setup so complicated as to take half the intermission preparing it and learning the routine. Start off the evening positively by teaching the attendants their system before the audience starts to arrive. Even if you do only a little business before the show, get the refreshment stand crew used to their stand, their prices, and procedure during the quiet time, so that when intermission busy-ness hits, they're familiar with their patterns and can handle them well. If you're dealing with liquid of any sort, a good number of cups should be poured and ready as the intermission audience arrives—this can be done by the house manager during the closing moments of the act, so that the stand is ready when the volunteers race out of the house ahead of the audience. One attendant can then fill new cups, based on the length of the line, as the other passes out those already poured and takes in the money. As the line diminishes, so should the zeal of the pourer, to avoid waste. As the line is satisfied, the attendants clean up the counter area, give the money to the house manager, pick up cups and papers left around the lobby, and go back in for the next act, leaving any final cleanup for the house management staff.

During each act, the lobby should be cleared of any debris, so that the audience coming out for intermission or after the show is not greeted with overflowing ashstands, muddy floors, or a lineup of used soft-drink cups. In no case should the refreshment stand be open after the performance. You will do no business, really provide no service, and only complicate your operation.

Many theatres, of necessity, use the same counter for cloakroom and for refreshments. If this is unavoidable, be very careful of laying coats in spilled cola, or mixing checkroom tips with refreshment income. The bustle of activity at such a combined area is conducive to spilling, and it is invariably the expensive coat that gets spilled on. Advise and exercise caution.

Chapter VIII

BUDGET

One of the students of my recent community theatre seminar brought in this budget report on one of the theatres she was researching: At the end of the previous season, their books showed a loss of some $1,700. A Board discussion of the importance of a balanced budget apparently ensued, and ideas of how to make up the loss were tossed around. At the end of the debate, the president of the group came up with a solution they all thought was grand. He made a donation to cover the entire deficit.

* * *

Donations of any kind are welcome at any time to a nonprofessional, nonprofit theatre. But a balanced budget is welcome, too, and I fault this group for settling on a quick specific personal donation to close their season's books.

Your strongest evidence of organization and of management is shown to the world, and to yourselves, in your ledger sheets. Good budgeting procedure, followed rigorously, will keep you and your members aware of your strengths and weaknesses, in income and in expenditures, and show you day by day where and possibly how you must restrict spending, if necessary, and increase receipts, if necessary. And—positively—show you which areas are solid and well-budgeted and well run.

Your business manager (or treasurer) and your Finance Committee are the initiators and custodians of the budget, the books, and the financial reports. It is their responsibility to draw up each season's budget, based on the number and type of shows you are doing, to keep the books, and then to report to each monthly meeting how well the theatre is sticking to that budget. It is perfectly in order to revise the budget, month by month, to keep the future reasonably budgetable. An unexpectedly sold-out show can give you more working capital for the next play; a poor turnout, on the other hand, may restrict the rest of the season even to the point of substituting a less-expensive show into the schedule. A careless department head spending over his budget may make it hellish for his followers, whereas an in-novative or cautious leader of an area may give his successor more money to work with.

For instance: If you had estimated that Show #1, a name musical, would take in $2,000 at the box office, but inclement weather kept the audience away, garnering only $1,500, adjustments are in order immediately, not at the end of the season. Two alternatives present themselves for the next, and remaining, shows: increase income or decrease expenses. A broader-than-usual publicity campaign may be mounted, using all the methods described in Chapter V, plus those of your own that you have found to be effective. Put your best promotional minds to the problem and build up the audience and thus the income. Or —examine carefully the expense budget for the rest of the year to see if any areas can be trimmed a lot or several areas trimmed a little in their allowed expenditures. One or the other, or both, must be implemented at the first Board or Financial Committee meeting at which it is evident that the budget has not been hewn to.

The same procedure will take place if expenses are up. If Scenery, for example, has spent more than its allotted piece of the budget (and this large, necessary budgetary department is the one most often to stretch beyond its limits, with the number of different elements that must be bought show by show to produce fine sets)—$700 instead of $450, let's say—adjustments must be made immediately. It is not required that the sets for the rest of the year be less expensive just to "teach the technicians a lesson," as you may well be hamstringing the whole visual appeal of your theatre. Certainly the people in charge of buying materials for scenery must be made aware of their carelessness and told to keep it down to budget size from now on, but cutting their budget may not be the answer. As with the diminished box-office example above, examine both sides of the ledger—how may we increase income, and how may we cut costs in *any* department, or both?

If the box-office income is down and continues down for several shows, your question to yourself had better be: Do they want us? A theatre playing to a consistent 75 percent capacity (or less) is either running its shows too long or not providing what the audience wants. Do they in fact want your theatre? If you really believe they do, see about limiting your run a little to provide more full houses, and get at that budget. Without the guide of a predrawn budget balancing at least in theory, you could continue blindly through the entire season, assuming that the next show will equalize the income/outgo columns, and wind up at the end of the year with no hope but to close the theatre or to beg for a donation.

Again, donations are welcome, and should be constantly solicited, but after a while even the most generous local benefactor will grow tired of deficit financing and withdraw all support forever from this mismanaged group. The time for the appeal for gifts is *before* you go in the hole; an-

nounce glorious plans of positive uses for the donated money—to mount an extra-special show, to buy needed equipment for the shop, or to refurbish the lobby. But to ask for money to cover bad debts becomes very old very soon. Set yourself a workable budget, and then stick to it. Or flop.

SAMPLE BUDGETS

The following three Figures (27, 28, 29) are accurate budgets, or financial reports, of community theatres whose break-even points are respectively $4,300, $35,000, and $160,000. Your operation should fall into one of these categories or be easily fitted between two.

Look them over, learn where they apportion

Fig. 27. *Community Theatre Budget—$4,300.00*

FINANCIAL STATEMENT 1970/71
4 Plays (including one kidshow)

INCOME

Single Ticket sales	$3,755.00
Season Memberships	260.00
Patron Memberships	357.00
	$4,372.00

EXPENSES

Utilities	$ 727.00
Telephone	102.00
Insurance	509.00
Publicity	457.00
Royalties	625.00
Program Printing	458.00
Refreshments	127.00
Scenery	433.00
Costumes	277.00
Building Maintenance	69.00
Postage	49.00
Meetings and Conventions	277.00
Miscellaneous Production	291.00
Miscellaneous	201.00
	$4,602.00
	$230.00 LOSS

Actually, this is a financial statement of the year just past, but it can serve as a guide to the setting of the budget for the next season.

or spend money, and apply their successes or failures to your theatre.

Figure 27 represents a theatre in a town of 45,000 in the East with forty years of operation. The season consists of four productions; two recent Broadway comedy-dramas, a children's play, and an American classic. The budget was fairly evenly divided among the four shows. Season tickets cost $5 for a single, $8 for a couple; Patron Tickets are $15. Single admissions are $2.50.

Shows #2 & 3 together did not equal the box-office receipts of show #1, so the theatre wisely doubled its publicity budget for show #4 and came close to matching the income for the first play. But show #4 was a multiset costume show, and the scenery ran more than on the first three plays combined, whereas costumes (mostly rental) required the expenditure of $277, the first money put into that department all season.

Although a final deficit of $230 isn't terrible, it is not a statement of good management on a $4,300 budget to lose that much. A less-expensive show might have been substituted in the fourth slot, assuring a smaller outlay of money. But they *did* increase their publicity, and felt it their duty as the theatre of the community to bring back a great play from the past and to vary their diet of contemporary hits. They gambled, they stuck true to their artistic and organizational concept, they produced all the plays they had promised their members, and they lost $230. They must be credited for their truth of purpose, but should begin earlier in the next season husbanding their funds and making adjustments in case of deficit. Forty season tickets, for instance, is a rather small number for a group in operation that long in a town that size. The working capital such tickets can provide, spread over the entire season, is a marvelous cushion, and it should be sought before the season begins. Notice that there is no budget department for Membership Campaign. A small investment in brochures and publicity for season tickets will generally pay off to a larger tune than merely $260.

Figure 28 is the financial report of a midwestern community theatre in a town of 5,000, a suburb of a major city with an overall population of 1,500,000. It has been in business for forty years, and this season consisted of three Broadway musicals, a recent Broadway hit, and an American classic of the 1930's. The musicals, as is fairly typical, outdrew the straight plays nearly two to one, but also cost a lot more to produce. Season tickets cost $12; single tickets are $2.50 and $3.

The loss of $316 on a $35,000 budget isn't bad, when you consider that expenses include a mortgage payment, new technical equipment, and such salary-reducing items as an answering service. They have also put a good bit of money into studio shows and teen-agers' theatre, with small financial return. But such shows are investments as you present shows appealing to younger audiences and devotees of non-commercial theatre, segments of your community you cannot ignore.

Musicals do cost money, however, and often the income is not enough, especially with several back-breakers in the same season, to offset the cost. One musical, budgeted at a slight loss (royalties alone on one musical can cost more than a season of straight plays), can win friends who will come back to the nonmusicals, too. Three may push your personnel, and your budget, beyond recovery. That accounted for the (small) loss here; the next season, one less musical might be produced, to see how many people come *only* to musicals and how many can be wooed into buying season tickets with only one or two musicals scheduled. Less money spent on production, plus nearly as much brought into the box office, can effect a balanced budget.

Figure 29 might seem to reflect none of your problems or benefits by its very magnitude, but look it over for a while. True, it is from one of the largest and longest-running community theatres in the country, but they were not always so, and their handling of money is in every way typical of the way they have run things from their earliest, slimmest days. Their season tickets run $15 for six shows; single admissions $3 through $4.50.

The budget is examined month by month, and the projections of income and expense adjusted as need be with a realistic look at what can be accomplished by intriguing an audience into the theatre and by more carefully guarding the expenditures. The scenery figure is much higher than anticipated (as often happens), but it was allowed to stay high and the schedule of plays to remain intact, because of the windfall in student-ticket income and in the Miscellaneous column. Had the income gone down, on the other hand, you can be sure the expenses would have been pulled in more stringently and something lopped off.

An examination of the budget of this large non-profit, nonprofessional theatre, putting its somewhat large budgetary items into the perspective of your budget, can help your planning as much as all the words in this book.

Fig. 28. *Community Theatre Budget — $35,000*

FINANCIAL REPORT 1970/71
5 Plays (including 3 musicals)

INCOME

Major Plays (Single Tickets)	$21,710.80
Season Tickets	1,109.00
Teen and Studio Theatre	3,833.85
Program Ads	3,295.00
Refreshments	90.02
Patron & Sponsor Memberships	270.00
Teen Theatre Registrations	310.00
Insurance Adjustments	268.40
Membership	240.50
Mortgaging & Refinancing	3,180.79
Building Rental	646.00
Royalty Refund of Canceled Performance	225.00
Miscellaneous	39.50
	$35,218.86

EXPENSES

Salaries	$ 6,140.00
Custodian Salary & Supplies	1,280.72
Utilities	2,789.94
Insurance	1,108.60
Printing (including programs), Postage & Publicity	4,049.73
Royalties and Scripts	5,774.86
Ticket Printing (includes 2 shows from previous season)	433.42
Scenery	4,240.97
Costumes	996.10
Props	428.52
Office Supplies	377.36
Real Estate Taxes	457.36
Answering Service	496.65
New Lighting Equipment	4,907.75
Mortgage Loan Interest	1,830.00
Miscellaneous	223.13
	$35,535.11
	$316.25 LOSS

Financial statement on which the new season's budget may be based.

Fig. 29. *Community Theatre Budget—$160,000*

ANNUAL FINANCIAL REPORT OF COMMUNITY THEATRE
1970/71
7 Plays (including 1 musical)

INCOME	BUDGETED	ACTUAL
Membership	$ 92,858.00	$ 89,622.00
Single Tickets, Adults	40,500.00	39,160.00
Single Tickets, Students	5,800.00	13,875.00
Group Rates	1,100.00	1,007.00
Program Ads	7,000.00	9,049.00
Refreshment Stand	2,900.00	2,992.00
Building Rental	1,000.00	985.00
Classes	1,000.00	1,492.00
Miscellaneous	3,060.00	11,155.00*
	$155,218.00	$169,337.00

*= Grant, theatregoing tours and donations

EXPENSES	BUDGETED	ACTUAL
Staff Salaries	$ 50,700.00	$ 47,735.00
Guest Staff Salaries	5,000.00	5,095.00
Custodian's Salary	5,850.00	5,080.00
Box Office & Accounting Staff	9,200.00	9,211.00
FICA	3,000.00	3,055.00
Utilities	7,200.00	6,089.00
Telephone & Telegraph	2,100.00	1,791.00
Insurance & Taxes	4,500.00	4,937.00
Publicity	1,600.00	2,740.00
Royalties & Scripts	11,700.00	12,266.00
Box Office Supplies & Ticket Printing	1,920.00	2,277.00
Program Printing	6,700.00	5,797.00
Scenery	5,300.00	9,399.00
Costumes & Makeup	5,500.00	5,816.00
Properties	500.00	1,175.00
Lights & Sound	600.00	1,819.00
Maintenance & Repairs	6,000.00	5,075.00
Building Supplies	1,500.00	1,659.00
Newsletter Mailings	1,700.00	1,064.00
Membership Drive	2,000.00	1,468.00
Social	650.00	594.00
Depreciation	16,000.00	18,082.00
Miscellaneous Production	500.00	1,175.00
Miscellaneous	5,050.00	3,445.00
TOTAL EXPENSES	$154,770.00	$156,503.00
TOTAL INCOME	$155,218.00	$169,337.00
	$448.00 Budgeted Profit	$12,834.00 Actual Profit

The Finance Committee has the opportunity to check the accuracy of their budget predictions, and the ability of the various departments to function under a strict budget, by comparing the budgets as set at season's beginning with the actual figures of income and expense at season's end. Budget for the new season is drawn up with the previous year's relationship of budgeted expenses and income to the actual expenses and income in mind. When a department has gone well over its expense budget, the Finance Committee probably cannot raise the new budget to equal the overage, unless the income budget can be raised proportionately, but will have to exercise more strict control over the high-spending department, with this budget/financial report as a guide.

SAMPLE MONTHLY REPORT

To more clearly illustrate this month-by-month control, I include all the pages of another theatre's report (Figure 30), this one a monthly statement, midyear, of a 17-year-old community theatre in a midwestern town of 50,000. This theatre owns its own building, a 299-seat proscenium house, and boasted 3,700 season ticketholders at the time of the report.

Each month, the managing director and the (volunteer) business manager prepared such a report for the Board meeting. Each report was discussed, and decisions on the financial future of the organization, both immediate and long-range, were made based largely on these figures and the defense or praise of them.

Taking it page by page:

Page 1—A short, clear statement of the theatre's financial state at the moment.

ASSETS:

There are three major banks in this town, and, in an effort to patronize as many businesses as possible, the theatre deals with all three. The Subscription Members Fund—money derived solely from season tickets—is kept in the ——National Bank in a savings account and in Certificates of Deposit. The General Fund, a checking account from which current operating expenses are paid and into which all income (except season-ticket money and building fund donations) is deposited, is maintained in the _____ County Bank. The Building Fund is the depository for pledge payments made against a loan from all the city's banks, held by the _____ Bank.

Subscription Members Fund—To get the greatest benefit from all that preseason money, let it sit and earn interest for you in a savings account or in Certificates of Deposit. CD's are high-interest-paying notes (higher than a savings account) through which you agree to leave a certain amount of money in the bank for a specified period (three months, six months, or longer). The business manager of this theatre feels a moral responsibility toward the season ticket holders to keep their money in trust in case the theatre should close, several shows be cancelled, or something make the tickets unusable before their value has been given the buyer. So he insists, rightly I believe, that no matter what straits the theatre is in, the money remain inviolable (and earning interest) until after each production has closed, at which time a certain portion of it is transferred into the General Fund operating-expense check-ing account. This transfer can be effected in one of two ways—either in direct proportion to the number of plays in the season, or in direct payment (from the theatre to the theatre) for the number of season-ticket coupons used on the play just closing. In the first instance, one seventh of the Subscription Members Fund (because there are seven plays in the season) would be transferred after each play regardless of how many season ticket holders attended the show. In the second case and the one this theatre follows now, the coupons exchanged for actual tickets are counted, and the actual value of each coupon (one seventh the cost of the season ticket) totalled and that amount transferred as an exact statement of payment for service rendered. (In the first case, a musical playing to 2,000 season ticket holders would garner the same subscription member income as a classic that might draw 800 people. This is legitimate but not as clear a statement of what the play actually earned as the second method.)

In case the theatre closes in midseason, under the second system especially, the season ticket holders could receive back the face value of their unused coupons.

At the end of the season under the second plan, an amount of money—sometimes surprisingly large—will remain in the Subscription Members Fund. Interest earned through the year is there, both through the savings account and from the CD's, which are transferred into the savings account at the end of their three-, six-, or nine-month holding. Estimating how many coupons are generally exchanged for each type of play, and looking ahead to the closing dates of the plays, the business manager buys CD's in amounts of money for periods of time to release the approximate money needed on the approximate date needed. But there is also what's called breakage. This is money not claimed by the General Fund because a certain number of coupons were never redeemed, as the holders did not attend some of the plays. This unearned money continues in the savings account, earning interest, until the board votes on its disposal—into the General Fund if the budget is in trouble, into purchase of new equipment, into reducing the mortgage debt in the Building Fund, and so on.

General Fund—will be more fully dealt with when discussing pages 2 and 3 of this report.

ACCOUNTS RECEIVABLE:

Here the accounts in the three banks are reflected through the money still due them from

10956

MONTHLY FINANCIAL REPORT OF COMMUNITY THEATRE, JULY 1–31, 1967
7 Plays (including 1 musical)

Assets

Subscription Members' Fund:

Savings Account in _____ National Bank (includes Interest and breakage from unused Season Tickets, 1966–67)	$16,366.46	
Certificate of Deposit from _____ National Bank	1,537.74	
3 Certificates of Deposit from _____ National Bank	10,000.00	
		27,904.20

General Fund:

Checking Account in _____ County Bank	447.20	
		$28,351.40

ACCOUNTS RECEIVABLE

Building Fund:

Pledges not yet redeemed	$ 4,333.00

Subscription Members Fund:

Season Tickets not yet paid	660.97

General Fund:

Program Ads receivable	445.00	
		$ 5,438.97

ACCOUNTS PAYABLE

Building Fund:

Mortgage Loan payable (plus interest) to _____ Bank	$12,605.59

Fig. 30. *Complete Monthly Financial Report of a Community Theatre*

GENERAL FUND—Income

DEPARTMENT	MONTHLY BUDGET	ACTUAL THIS MONTH	BUDGET YEAR TO DATE	ACTUAL YEAR TO DATE	ANNUAL BUDGET
TICKETS					
Major Shows	$3,000.00	$ 622.50	$21,000.00	$18,428.43	$36,000.00
Children's	500.00	588.70	3,500.00	2,124.65	6,000.00
Studio	8.33	18.70	58.32	67.20	100.00
	3,508.33	1,229.90	24,558.32	20,620.28	42,100.00
PROGRAM ADS	375.00	205.00	2,625.00	2,150.00	4,500.00
REFRESHMENTS	125.00	66.00	875.00	735.95	1,500.00
CHECKROOM	33.33	—	233.32	189.00	400.00
AWARDS BANQUET	66.67	24.00	466.68	879.00	800.00
SUSTAINING MEMBERS	291.67	1,050.00	2,041.68	2,250.00	3,500.00
ARTS COUNCIL GRANT	208.33	—	1,458.32	—	2,500.00
DONATIONS	416.67	—	2,916.68	2,600.00	5,000.00
BREAKAGE FROM SUBSCRIPTION MEMBERS FUND	250.00	—	1,750.00	—	3,000.00
ACTING CLASSES	83.33	319.75	583.33	1,879.75	1,000.00
MISCELLANEOUS	41.67	109.00	291.67	946.47	500.00
TOTALS	$5,400.00	$3,003.65	$37,800.00	$32,250.45	$64,800.00

FIG. 30. *Complete Monthly Financial Report of a Community Theatre*

GENERAL FUND—Expenditures

DEPARTMENT	MONTHLY BUDGET	ACTUAL THIS MONTH	BUDGET YEAR TO DATE	ACTUAL YEAR TO DATE	ANNUAL BUDGET
SALARIES & WITHHOLDING	$2,360.83	$2,301.30	$16,525.82	$16,107.82	$28,330.00
UTILITIES	233.33	8.39	1,633.32	2,000.08	2,800.00
TELEPHONE	62.50	–	437.50	412.08	750.00
INSURANCE	83.33	–	583.32	1,418.14	1,000.00
PUBLICITY	191.67	–	1,341.68	1,020.06	2,300.00
SCRIPTS & SCORES	22.92	–	160.43	399.41	275.00
ROYALTIES	208.33	275.00	1,458.32	1,760.00	2,500.00
TICKET PRINTING	83.33	–	583.32	349.50	1,000.00
PROGRAM PRINTING	241.67	–	1,691.68	1,094.20	2,900.00
REFRESHMENT STAND	70.83	–	495.82	197.75	850.00
MAKEUP	16.67	.65	116.68	38.96	200.00
SET BUILDING	108.33	1.93	758.32	622.47	1,300.00
SET PAINTING	33.33	–	233.32	243.94	400.00
COSTUMES	112.50	–	787.50	615.96	1,350.00
PROPS	15.00	6.22	105.00	106.85	180.00
SOUND AND ELECTRIC	18.75	7.20	131.25	126.19	225.00
HOUSE	33.33	–	233.32	203.49	400.00
NEWSLETTER	45.00	–	315.00	297.62	540.00
PRODUCTION PHOTOS	7.09	1.80	49.61	12.80	85.00
STAFF INSURANCE	39.58	–	277.07	476.82	475.00
OFFICE	41.67	7.84	291.68	370.99	500.00
POSTAGE	29.18	100.69	204.22	434.42	350.00

FIG. 30. *Complete Monthly Financial Report of a Community Theatre*

GENERAL FUND—Expenditures (cont.)

DEPARTMENT	MONTHLY BUDGET	ACTUAL THIS MONTH	BUDGET YEAR TO DATE	ACTUAL YEAR TO DATE	ANNUAL BUDGET
AWARDS BANQUET	66.67	—	466.68	96.57	800.00
MEMBERSHIP DRIVE	33.33	10.00	233.32	107.70	400.00
STUDIO SHOWS	8.33	—	58.32	84.68	100.00
PLAYREADING	2.09	—	14.61	21.07	25.00
DONATION TO BUILDING FUND	416.67	—	2,916.68	2,500.00	5,000.00
BANK LOAN INTEREST	83.33	—	583.32	709.28	1,000.00
STAFF TRIPS & CONVENTIONS	83.33	12.25	583.32	61.41	1,000.00
ORGANIZATIONAL DUES	8.33	—	58.32	56.00	100.00
WIGS	8.33	—	58.32	47.94	100.00
NEW BOOKS	8.33	—	58.32	78.10	100.00
BUILDING MAINTENANCE & CAPITAL IMPROVEMENTS	227.09	5.00	1,589.61	562.37	2,725.00
CHILDREN'S THEATRE DEVELOPMENT	104.17	—	729.18	—	1,250.00
MISCELLANEOUS	83.33	13.32	583.32	1,114.38	1,000.00
TOTAL EXPENDITURES	$5,192.50	$2,751.59	$36,347.50	$33,749.05	$62,310.00
TOTAL INCOME (from Pg. 2)	$5,400.00	$3,003.65	$37,800.00	$32,250.45	$64,800.00
INCOME OVER EXPENDITURES	$ 207.50	$ 252.06	$ 1,452.50	−$ 1,498.60 (loss)	$ 2,490.00
Plus: BALANCE 1/1/67				$ 2,211.61	$ 2,211.61
CHECKBOOK BALANCE 7/31/67: $713.01 = (Date of this report)				$ 713.01	$ 4,701.61

FIG. 30. *Complete Monthly Financial Report of a Community Theatre*

SHOW-BY-SHOW BREAKDOWN (for reference only)

CHILDREN'S PLAY #1	1967	1966
Income	$1,535.95	$1,875.49
Expenses	603.34	395.46

MUSICAL (incomplete)

Income		
Single Tix	$2,961.21	$2,520.03
Season Tix	5,575.00	5,899.29
	$8,536.21	$8,419.32

Expenses		
Sound & Electric	20.51	
Scripts & Scores	321.26	
Royalty	900.00	
Publicity	240.50	
Ticket Printing	120.00	
Building	192.56	
Set Painting	72.00	
Costumes	118.48	
Piano Tuning	42.00	
Props	14.44	
Makeup	33.85	
Wigs	11.65	
	$2,087.25	$2,840.41

CHILDREN'S SHOW #2 (incomplete)

Income (Tickets)	$588.70	$624.99
Expenses		
Scripts	10.00	
Publicity	33.33	
Props	10.35	
Set Building	110.00	
Makeup	.65	
	$164.33	$655.89

SUMMER PLAY #1 (incomplete)

Income	$622.50	$3,262.84
Expenses		
Set Building	.83	
Props	.57	
Scripts	15.10	
	$ 16.50	$1,180.10

FUTURE SHOWS:

Expenses		
Scripts	$64.65	

FIG. 30. *Complete Monthly Financial Report of a Community Theatre*

various sources. A healthy list of receivables should stir the theatre to try to collect it; a small loss at the box office or a small overspending by one of the departments need cause little concern if the receivables are indeed collectable and not bad debts.

ACCOUNTS PAYABLE:

This section should actually be larger, but this theatre does not use the Purchase Order form of buying, thereby fooling itself (sometimes by large amounts) into thinking it is in better financial shape than it really is. Even if all bills that have arrived have been paid at the time the report is made, chances are that an actively producing theatre has a number of charges at local stores and suppliers not yet billed, which should be reflected here. See Purchase Orders later in this chapter.

Page 2—GENERAL FUND—Income.

The operating fund checking account receives income from varied sources, all reflected on this page. The far left column details those sources, the far right column the estimate of how much each can expect to receive over the year, based on the number and type of shows and the reception those types have met in the past. Between those two columns are statements of how the theatre is actually doing.

The second and third columns show what has been taken in since the last monthly report and what *should* have been taken in, based on one month being one twelfth of one year. Since few theatres run precisely twelve shows, with all income from each contained precisely within the confines of one month, the figures showing actual income will seldom come very close to the monthly budget, but will go well under during a nonshow month and well over when a show has produced income.

So the next two columns are necessary to show how the theatre is faring thus far in the fiscal year. (January through December is the required fiscal year for nonprofit organizations reporting to the government, making July through June or September through May theatre seasons clumsy to report.) The Budget-Year-to-Date and Actual-Year-to-Date columns show how much the theatre should have received in each area by this time in its January-to-December course and how much it *has* received. These are the columns that must be studied each month with an eye to how many shows are left and what kind of income they can realistically be expected to bring in. If

not enough to offset currently low income as compared to the budgeted and expected income to this date, something must be done to try to increase it or proportionately to reduce the expenditure budget on some items on the next page.

Most items on the Income Page have been discussed in previous chapters. A few bear a closer look:

The *Major Show* income figures include season-ticket money transferred from the Subscription Members Fund show by show.

Refreshments indicates money *paid* to the refreshment stand, not the *profit* from the stand. Amount of profit is found by deducting from this figure the amount listed under Refreshments on the Expenses page. Do not do the arithmetic before the report is made—show what has been spent and what has been earned in this way.

Awards Banquet is basically a break-even affair each year to celebrate the closing season and to reward those participants in each area deemed superior or "best." Income from banquet tickets should pay for the meal itself as well as for any decorations, the awards, statuettes, and so on.

Sustaining Members are those patrons of the arts who pay substantially more than even Patron Members for extra privileges, but more especially for the support of a worthy artistic enterprise. (Patron Membership money, from the time this theatre began, has gone straight to the Building Fund, years before a new building was even a dream. They now boast a beautiful theatre building downtown, built in their thirteenth year. The larger Sustaining checks are welcome and immediate additions to the operating expense General Fund.)

Arts Council Grants are more possible than ever now for well-managed nonprofit organizations, especially for new programs or for plans including children. Talk to your state's Arts Council and see how you may qualify. Investigate, too, local foundations, including family foundations, for possible grants for specific projects or just general support of their local theatre. Industries, too, are finding themselves with money to give out for artistic enterprises—talk to the public relations men at your large local firms to suggest they finance an entire show or at least subsidize their employees' tickets to your plays. (State Arts Councils' addresses are listed in the Appendix)

Page 3—GENERAL FUND—Expenditures.

This page is the correlative of the previous page, balancing, hopefully, the income with an equal or smaller figure for operating expenses. The columns are exactly the same as on the Income page, and many of the departments have been spoken of already.

Salaries includes all state and federal withholding taxes and FICA (Social Security) payments for salaried employees, as well as the actual salaries themselves. Remember that a director earning $10,000 a year cannot be put into the budget at exactly $10,000. His paycheck totals will come to less than that after deductions, and payments must be made of all monies withheld, plus the employer's share of FICA, to a nearby Federal Reserve Bank at specified times. This will require more bookkeeping, reports, and on-time payments, or fines are levied. I know of a community theatre at this moment in great financial trouble because no one kept up these deposits and payments, and the back money owed and the fines accrued ate well into the next year's budget before a penny was spent on producing a play.

Utilities for one's own building often equal rent paid on a hired hall. But, like all rental payments for anything, all that is left in one's possession at the end of the year is a stack of receipts. Think, think, think about the possible purchase or building of your own theatre. It is yours, all day every day, for whatever activities you need or choose to sponsor, and the office, shop, stage, and auditorium are shared only at your choice.

Insurance is mandatory before you even hold your first set of tryouts. Public Liability Insurance, especially. Find an insurance man within the group, if possible, who will care 100 percent about the right insurance for your budget and your needs at this stage of the life of your theatre. Cover everyone who sets foot in your building as volunteer, visitor, audience, or off the street to use the phone. Workmen's Compensation covers only salaried employees. Some policies cover volunteers doing precisely what they are assigned, period. Some will not cover visiting theatre groups you have brought in for a special performance, or your group on its own tour. (A lawsuit is still pending against a community theatre from whose stage an actress fell during the performance of a visiting play during a community theatre festival. The home theatre's insurance company refused to pay.) If you are a group within a school, does the school's policy cover all your people in all their activities? What about volunteers from the town? Be sure.

Be equally sure that everything you borrow for shows or any other purpose is fully covered. As a nonprofit group on a tight budget, you will find yourself having to borrow to stay alive. Describe your needs honestly and fully to the insurance representative, and be sure you can replace or pay for that office equipment, those drapes, that sofa, that dress, or *don't borrow it.* Try not to borrow anything too expensive, anyway, for the value of the items likely to be borrowed will determine the cost of your insurance premium. Keep both very low.

Royalties must be paid. Even in a free, unadvertised reading of a play solely for your members. The playwright, that original creative artist, must be paid for his work. Don't avoid your responsibility to him, and don't take a chance on being caught—as the publishers have their ways of finding wildcat productions—and being fined or sued and closed. Most royalties are very low. Pay them.

Production Photos of each play are a valuable asset to your archives and can be used for lobby exhibits, convention displays at distant cities, in future programs, in brochures, and just in reminiscing. They cost little. Get a good photographer, set a date early in the run for the entire cast and crew to stay after the performance, and take at least a dozen good representative shots of your show with all sets and most costumes included. Once the show is struck, you can never bring it visually to life again. The cost of photos is very small for their worth.

Staff Insurance in this case is a sickness and accident policy covering your paid creative employees in case of long-term sickness or accident preventing their producing for you, and ultimately causing you to hire someone else, at least for a show or two. Your budget can't stand paying two salaries for the same job of work, and you don't want to leave your employees stranded with medical bills and no income through no fault of their own. Pay the small premiums on so-called income-protector insurance for them, and make it an untaxable fringe benefit of working for you.

Playreading money offers a broader latitude to your play-selection committee by making more and newer scripts available to them, with purchase officially authorized by budget.

Donation to the Building Fund is a chancy proposition, but this theatre seems to feel, and rightly, that their operating budget is secure enough that they can schedule a large chunk of money to help wipe out the mortgage-loan debt. In case of trouble, this item could be reduced or eliminated altogether. The next listed expenditure, however, cannot be elided.

Bank Loan Interest on the mortgage must be paid on time, and though it is perhaps wrong to reduce the operating budget, which should be given to the production of plays and the continuing running of the organization, where else would this payment come from?

Staff Trips is another item representing a fringe benefit, untaxable, to the staff. To keep their own creative juices flowing and their minds in touch with other theatre minds around the country, they must be financed on a trip to New York or another theatre center to see the current plays, and to theatre conventions.

Organizational Dues are paid to enroll your theatre in state, regional, and national theatre groups, whose conventions, publications, and facilities can be a boon both to your professionals and your volunteers. The American Community Theatre Association, a division of the American Theatre Association (formerly American Educational Theatre Association) is a virtual necessity for the exchange of information during the year and at convention time, and whose "floating conferences" and play festivals alternate year by year, with a community theatre production sent every four years to the World Amateur Theatre Festival in Monaco.

New Books are additions to the theatre library and include technical books, biographies, and the like, making this a separate entry from playreading.

After the expenditure columns have been totaled, totals from the Income page are inserted and the differences between the two noted column by column to show how much more has been made than spent, or vice versa, compared to what the budget says you should be doing. Another check on your financial status.

Then, to finish the page off as a check for accuracy, the General Fund balance from the opening of the fiscal year is added to the last two columns—to the last column to show what your balance should be at fiscal year's end, and to the Actual-Year-to-Date column to show what your checkbook balance should be today. If this figure *is* the same as your checkbook balance, your report is accurate and reflects, with the exception of the Accounts Payable lacks mentioned earlier, the state of your operating budget today.

Page 4—Show-by-Show Breakdown.

This is a page of unofficial reporting, including only those items of income and expense directly applicable to the production of the plays, for comparison, one with the other and with the equivalent plays of the previous season.

Once all the bills on a particular show have been posted, the itemization of the show no longer appears on the monthly statements but will always be available in the files for reference.

This manner of reporting the finances to the Board (and the membership, as all books and financial reports should be available at any time to any member for perusal and comment) is a workable one, but it is surely not the only way of recording and reporting finances. Use whatever part of it works for your group, add and innovate as you will, but devise and keep a system that you can live with and that reflects accurately how you're doing financially.

Other entries that appear in other nonprofessional theatre budgets include: historian, librarian, scenery items broken down more fully (lumber, paint, canvas, etc.), auditor's fee, piano tuning, piano moving, storage, rental of costumes to other theatres and for parties, etc. . . . and you will have your own special entries that don't appear here. Use them. Let your financial report reflect your group accurately and completely.

AUDIT

At the end of each fiscal year, balance the books as you have each month, and immediately submit your final report together with the full set of ledgers to a Certified Public Accountant for an official legal audit. In many states, it's a law, but whether it is or not, you want to have the imprimatur of a professional on each year's books to reassure yourself that you're keeping accurate records and for ready availability to anyone who is interested or doubtful of your organizational and managerial status as regards money. It's an added cost, but worth it.

PETTY CASH

Not shown on any of these reports is one of the most wearisome yet necessary parts of any theatre's financial life—the petty cash fund. You must provide ready small cash allotments when you send volunteers (or even staff) out for small purchases, or when they have made small outlays of personal cash and want, rightfully, quick reimbursement. Direct one person on each production to take charge of petty cash disbursement and recording—probably the technical director, or whichever of the staff or volunteer ranks fills a comparable job for you. Give him a cash box with a lot of coins and small bills, totaling $100, and a batch of petty cash slips. (See Figure 31.) As he doles out each amount of cash, he gives at the same time a slip on which will be written the pertinent information and the correct total of cash spent under Petty Cash, with the paid receipt stapled to it. The person on the buying trip returns to the tech director remaining cash plus

```
┌─────────────────────────────────────────┐
│            PETTY CASH SLIP                │
│                           Date_____  │
│  ITEM:_____│
│                                           │
│  AMOUNT ($5 or under):  $_____      │
│                                           │
│  DEPARTMENT_____│
│                                           │
│  Signature:_____│
└─────────────────────────────────────────┘
```

FIG. 31. Petty Cash Slip
The slip is filled out fully and turned in with any change and with a receipt equaling the amount listed on the slip. All slips and their receipts are stapled to the Petty Cash Report when it is filled out.

a correctly filled-out slip (with receipt) whose combined total equals the amount he was originally given. These slips are kept in the cash box with the remaining petty cash until almost all the cash has been spent; the slips are then totaled and a report form filled out. (See Figure 32.) The slips and completed form are given to the business manager who, as quickly as possible, restores the original amount of cash to the cash box. This immediate replacement of spent funds is one of the most niggling, time-consuming, yet vital jobs the business manager fills. Asking volunteers to spend their own money, and then taking days to repay them, will lose friends permanently. Even on a many-thousand-dollar budget, that $100 in-

MOUNT HOLYOKE COLLEGE
REQUEST FOR PETTY CASH REIMBURSEMENT

Department _____Theatre Arts_____   Date ___November 20, 1971___

Amount of petty cash requested at beginning of college year $ ___100.00_____

Expenditures (Receipts must be attached for all expenditures
                of 50¢ or over.)

Item	Amount	Department
thread, pins, zipper	$ 1.32	costumes
tacks, wire, extension cord	4.12	sets
construction paper, magazine	1.65	props
Gold paint, brush	3.79	props
rubber bands, pencils	1.70	office

Total Expenditures (Reimbursement check requested for this amount)... $_____

Balance of Cash on Hand . . . . _____

Approved _____
                    Head of Department

FIG. 32. Petty Cash Report Form

and-out cash box is an area of tremendous importance.

When making the monthly report, the business manager should not lump all these expenditures under the heading of petty cash and include it as such in the report. He should assign the expenditures to their proper departments (Set Building, House and Grounds, etc.) so that a true reflection of where the money is going is indeed shown in the report. If you go through several hundred dollars in petty cash on a large show, and the greater part of it goes for Costumes, say, but is never reported except as petty cash, neither the costume designer nor the Board has a clear picture of what costumes are really costing the theatre.

A limit should be placed on how much may be taken from the petty cash box for one purchase. Probably $5. Anything more, even on the largest budget, cannot be considered petty. Purchases of $5 or more should be charged, and a Purchase Order form used.

Purchase Orders

Another nuisance, but a necessary nuisance, is the use of the Purchase Order.

When anyone, staff or volunteer, sets out to buy something for the theatre, even at stores where you've long had a charge account, he must be armed with a Purchase Order number or be able to phone from the store to get a number from the theatre. (As with petty cash, Purchase Order numbers must be available to your people at all hours.) The business manager sets up a simple loose-leaf notebook with blank pages on which he lists consecutive numbers, beginning at 1, at the left-hand margin. (See Figure 33.) He then provides the tech director (or the secretary, during the day) with a book of Purchase Order blanks (Figure 34), a piece of carbon paper, and the loose-leaf Purchase Order record book.

As anyone sets out to buy, in person or by phone, anything costing over $5 (if that is your petty cash limit), he first gets a Purchase Order number from the keeper of the book. The purchaser makes sure that the store he buys from includes that number on the invoice, the receipt, the billing order, on anything on which this purchase is recorded. Thereafter, this number equals that purchase. The purchaser also gets as complete a price quotation as possible for this purchase and reports back to the tech director everything about the transaction (if he knows ahead of time precisely what he wants and where he's

going to find it, he gives that information *before* he goes or calls, at the time he is given the Purchase Order number). The tech director fills out a Purchase Order Form, as in Figure 34, including specifics on the purchase, and for which budgeted department each item is being bought. Then—*and most importantly*—he includes the price of each item on the Purchase Order form. If the exact price is in dispute because of possible discounts or bulk buying, he puts down an approximate figure, as close as the clerks can give him. One copy of the Purchase Order form is sent straight to the business manager and one kept in the loose-leaf Purchase Order Book, after all the information from the forms is transferred to the properly numbered line in the book, as in Figure 33.

The tech director can keep track of what is being spent by each department and can alert the business manager in case of heavy spending in any area, including his own. The business manager, meanwhile, keeps his copies of the PO's. As each bill comes in, he staples the proper Purchase Order form to its same-numbered bill. He can then see by the Purchase Orders whose bills have not come in by Monthly Financial Report time, and by double-checking in the loose-leaf book, which amounts are still outstanding, for inclusion in the Accounts Payable area of page 1 of the report.

It's a lot of trouble, but, especially when many people are buying for various departments, it keeps a check on what is being spent, so that a show that seems to be making money doesn't suddenly prove a loser as an unexpected bill for several hundred dollars arrives the following month. Nothing should be unexpected under this system, and though you can't be exact to the penny with a Purchase Order system until the final bill comes in, you can be exact to the nearest dollar or five dollars, keeping you far straighter in your accounting.

Donations and Services

It must be restressed that a nonprofit organization cannot expect to keep alive by paying its own way fully in the open market. You must learn to beg gracefully and to prebalance a season's budget by spotting early the needed expensive items that can be borrowed or bought at cost from friendly suppliers, and services that can be given by friendly experts. It must be restated, also, that the time to beg is not after the financial report has been printed in red, but by careful

P.O. Number	ISSUED TO WHAT COMPANY?	ITEMS PURCHASED (BE SPECIFIC)	DEPARTMENT AND SHOW	AMOUNT
289	JONES LUMBER	12 1x3x10' 6 2x4x8'	SCENERY "ODD COUPLE"	$14.40 (minus possible discount)
290	SAMUEL FRENCH	Royalties	ROYALTIES "DARKNESS at NOON"	$200.00
291	LANG'S FABRICS	Material	COSTUMES "ODD COUPLE"	$83.57 37.29 (minus possible discount)
292	V.T. Supply	Hardware (nails, screws, hoots)	Scenery "ODD COUPLE"	$22.40
293				
294				
295				
296				
297				
298				
299				
300				
301				
302				
303				
304				
305				
306				
307				

FIG. 33. Purchase Order Master Book

An inexpensive loose-leaf notebook, whose pages have been lined as illustrated, holds the record of all Purchase Order numbers as given by the Technical Director to crew members charged with buying items for the theatre. The actual amount spent against each P.O. number is entered as soon as it is known; until then, an approximate cost is put down, so the theatre has an up-to-the-minute record of where each department stands in regard to its budget (within a few dollars). When making out the Monthly Financial Report, the Business Manager can determine from this book which bills are still outstanding, and, therefore, what to enter in the Accounts Payable section of his report.

MOUNT HOLYOKE COLLEGE   Order No. *#289*

PURCHASE REQUISITION   Order Date *March 4, 1972*

Please { ~~purchase~~ / confirm } the following items:

Deliver to: *Lab Theatre*
Charge: *Theatre Arts*

Quantity	Description (indicate source of supply if known)	Price
12	1 X 3 X 10' #2 PONDEROSA PINE @8¢	$9.60
6	2 X 4 X 8' " " " @10¢	4.80
		$14.40
		(possible discount)

Purpose or use *SCENERY (ODD COUPLE)*   From _____ (to be filled in by Purchasing Dept.)

When Wanted *Now*

Dept. signature _____

Date *MARCH 4, 1972*

JONES LUMBER
85 WOODBRIDGE ST

Form 180. 9-71-10M-HP

FIG. 34. A Purchase Order Blank

Although this form is used by a large institution, it can serve almost without change for a theatre of any size. Adapt it to your needs, and insist that a Purchase Order number accompany each purchase except those made with Petty Cash.

preseason and then month-by-month examination of the problems, lacks, and needs in the theatre as reflected in potential loss of income or in overspending. Wrap yourself in the nonprofit flag of community culture and go out and tell that wholesaler, that accountant, that antique dealer what you will need next month, and how you can't afford any more than a sincere Thank You in the program. Keep track of these donations of goods or services, do give them program credit, and follow up with a note of thanks suitable for income-tax deduction.

In drawing up your budget, make an effort always to underestimate income and overestimate expenses. Why kid yourself? There is going to be a snowstorm some night, severely limiting your audience, or one show that you think is a great attraction will play to poor houses. And that simple one-set comedy is going to demand that you build twelve new flats and two new door units, throwing the scenery budget out the window. Better to plan for the worst in making out a budget, and then possibly surprise yourself as the weather holds and the shop crew learns frugality and the audiences come in droves. But however you do it, the theatre must work on a balanced budget; whether by better publicity to bring in more income, by cutting costs, by begging donations to cut expenses, or by some new method of your own—you must constantly manage the budget . . . or flop.

Part 3

BACKSTAGE ORGANIZATION

Here it comes—the section all the theatre artists are dreading. The organization of the backstage. The locking into a vise of all that creative talent, right? The bloodletting that sacrifices talent for routine, right? The setting of deadlines to disturb the natural flow of creative energy, right? Wrong.

Let me repeat myself: Without organization, the brightest talent will be dulled, the grandest ideas die aborning, and the theatre arts soon turn into anarchy as each artist does his thing with no central concept, no chain of command, no common set of deadlines with which to bring the entire work of art, the production, to fruition at the same time—opening night—for the same purpose—the involvement of the audience.

Without a common goal, which must be the appeal to an audience, individual moments or elements of the play may be works of genius, but they may be placed side by side with works of sheer self-indulgence or just bad work. The true theatre artist or craftsman *wants* and *needs* a schedule telling what is expected from him when, whether imposed on him or suggested by himself. Whichever method he and you agree to, his priorities and deadlines will guide him and always remind him that his creative work cannot (or bloody well should not) stand alone but is only successful as it meshes with a dozen other departments to create one common work of art called the production. This is true whether he's the director, designer, prop chief, or any department head.

Go back to Figure 3 and look over the DO LIST (sometimes called a DUE LIST) used during preproduction. This is a strongly stated schedule of needs and dates, not an unbreakable regimen—schedules and deadlines are negotiable as trouble occurs, as long as everyone realizes that once a deadline has not been met, the production *as a whole—not just that department*—is behind and therefore in trouble, and thought must be given to the Rule of Three.

THE PRODUCER

Who is responsible for unifying all the backstage departments into one productive, producing body? It's up to you and your chain of command to determine. Often it's the director, though some theatres work better with a man they call the producer or production manager. If you hire a new director for each play, you may be happier maintaining backstage control with a producer who is a member, who knows your theatre, your organization, your personnel. The one-time director has no interest in the long-term plans of your theatre organization; his main interest is probably the actors and their relationships to the other departments, rather than the needed equal emphasis on all areas at once. This producer (call him what you will) runs the production meetings, checks on the due lists, and is responsible for the amounts of freedom and restraint given to each artist and each craftsman in the backstage organization. He works side by side with the business manager, whose budget must be adhered to if the theatre is to continue after this production.

PSYCHOLOGY OF VOLUNTEERS

In the professional theatre, there is no question about showing up on time, completing a job when it is called for, following the regimen and the concept and the style

111

as set down by the overall boss, be he director or producer or a combination of both. The pro does it to the best of his ability, on time, or he's fired and never hired by this producing body again. In the nonprofessional theatre, however, it's vastly different. Of course, in the best-organized little theatres, the pride of professionalism pervades all departments, and the threat of being fired is not necessary to keep a tight ship and produce a quality play with all deadlines met and every part of the team contributing to the health of the whole. But most nonprofessional theatres are built on only a small core of people with such dedication to professionalism and must constantly work to enlarge that core. To do so, they should be very aware of the psychology of volunteers.

This is, after all, recreation or unpaid labor, an ego-trip or a social experience or therapy for many of them, and the final product doesn't mean as much as their individual involvement and rewards. Fine; there's nothing wrong with anyone coming to the theatre for any of the above reasons or a dozen more. But you will fail your volunteers and therefore your organization and therefore your show, if you do not take those disparate entrees to the theatre and unify them with a caring about the production itself, about its need for unity, deadlines, and a common creative goal. You may achieve this unity with subtlety or with an outright lecture on the need for teamwork. But somehow your volunteers must be galvanized with a love for the production, creating a team of zealots the like of which the professional theatre will never see.

Treat them well, use their time wisely, and they'll be theatre devotees as long as they live. If a crew call is for 7:30, have the shop leaders ready to work at 7:30, not just arriving and then having to unload the lumber and find the plans and finally get started at 8. At the other end of the evening, too, if you have promised a 10:30 dismissal, don't make it a nightly practice to plead with them to stay until midnight. Once or twice, sure, when the show is in trouble, everyone is excited about staying and helping out; but keep such thoughtless misuses of promised time to a minimum.

The head of each department should always keep in mind and at hand some simple but necessary busywork to give someone who's not awfully good with his hands, or has only an hour to give, or to pass on to an entire crew if a large project is just finishing and there's nothing you can start them on for a while. Tasks as basic as sweeping the floor, emptying the wastebaskets, sorting buttons or stage hardware, taking decor off a dress or a flat, coiling line, polishing shoes, taking thread out of a hem, cataloging flats. Be careful not to put the same people onto busy work every night, unless it's really all they can handle, but to balance it with highly creative craftsmanship they can be proud of and can actually see the results of on stage opening night.

At all times tell every crewman just what he's doing. Don't put him to work blindly sweeping the stage without advising him why it's necessary; don't give a girl skirts to baste without careful instructions in how to do it and a few words about what it is contributing to the costumes for the show. Don't put a new volunteer to cutting out corner blocks without showing him an actual corner block on an actual flat and letting him know its use and importance.

Compliment work done well; don't yell about poor work—point out pleasantly why it's not acceptable and help the volunteer to do it over properly; then compliment him when he gets it right.

Thank your volunteers for their work when they leave, and encourage them to come back. Even if they're only good for picking up debris or washing paintbrushes, that's a load off your back, and they are indeed valuable in that area. Make them *feel* valuable, and they'll come back. Make them feel like slaves or useless drones, and they won't. Include them in parties, spell their names correctly on the program, include them in annual awards (too many theatres, caught in the award excitement, give statuettes only to actors, forgetting the mammoth amount of talent and sweat and man-hours that have put those actors on the stage). Yes, fuss over them. You will always have people trying out for the glorious acting roles; you will soon have no one volunteering for nonacting assignments if they don't feel wanted or needed or a part of the creative team.

Backstage, where the heart of the play is found, our Manage or Flop maxim is more true than anywhere else.

Chapter IX

DESIGNERS AND THEIR CREWS

The finest designer I have ever worked with in community theatre started off our first show to-gether—a mammoth musical—with something every director loves to hear. I'd preface each suggestion or question on the set with "Is it pos-sible . . . ?," and he'd answer each with a cheery "Anything is possible."

When we got close to dress rehearsal, however, he came to me and asked if we could cut two sets entirely from the play. "But you said anything was possible," I argued. "Anything is possible," he said, "with enough time."

* * *

Let it never be forgotten that designers—set designers, costume designers, lighting designers—are highly creative artists in their own right and must be given as much freedom as is possible. Once given the director's concept of a produc-tion, they can bring ideas from their own creative souls that go far beyond anything the director has conceived—they can bring that concept to life visually, making a far better production than could ever have been dreamed of—and their suggestions for basic style can start the director thinking in altogether new and exciting ways. Several years ago I directed *A Midsummer Night's Dream,* costumed in the Empire style of Regency England, purely as a result of a sugges-tion from my costume designer, and found more beauty, more ways of expressing the love and the magic and the comedy than I would have been able to in any other style. So listen to them, even if their ideas are counter to what you started out with, and be well aware that the visual aspect of your play—as presented by your designers—is one of the chief means of getting across the au-thor's ideas and feelings to your audience.

The director-designer relationship is the most vital, and can be the most exciting, in the whole creative world of the theatre. Include designers in all preproduction discussions, try out ideas on them and listen to theirs in return, show their sketches at auditions and at rehearsals, con-stantly, to remind the actors of the visual envi-ronment they will be working in. A director-designer team that works produces fine art; lack of communication within that team will present you with a mess.

And in that communication, *remind* the de-signers and their crews that they are a part of that team, not independent creative artists working on their own projects, and that deadlines must be set and met.

No matter how marvelously an actor is doing in rehearsal, if he never sets foot on that 10-foot platform until two days before opening, his scenes there will be less sure, less patterned, less effective for the late addition of an important physical aspect of his work. The strongest actress will lose strength if put into unusual shoes or a difficult-to-maneuver skirt only at dress rehears-al. The best comedy business, honed for weeks in rehearsal, will turn to jelly if the comic actors find themselves surrounded with furniture of vastly different size and shape from that they've been working with. Impress on your designers the need for priority, and begin your priorities with what-ever the actors actually touch and wear and step on.

Approach this problem carefully, since you'll hear, as I have, again and again—"You think only about the actors—remember there are other elements of this production, too." And that's a danger—working with the actors night after night, in depth, a director is liable to think of them as the beginning and the end of his play. But the crews must remember, too, that the actors carry the major responsibility of the perform-ance—to convey the author's words, and, there-fore, his feelings and his theses, to the audience, and that they must be comfortable, within reason, to be able to do so. The most beautiful drop in the world, painted with loving care and delivered early, can't help that actor as he stumbles up some stairs he has never seen before preview per-formance. The loveliest headdress won't con-ceal the fact that the actress is concentrating more on balancing this new piece than on the song she is singing. And the most inspired lighting effects are of no use if the actor can't find his way around the stage.

So, new and unusual and possibly difficult design elements in the set must be at the director's and the actors' disposal as first priority. This is not to say that the director should ask for needless props and costumes early—that's selfish and not to the purpose of the production. The best designers will know the importance of the availability of the proper shoes and that heavy door, and will give them to you early in rehearsal. New or selfish designers must be brought into the idea of the production team from the beginning, so that the audience won't go out of the theatre, in one critic's words, "whistling the scenery." A beautiful set ill-used can't save a show. Well-used, it takes its place with the dialogue and the emotions and the movement and the lighting and the audience's comfort to make a great evening of theatre.

Having begun with suggestions for solving one of the biggest complaints usually found between directors and designers, let's go back to the basics of what designers and their crews do.

Each in his own field helps bring to life the concept of the play as written by the author and interpreted by the director.

THE SET DESIGNER

His chief assistant: the Technical Director.
  Their crews:
    Preparation:
      Set Building
      Set Painting
      Prop Gathering
      Prop Building
    Running:
      Grips (moving scenery along the floor, by hand and on castors)
      Flymen (flying scenery)
      Prop running

All scenery, set pieces, furniture, and props are under the creative control of the set designer. He designs each piece or approves its selection by his technical director or prop crew. Everything visual, except costumes and lighting, is in his milieu. (Many designers handle both sets and costumes, and, in my opinion, the best set designers are those who also design their own lighting. More later.)

After consultation with the director, the set designer brings a first sketch, which may be on the back of an envelope or a napkin or may be more formal. This is his proffering of his feeling of the show, expressed visually. There may be no doors, or windows, or levels—just a few lines expressing through his specific medium the concept of the play. He and the director discuss the feeling given by the sketch, and if suitable talk about more practical elements, such as doors, for instance. The designer next brings in his finished sketch of the setting(s). This is in color, with a realistic representation of how he wants the set to look from the first dress rehearsal. When accepted, this sketch becomes his contract with the director, who will conceive the movement and staging of the play with that feeling, that design in mind.

The set designer, then, through the technical director, sees to the building and securing of everything in the sketch—from draperies and rugs to furniture and decor to the basic flats, doors, windows, etc.

He provides the TD (Technical Director) with whatever working drawings are needed for the accurate building of the set; he shows, by his own sketches or by extracts from books and magazines, the furniture he wants; he works closely with the prop crew, telling them what to look for from the stage manager's prop list, or approving what they bring in, or both.

He sets with the director the deadlines for various priority elements, and sees, through the TD and his preparation crew, that the deadlines are met.

Deadlines may include publicity pictures for newspapers and/or the theatre lobby. To do any good, pictures must appear in the paper before the play opens, which generally means they must be taken before dress rehearsal; therefore, before the entire set is finished. And they must make a strong visual impact on potential ticket buyers, to make them want to come to the performance. So, together, the set designer and the director select an area of the set that will be ready for pictures a week or so before dress rehearsal. There must be no bare lumber, no paint puddles on the floor—the area, even if only six or eight feet wide, must show the camera a stageworthy play in the way only a photo can—visually and emotionally. No dialogue, no movement—here the combination of the designer's creative concept of the scenery and the director's skillful staging of several of the more interesting characters on that segment of set must sell the play.

A week before tech rehearsal, each designer and/or his chief assistant works with the director and *his* chief assistant, the stage manager, to produce the cue sheets from which the running crews work, under the stage manager, to run the show. This includes the costume designer, who works out location of all costume changes, especially *quick* changes, assigning dressers to the actors when necessary for speed and efficiency in the changes. The preparation of cue sheets is discussed in Chapter X.

By three days before tech rehearsal, the sets and props must be completely ready. At that time, the director can begin truly melding his actors and their action into the physical setting, so that dress rehearsal will not see the disintegration of the performance as actors adjust, badly, to new elements. This also gives the designer an easy period in which to do any touch-up required, to make any adjustments in his own visually expressed concept, as he and the director see that an element won't work. He will avoid the (bad) tradition of working all night following the dress rehearsals, often up to opening, completing things that should have been ready before.

The designer's eye must be sharp during this period, for polishing his contribution to the play. By setting a deadline of three days before tech rehearsal, his senses won't be numbed to what is onstage during tech by the artless sweat of completing the bare-bones necessities, making the tech rehearsal a tense, tiring, and totally noncreative period. With the first tech rehearsal the preparation crews are finished, and the tech director and his running crews begin to man the running of the play each night. They sweep the acting and offstage areas used by actors, set the opening scenery and props, pull the curtain, make any set and prop changes or adjustments called for, and batten down the set at the end of each evening, paying special attention to the covering up or locking up of expensive and breakable borrowed props and furniture.

Throughout tech and into dress rehearsals, the set designer sits in the house, taking his own notes of necessary changes, improvements, and completions and staying available to the director for questions and notes on *his* needs. Both do their best to ensure that nothing is changed or added after the final dress rehearsal, as there is no surer way to ruin an actor's opening-night concentration and timing than to throw in a new color, a new object, or anything he has not absorbed into his pattern during the rehearsals.

THE COSTUME DESIGNER

His chief assistant: the Costumer (or Costumier).
   Their crews:
      Preparation:
         Costume Sewing
         Costume Gathering
         Costume Painting and Dyeing
      Running:
         Wardrobe Mistress
         Dressers
         Makeup

Much of what has been said above holds true for the costume designer, too, whether he designs every costume from scratch or does the no-less-creative job of coordinating costumes and street clothing that already exist into an artistic onstage statement of these characters in this setting and in this style.

The costume sketches, like the set sketches, begin with a visual representation, however simple, of the feeling this artist has of the characters and their clothing. Later they are translated into full sketches, with color and swatches of material, of how the characters will look onstage.

Including their makeup.

The best costume designers are also designers of character makeup, the costume not stopping at the neck. The sketch reflects the total feeling of the inner life of the character manifest externally in line, color, texture, and facial structure. Such sketches, when approved by the director, give the actors a stronger feeling of what sort of characters they are attempting to create.

The costume designer's chief assistant, the costumer, supervises the buying of fabric and the buying or borrowing of existing clothing, the cutting of it to pattern (sometimes the creation of the patterns themselves), the fittings, and the alterations.

Under both of them are the seamstresses, the costume painters and dyers, the gatherers, and the many unskilled workers who can sew on buttons or rehem a skirt or sew on trim.

Priorities in costuming, too, are important, remembering that unusual costumes must at least be represented by rehearsal skirts or jackets or shoes from the very beginning of rehearsal, and that photo-call costumes must be ready for newspaper pictures well before dress rehearsal. On a recent production of *Mourning Becomes Electra,* the costume designer insisted, rightly, that the actresses wear corsets and hoop skirts from the very first rehearsal and that the actors wear tightly buttoned vests to give them the feeling of the heavily-cinched post-Civil War line. Conversely, on a large musical I was associated with, every costume for a forty-five-second chorus appearance was made down to the last snap two weeks into a five-week rehearsal, but the leading lady went into dress rehearsal a full three costumes short. Good management brought about the first event; pretty awful management allowed the second.

On that historic third day before tech rehearsal, the costume designer stages a Dress Parade for the director, in which each actor models each costume he will wear onstage. The actors are brought on in groupings, by scene, by family, or other relationship, for the director and costume designer together to check the basic fit of each costume, the freedom it allows actors for any extreme movements that are part of the blocking or choreography of the show, and its suitability for this character in this situation. If the sketches were correct and correctly approved, nothing should be rejected at this late date; but if the costume designer had to substitute something of a different line or color because of time or unavailability, adjustments may have to be made. Notes are taken, and the three-day grace period is used for final alterations and substitutions.

The costume designer need not attend tech rehearsal, unless to check a few light settings and colors for their effect on costumes; but from first dress rehearsal on, the costume designer turns the backstage workings over to the wardrobe mistress and the dressers, whose charge is the hanging of every costume in its proper dressing room or quick-change booth, by cue sheets set up by the costume designer (or the costumer) with the stage manager and director, and the effecting of all costume changes. The costume designer, like the set designer, sits in the house during each dress rehearsal taking his own notes and those of the director regarding costumes.

The Lighting Designer

Chief assistant: Chief Electrician.
   Their crews:
      Preparation:
         Hanging Crew
      Running:
         Switchboard Crew
         Floor Crew (if needed, to replug, reposition, or re-gel certain lights)

As previously stated, I honestly believe the best set designers conceive their scenery with stage lighting as well as pigment in mind and actually do their own lighting design. But there are many fine set designers who do not know much about lighting, except to holler that it's wrong or smile that it's right; and some superb lighting designers cannot draw a cat. So use your creative people as their abilities best allow. If a combination set/lighting designer, fine; if two separate artists, fine again.

The lighting designer should be in on all discussions between the director and other designers from the beginning and should discuss the needs and offerings of his art at each meeting. His first job, as with the other designers, is to present his feeling about the production. Realistic lighting or strictly mood? Or a combination of both? Bright colors or dark; bright lights or dim; full illumination or area lighting? After his concept has been approved, he moves to the more practical matters of onstage lamps, light sources, what can be accomplished with the number of instruments and dimmers at his disposal (or shall he rent or borrow more?). How many cues in the production? What colors are the other designers putting onstage for him to light? What color gels will present those colors of pigment and dye to achieve the effect the designers want? What gels will turn them to mud and must be avoided?

He then designs his light plot, showing the designers and director the lighting areas this plot will provide. He shows them the gels he proposes using, and, if there is any question, tries them out on a swatch of material or painted surface to reassure himself and everyone else that they are the proper choice.

Then, through his chief electrician, he begins to hang and angle and gel his instruments, even before the set is up. With the erection of the set, the electrical preparation crew will focus the lights, check the effect, and make adjustments as needed.

The director and his stage manager will work out cue sheets with the lighting designer after the play has been blocked and the director has decided what he needs in each scene. A day or two before tech rehearsal, the lighting designer will present to the director and set designer his first lighting run-through, taking each cue, as provided by the director, and embellished by his own creative feeling for the play, as the stage manager walks through the actors' moves. During this run-through they discuss cue timing, intensity of each cue, the effect of the color on the set (and costumes, too, if the costume designer wants to place some of the costumes onstage under the lighting), and the overall dimension provided by the lighting on that faraway field of action on which people and objects tend to flatten terribly unless properly costumed and lit.

The lighting designer will stay with the show during all tech and dress rehearsals, making corrections as he sees their need or as instructed by the director or set designer. He will, with his crew of electricians who run the switchboard, sharpen the timing of each cue and double-check to see that the cue sheets are accurate for the reproduction of agreed-upon intensities and colors and timing, night by night with no guesswork or fallible intuition.

THE TECHNICAL DIRECTOR

We have discussed the technical director only in his function as chief assistant to the set designer. In large theatres this is accurate, but in many small theatres the tech director fills broader and more creative jobs. Often he is the only paid employee other than the director, the only person backstage with firm technical training and experience, and it is he who guides the designers and all their crews, perhaps even serving as set designer or lighting designer himself. If so, many of the above paragraphs are for his eyes.

Even in large theatres, the tech director is often the lighting designer, or the chief electrician; this is fine, as long as his main duty of getting the set up and dressed is not slighted.

We have not talked of sound recording or the playing of sound during the performance; this, in nearly every case, is under the command of the tech director, with a sound preparation crew for preshow, and a sound running crew from tech rehearsal on.

To cover all types of theatre, the best statement on the technical director is: He is in charge of every nonacting onstage aspect of the production. With a good TD, every designer is stronger and more able to devote himself to the more artistic aspects of his work; with a weak one, or an overbearing one, troubles can develop in those quiet, dark corners of the stage out of sight of the unknowing director out front. Unlike the designers, his job continues well past dress rehearsal and through the entire running of the production.

If you have only one professional slot to fill in your organization, it might be well to consider hiring a top-flight, interested, and personable TD.

He can build up the numbers of crew people volunteering, can keep a happy and educational shop, and can unify the many elements of backstage theatre.

MAINTENANCE OF THEATRE EQUIPMENT AND BELONGINGS

Each designer, whether paid or volunteer, must take responsibility for the maintenance of everything that could fall under his aegis on a play, for himself and for future designers. The storage, cleanliness, and availability of everything in his sphere must be of as prime concern to him as the elements actually used by him in his design of the play. The technical director is actually an assistant to each designer in this area and helps with the maintenance of all the tools for each.

Following are some ways this maintenance can best be accomplished.

KEEPING YOUR STOCK VISIBLE—RECORD-KEEPING

Your designers can do a better job of utilizing existing stock if they know what is *in* the stock. There are countless instances in nonprofessional theatre in which time and money have been spent finding design items when exact duplicates were buried in theatre storage rooms. Proper storage and/or the keeping of records would have eliminated the waste. Proper record-keeping will ensure proper organization and management of the designers' stock—costumes and sewing accessories, lighting instruments, cable, lamps, gel frames, flats and other scenic pieces, and props of all description. And the time taken to enter new acquisitions and delete those used up, thrown away, or altered in description will be far less than that wasted looking through stock for things not there to begin with, or looking elsewhere for something you have hidden, especially if, as with many small theatres, your stock is stored in many separate buildings around town.

With or without good record-keeping, time and care must be taken to store all theatre belongings where they will be kept clean, free of temperature extremes, and visible. Throw away the useless one-time props, costumes, and set pieces, leaving proper room for the reusable items. Group like items together—clothing of the same period, or from the same show (for possible rental to other theatres), sofas and chairs, lamps, desk

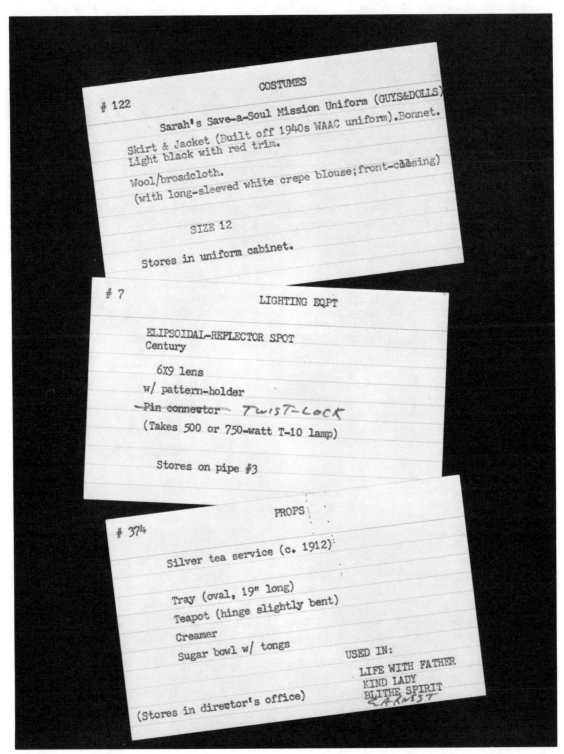

FIG. 35. Record Blanks for Inventory of Props, Costumes, Lighting Equipment
Affix the record number to the actual item in a permanent way, but (certainly in the case of props) so that the audience cannot see evidence of the number. Include on the cards as much information as will help a crew head decide in advance whether he wants to consider the item, without having to plow through the storage room. Add or delete as the item is changed from show to show. To avoid using the same prop or costume so often as to make it familiar to your audience, list the shows it appears in.

accessories, kitchen equipment, hats, canes, and so on. Label the shelves or the cabinets so that each new designer or crew knows where to look for and where to return the tools of his trade. Several times a year, have a designer from each area, with a willing crew, clean out his specific storage area, ruthlessly throwing out junk and recataloging (if you keep records), relabeling, dusting, and straightening so that everything is again visible, clean, and ready to be used.

Index cards are the best format for this sort of record—they may be kept neatly together in a little tin box (one box for each design area), with new cards added for new acquisitions, amendments made to the cards as needed, and elimination of a prop or costume reflected by simply throwing its card away.

For props, costumes, or lighting equipment, the card is filled out as for any stock inventory in any sort of operation (see Figure 35); for scenery, the same sort of format is possible, but a more practical method is to cut out scale models of the flats (perhaps 1/2" = 1'), mark them with the serial numbers borne by the actual flats, and keep the models in a special large tin box. (See Figure 36.) Platforms, step units, doors, win-

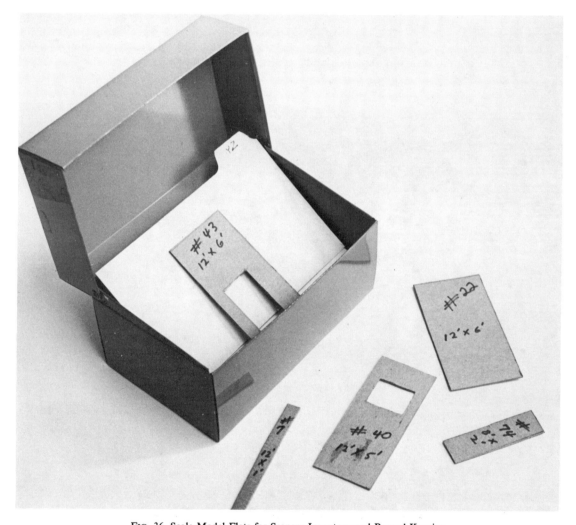

FIG. 36. Scale Model Flats for Scenery Inventory and Record-Keeping
Each flat is numbered on the back with large painted figures to correspond with the numbers on the model flats. (Scale ¼" = 1'.) Any changes made on the actual flat should be reflected in changes made on the model: Is a door opening made larger? Make it larger on the cardboard mock-up. Has the shop cut a window opening in a standard flat? Cut one in the model, noting that it may be covered again at any time to restore the flat to its original condition. If an old flat has run its course of usefulness, throw it out, but build a new one of the same size right away and assign it the old flat's number, keeping the tin box of flat models accurate and your stock ready for any show.

dows, fireplaces, and other three-dimensional set pieces are best represented by scale models (same scale as the flats) cut from scrap lumber and marked as the units themselves are marked. (See Figure 37.) A new designer moving into the theatre can assemble possible combinations of set pieces on his drafting table to see what exists that can be used, and to better order what new pieces must be built for his set. If your theatre rents out its belongings, a note should be made on the index card, or fastened to the model piece, to indicate the piece is out of the theatre and unavailable from X date to X date.

RENTING OUT

The potential income from renting out sets, lights, props, or costumes is not to be ignored. It takes time from your staff or volunteers, and there is always the danger of a handsome piece being permanently harmed, but it's another way of being known in the community, and it can bring in a lot of money.

If you decide to rent out some of your properties, assign a designer from each area to supervise the operation of the rental business, determining which pieces in his area are available for rental, for what price, and to whom. To other theatres only? Or for costume parties, school dances, political rallies? It's up to each designer, who will supervise the pickup and redelivery by the renting group, will receive the deposit, and will keep accurate records of the transaction. (See Figure 38.) As something is lost or returned in an unusable condition, he will see to it that the deposit is forfeited and may decide that nothing is to be let to that group again.

FIG. 37. Scale Model Scenic Units for Inventory and Record-Keeping

Stairs, platforms, fireplaces, etc. are represented by scale models (¼" = 1') in exactly the same way flats are (Figure 36). They are numbered and kept current with any changes, replacement, or disposition of the actual scenic pieces in your shop or storage area. The designer may decide to use these model pieces, both flats and platforms, in putting together a mock-up of the set; or he may simply refer to them to see how best to design his set inexpensively, using only—or mainly—what is already built and in good condition.

Scale models built by Christine E. Smith

LABORATORY THEATRE

MOUNT HOLYOKE COLLEGE
SOUTH HADLEY, MASS.   01075
536-4000 - EXT. 310

FURNITURE OR PROPERTIES TO BE BORROWED:

coffee table   hand puppets from "Balk circle"

lamp

follow spot

DATE TAKEN OUT: Nov. 23, '71

CONDITION: table has two scratches on top, rest in good condition

DATE RETURNED: Dec. 10, '71

BORROWER: NAME: Wm. Hueydinski PHONE: 542 - 0921

STREET: Hyman St. SCHOOL OR CITY: Central School

SIGNATURE William Hueydinski

FIG. 38. Form for Recording Rental-Out or Lending of Props, Costumes, Etc.
When items are returned in good condition, this form is given to the borrower as a receipt for the returning.

RENTING IN OR BORROWING

The stock of set pieces, costumes, props, and lights owned by a theatre can seldom fully supply a show, and your designers will require all the budget you can give them to add to the stock and produce a beautiful show. But that budget may not always stretch to include the purchase of everything needed. We have spoken before about the availability of items to be borrowed, and it bears repeating—there is virtually nothing except lumber and nails and fabric, which will be used up, that cannot be borrowed from other theatres, stores, and private homes. Remind your designers and their crews, and see how much money *cannot* be spent, by the practice of seeking and borrowing. And when something is borrowed it must be well cared for, returned promptly after close of show, and program credit must be given. To be sure everything gets back to the proper place, each designer should maintain careful records of the borrowing, checking off each piece as it is returned. (See Figure 39.)

Renting in is another problem, and I'm basically against renting anything if it can be borrowed, or if the budget and future planning will allow it to be bought and added to the permanent stock. Rental of most items needed by a show is

very expensive, and when the show is finished a hole in the budget is all you have to show for it. If you should have to rent in, however, maintain the same careful records and the same care of the items rented as you do with borrowed items. And, to avoid additional rental charges, get them back immediately after the final performance. But try to convince the designers that renting is a last resort, following outright purchase and borrowing.

I shall close the discussion of designers and their crews with one final limiting and one final freeing of their creative juices.

THE BUDGET

In answer to the question: "How much may I spend?," I have heard business managers and treasurers answer "As little as possible." This is foolhardy, and every department head must know precisely what he has at his disposal for the proper management of his funds and his job on the show. This is especially true of designers, who, again, are probably the most creative forces on your production, but not always the most frugal. If a certain color of fabric is the only one that

PROPS
BORROWED OR RENTED FOR *The Hostage*
(Production)

ITEM(S) (Be specific)	BORROWED OR RENTED?	FROM WHOM? (Complete address)	BY WHOM?	DATE	CONDITION	DATE RETURNED (with your initials)
3 WORLD WAR I RIFLES	B	The Gun Shop 12 Main St.	Sam	4/12	RUSTY BUT INTACT	5/10 SG
DART BOARD 16 darts	B	MR. CRIMMINS CHEMISTRY DEPT.	Sam	"	GOOD	5/10 SG
IRON BEDSTEAD SPRINGS, MATTRESS	R	JOE'S SECOND HAND SHOP – 193 APPLETON	Sam	4/13	PAINT PEELING	5/10 SG
steins (6)	B	(46 North St.) Dew Drop Inn	Connie	4/14	good	C.B. May 10
shawl (white crochet)	B	Josephine Cusack 295 Murray Ave	I.E.L.	"	ONE TINY SPOT	5/10 IEL
painting	B	Mr. John Maley 3065 Fairview Rd.	Connie	4/14	some cracks in paint	
wooden leg	Borrowed	The Old Mariners Museum (Hogg's?)	Connie	4/14	slightly chipped worn on bottom	

FIG. 39. Form for Recording Rental-In or Borrowing of Production Items

The form shown is exclusively for props, but the costume chairman has a similar sheet, filled out in exactly the same way. Nearly everyone will be happy to lend you props for a show, if he knows he will get them back in good condition and promptly. But it takes only one negligent volunteer on one show to ruin future borrowing possibilities for the entire theatre. Make complete and accurate entries on these forms, take care of the borrowed items, and return them when you have promised. None of these in-house forms need be a work of art—handmade or mimeographed, their purpose is function, not for filing with the Library of Congress. No money need be spent, as long as they serve their purpose and are completely legible.

will really do for this play, and it costs a great deal of money, the designer must—repeat must—be the one to decide that it's worth scrimping somewhere else to have the piece he wants. But, if he has no budgetary guideline, he may well buy that fabric, plus several other expensive items, scrimping nowhere, and spend more than the box office can take in.

So the designer must be presented with a carefully considered budget and instructed to stick to it. And *made* to stick to it. Again, this is not limiting his creativity just for the sake of rules and regulations, but he, like all of us, must realize that without his own budgetary management the theatre will flop, and he will have no more forum in which to demonstrate his art and express his love of the theatre.

But keep him creatively alive and determine in advance that he may be allowed some. . .

LUXURIES

A low-budgeted nonprofessional theatre owes it to itself and its future to restrict its spending to items that can be used on later shows. Step units, doors, platforms, special costumes such as uniforms should generally be included in the design only when their cost can be prorated over several plays or several seasons. Flats and set pieces should be made to exact foot-and-inch measurements so as to fit into other floor plans easily (and for easy storage). With a new paint job, and a new façade changing the line, most can serve again. A high curving staircase may be beautiful in a particular show, but can the cost of its building (and the trouble of its storage) be justified? Probably not. However . . . remember, always, the creativity of your designers, and learn where to break the rule of recirculation of the stock. On each play, allow each designer to design as he has to, and then bring the sets and costumes into existence partly from existing stock, partly from pieces that can be made and reused, and partly (here's the luxury) by stretching the budget to build or buy a few new pieces that can't possibly be used again but will beautifully express the designers' concept of this play. You will have invested wisely, as you will have a better show and keep your designer with you. Admittedly it's a luxury, but it's also an art form, and not strictly a business graded in dollars and cents.

Chapter X

STAGE MANAGEMENT

This story may be apocryphal, but I am told it's true: On the second night of a college production a few years ago, a strange girl showed up backstage at check-in time. "Hi!" she said. "I'm the stage manager's roommate. She has a date at Dartmouth tonight, so I'm going to stage-manage the show for her."

* * *

The stage manager's duties are really only two, and are simply expressed:

Until opening night he makes the director's life as easy as possible:

Thereafter, he runs the entire backstage, maintaining the performance to the exact pattern the director has set in rehearsals.

The organization and management we have spoken of have been in preparation for the chief reason for theatre—the performance. And the organization and management of the performance and of all auditions and rehearsals leading to it are in the hands of the stage manager.

His duties are unnumbered and may encompass everything from moving chairs for rehearsals to serving as a sounding board for the director's ideas in a late-night coffee-drinking script-searching session. He is not a stagehand, though he will feel he is in the audition and rehearsal days; he is not the director, though at times he will act as surrogate for the top man, especially in disciplinary cases. He is in every way the strong right hand of his director, and he must learn, before anything, how his boss works, how he approaches his cast and his script, what he wants and when, and precisely how he thinks. The stage manager, keeping in mind the smooth running of the play at every stage, and the director's needs and wants as his chief momentary concern, will anticipate and circumvent trouble before it happens. He remembers Murphy's Law: "If something can go wrong, it will," and stays fifteen minutes ahead of the rest of the world, from his first day of work until the set is struck. What time must the building be vacated? Remind the director, so he can sew up auditions or rehearsals without eliding something he wanted

to save for the end. Who is due at a certain time for a meeting or a rehearsal? Start phoning for him five minutes early. Who is needed for the next scene? Send the assistant stage manager for him before this scene is finished, so that no time is wasted in the search. Does the director prefer a loose-flowing audition or rehearsal? Help him, but stay ahead of him in getting everyone where he must be, and still finish before midnight.

It may seem at times that I consider the director some sort of god and the stage manager his handmaiden, racing ahead to remove pebbles from his path, lest he trip. Not so. But the director, who has probably worked a full day himself, must keep his mind alert to the artistic bringing-to-life of the play and the psychological balance of the creative humans under his direction. Anything the stage manager can do to remove needless distractions is all to the good of the play.

Bert Gruver's *The Stage Manager's Handbook* (see Bibliography) should be read and digested and constantly referred to by every stage manager of every play in every theatre. This chapter, then, will presume that Gruver is at the stage manager's elbow, and will concentrate on delineating his duties in the nonprofessional theatre.

PREREHEARSAL DUTIES

The stage manager begins making life easier for the director even before auditions, handling all detail and administrative work and checking each step with the director for accuracy:

• Enough scripts must be available for auditions and for the actors who will ultimately be cast; the designers need copies of the script, and perhaps those in charge of props, sound, etc., will need scripts as well.

• Any cuts, changes, or additions made by the director must be inserted into all scripts.

• Any reference material needed by the director is secured for him.

• Notification of audition time and place must

124

be given to the publicity chairman. If a mailing or phone list of potential actors is available, all on it are contacted.

● A preliminary prop list, based on his understanding of the script, is made; in discussions with the director this list is solidified and passed on to the prop chairman.

● Audition sheets are prepared, giving the actors the information they should have and securing from them information the director must have. (See Figure 40.)

● In short, *anything* the director needs or wants (to free his mind for the creative work of the preproduction days) is done by the stage manager.

AUDITIONS

Once auditions begin, the stage manager, like a good operating-room nurse, has the necessary implements in the director's hands before he asks for them.

The audition area has been arranged for by the stage manager—it is clean, quiet, and heated (or cooled) for everyone's comfort. The area in which the actors will appear—either the stage or a cleared area within a large room if no auditorium is available—is well lighted and set with several chairs. The director has an uncluttered table in the middle of the auditorium or toward the back of the audition room, with a small shaded light, enough to give him illumination but not enough to distract the actors when he takes notes. He has sharpened pencils and a list of the characters to be cast; the stage manager makes sure the director has his script (many directors constantly misplace this most necessary tool), plus a pitcher of water and a glass. If he smokes, there is an ashtray and a supply of matches—perhaps even of his brand of cigarettes or tobacco.

The stage manager, generally with an assistant, sets up shop in the lobby, or at the entrance to the room, with a solid table, a good supply of sharpened pencils, the audition information sheets, the audition cards, and the answers to all questions actors may have: dates of performance, of first rehearsal, hints on what the director is looking for in any cast and specifically in this cast, and so on. If the director wants it known, the stage manager will have information of what scenes will be read, and will have scripts or typed audition scenes available. A stapler should be kept handy to fasten to the audition sheets any additional material actors may bring, such as résumés or photos.

As at rehearsals and performances, the stage manager and his assistants will report for work at auditions at least a half hour early, to be sure nothing is missing and all is ready to go.

Most directors will want to say a few words to the applicants before beginning auditions. At that time, the stage manager will shepherd all actors into the audition area, whether or not they have finished their applications, to hear the director. An exciting addition to the auditions is the display of costume and set designs for this production, explained briefly by the director. Many actors have no idea of the work done by theatre artists other than actors; this will put into perspective the creative concept as expressed in design, and it may help to enlist actors to costume-sewing or set-building or painting. It may also help the more experienced people to project in auditioning the feeling of the show, having seen a visual representation of the concept. After the opening remarks, the stage manager hands the director all the audition cards that have been filled out and hurries the remaining actors into finishing theirs. Throughout the audition session, any new cards coming in are taken immediately to the director's table; if he likes them separated by men and women, the stage manager places them in the proper pile.

Some directors prefer that each actor read only with the stage manager, so that the attention is kept on one person at a time. In this case, the stage manager has rehearsed the scenes to be read and serves as a good, solid tennis backboard —giving loud, clear, intelligent readings for the actors to read against, not trying accents or large emotions, or in any way to steal the scene. If the actor gets lost on the page, the stage manager helps him find his place with no fuss, in every way giving the actor a chance to do well and the director every opportunity to see the actor at his best. (During such readings, the assistant stage manager is handling the desk and bringing the director new cards.)

If the director prefers to hear actors reading with other actors, the stage manager runs the desk, keeping himself always available to the director to make phone calls, to take messages to actors in the lobby or sitting across the auditorium, especially as to entries on their audition cards that are confusing or not complete. The director will probably require coffee, tea, or a soft drink during a long audition session—the stage manager anticipates the need, and has it there as the director needs it.

If an actor expresses a need to leave early, the stage manager finds out if the director wants to

```
                         AUDITION  INFORMATION                              A
                                  for
             Right You Are If You Think You Are, by Luigi Pirandello
                                  and
          Guys and Dolls, by Abe Burrows & Jo Swerling; music & lyrics by Frank Loesser
```

* Except for the roles of Big Jule & Lt. Branningan (and possibly Nathan Detroit) in GUYS AND
DOLLS, there is <u>no possibility</u> of anyone filling parts in both plays.

* RIGHT YOU ARE will begin rehersal immediately, and will be presented
                    Oct 22-24 & 28-31, evenings, for a total of 7 performances.
   Rehersals will normally be held Sunday thru Thursday evenings, 7:30-11 p.m., with major
roles called more frequently than smaller parts.
   A special, concentrated rehersal is planned for one of the weekends, rehersing 5 segments
out of a possible Fri night, Sat morning, Sat afternoon, Sat night, Sun afternoon and Sun night.
(This would be: Oct 1-2-3 <u>OR</u> 8-9-10). In addition to doing a full week's work in a few days,
this would give us all the opportunity to work Theatre as Theatre is worked - with no distraction
and with emphasis on the play. It's possible that samller roles would not be called, or called
for only a partially intense day....

* GUYS AND DOLLS will begin singing and dancing rehersals fairly soon, and will reherse
throughout October, not constantly but frequently, so all music is well learned by Nov. 1. Small
roles, or people with little musical contact in the play would of course reheares proportionately
less than those with larger musical involvement. Then, beginning Nov 1, the book will begin
rehearsing, and the songs staged, etc.... with the Sunday-thru-Thursday rehersal week applying,
with larger roles needed more nights then chorus and small parts.
   GUYS AND DOLLS will play 9 performances:
                    Dec 3-4-5 & 11-12-13-14, nightly, plus a matinee each of the 2 Saturdays,

---

You may try out for either play - or both plays - with the knowledge that you probably <u>cannot</u>
be in both -- see first note, above.
You may try out for either play or both plays at any of the 4 audition sessions:
                    Monday Sept 20, 2:30 p.m. and 7:30 p.m.
                    Tuesday Sept 21, 2:30 p.m. and 7:30 p.m.
You need come ONLY ONCE, unless you are asked to come back. However, you MAY come to as many
audition sessions as you like......

Both plays will be vast - we hope - late Tuesday night, and those who <u>are cast</u> called as soon
as possible; that night, it is planned. The cast list will also be posted on the Call Board
that night. If you're NOT cast, we can't call you, but you'll know by <u>not</u> being called by Wed
                                                                                          noon.
You may specify which play you'd rather be in, and which parts you would accept. Be sure you
are honest with yourself and with us on this: don't limit yourself to only accepting a lead
unless you realize this severely narrows your chance of being in the play: don't say you'll
only accept a chorus role and then find yourself unhappy you haven't a larger role. On the
other hand, examine your limitations as well as your strengths, and don't count on a lead if
you've only been in 3 plays before.....

Both plays are being done true to their periods: RIGHT YOU ARE, Italy 1920s: GUYS AND DOLLS,
New York gamblers of the 1940s.... We will follow the styles as far as scenery, costumes
and hair styles.... It'll likely not be necessary that any girl out cut her hair, tho Adelaide
should almost certainly be a brassy blonde; but men must realize that straight hairstyles
will be the rule.... No one will have to cut hair or beards until close to show time, but
makeup must be proper period. Perhaps a few well-tended short beards would fit into RIGHT YOU
ARE....

Music for the GUYS AND DOLLS auditions will be provided by our piano and pianist; you furnish the
sheet music, if you can -- AT ANY RATE, KNOW WHAT YOU'RE GOING TO SING BEFORE YOU GET TO THE
PIANO....   You <u>need not</u> sing anything from Guys and Dolls, but you may. You <u>need not</u>
sing an extire song; we'll probably stop you midways if you do....
```

FIG. 40. Audition Forms
```

CHARACTER DESCRIPTIONS -- Guys and Dolls   B

WOMEN ((ALL MUST HAVE COMPLETED THE MOUNT HOLYOKE THEATRE ARTS #145 COURSE, OR CURRENTLY BE
          ENROLLED IN IT))

* Miss Adelaide - LEADING ROLE - New York accent, vivacicus, braggy, very-nice, simple show
                  girl. Alto/2nd Soprano. Must be fairly good dancer. Also a good
                  conedienne, in dialog and in song. Sexy without working at it.
                  Fer auditions, prepare a happy, fast song.
                  Inthe play, sings: ADELAIDE'S LAMENT, BUSHEL AND A PECK and TAKE BACK YOUR
                  MINK (with the Hot Box Girls), MARRY THE MAN TODAY (with Sarah); SUE ME (with
                  NATHAN).

* Sister Sarah - LEADING ROLE - Conservative, intelligent, dedicated Salvan_ion Army girl,
                 Lyric Soprano. Pretty underneath all that uniform.
                 For auditions, prepare: High, alow ballad: PLUS
                                              Something lively (to audition for the scene in
                 which she gets drunk and flirty and fun and sings about it.)

                 In the play, sings: I'LL KNOW & I'VE NEVER BEEN IN LOVE BEFORE (with Sky);
                 IF I WERE A BELL: FOLLOW THE FOLD (with the Mission Band): MARRY THE MAN
                 TODAY (with Adelaide).

* General Cartwright - FEATURED ROLE - Rigid, efficient Salvation Army officer, over 50. She
                       loosens up a little, later on, but not much.
                       Sings with the Chorus: SIT DOWN, YOU'RE ROCKIN THE BOAT. For audition: sing
                                                                                  a fast number.
* The Hot Box Girls - SUPPORTING ROLES - have some lines, but mostly sing and dance with
                      Adelaide (BUSHEL AND A PECK; and TAKE BACK YOUR MINK, in which they strip to
                      very decent 1940s underthings); also appear in RUNYONLAND (staged movement).
                      Chorus girl types. Also sing in SIT DOWN, YOU'RE ROCKIN THE BOAT.
                      For auditions, prepare fast number.

* Mission Band   - 2, 3 or 4 Salvation Army girls, who must sing (FOLLOW THE FOLD and SIT DOWN,
                   YOU'RE ROCKIN THE BOAT) and will be made valuable if they can play band
                   instruments (portable)..... Make yourself plain and holy.
                   For audition, bring an instruments if you can; plus sing a religious number
                                                                      and a bouncy number.

FIG. 40. Audition Forms

CHARACTER DESCRIPTIONS -- GUYS AND DOLLS Continued   C

Men (no limitations on where the men come from ....)

* Sky Masterson - LEADING ROLE - Cool, sharp, gambler. Gets excited only when a big bet is
                  riding; falls in love in spite of himself, and then loves big.
                  Romantic Baritone/2nd Tenor. (Hits high D).
                  Good-looking in sharp Broadway way.
                  For auditions, sing; Romantic Ballad, plus Fast song.
                  In the play, sings: I'LL KNOW and NEVER BEEN IN LOVE BEFORE (with Sarah)
                  LUCK BE A LADY, with chorus; MY TIME OF DAY

* Nathan Detroit- LEADING ROLE - Nudnik, always-losing gambler. Fine comedy role - little
                  New York gambler, warm and loveable, and deeply in love with Miss Adelaide,
                  but more interested in Where'm I Going To Hold My Crap Game???
                  Baritone, but can talk a good part of his one real song - SUE ME (w/Adelaide).
                  If a singer, will also sing: OLDEST ESTABLISHED FLOATING CRAP GAME and
                  SIT DOWN, YOU'RE ROCKING THE BOAT.
                  For auditions, sing a comic song - he's chief comedian of the play.

* Nicely-Nicely Johnson - SUPPORTING ROLE. Ideally, he should be very fat, very loveable
                  have a high, high tenor voice and be able to dance pretty well.........
                  However, we'll be pleased to find someone with 3/4 of those attributes....
                  Nathan's henchman, always polite, always scared, and anxious to
For auditions: please. Horse-player, gambler, messenger, guide.
Belt a fast,   Sings the show-stopper: SIT DOWN YOU'RE ROCKING THE BOAT, with the Chorus
showy patter song.backing him up: also: GUYS AND DOLLS (with Benny): FUGUE FOR TINHORNS (I've
                  Got The Horse Right Here) with Benny and Rusty: and OLDEST ESTABLISHED with
                  the male chorus. (Also sings with the chorus: LUCK BE A LADY).

* Benny Southstreet - FEATURED ROLE - 2nd banana to Nicely-Nicely. Side-of-mouth-talking
                  smooth gambler. Dumb but nice. Tough but gentle. Comic role.
                  Sings: GUYS AND DOLLS (with Nicely): FUGUE FOR TINHORNS (with Nicely and
                  Rusty): and with men's chorus sings OLDEST ESTABLISHED and LUCK BE A LADY:
                  and with everyone sings SIT DOWN YOU'RE ROCKING THE BOAT.
                  For auditions, sing a LOUD showy song.

* Rusty Charlie - Mostly a chorus role, the he has a few lines. Mainly famous for singing in
                  the FUGUE FOR TINHORNS trio with Nicely and Benny to open the show.
                  Tough/gentle gambler.
                  Also sings: OLDEST ESTABLISHED & LUCK BE A LADY with the male chorus; and
                  SIT DOWN YOU'RE ROCKING THE BOAT with everyone...
                  For auditions: sing same type song as Benny.

* Arvide Abernathy - SUPPORTING ROLE - Sarah's grandfather; warm, canny old Salvation Army
                  man. Capable of coming a gambler or saving a sinner. Loves Sarah very much.
                  Romantic, old-man baritone. Sings MORE I CANNOT WISH YOU, solo. And, with
                  Mission Band, sings FOLLOW THE FOLD: with everyone, sings SIT DOWN YOU'RE
                  ROCKING THE BOAT.
                  If he played a band instrument, too, how nice...
                  For auditions, sing a romantic ballad.

* Men's Chorus - Crapshooters - 6 Gamblers, like LIVER-LIPS LOUIE, THE GREED, SOCIETY MAX, etc
                  Good singing voices: able to move somewhat. Not too many lines, but funny
                  Damon Runyon lines when you have them...
                  SING: OLDEST ESTABLISHED: ROCKIN THE BOAT: LUCK BE A LADY: dance or move to
                  a staged crap game, in CRAP GAME BALLET, and RUNYONLAND.
                  Sing any fast song for audition.

* Mission Band - See description on Women/s page.

* Havana extras - Good dancers, mostly, in Havana nightspots; also in RUNYONLAND: and spectators
                  at the Hot Box Night Club.

FIG. 40. Audition Forms

GUYS AND DOLLS AUDITION INFORMATION   C

Male Roles -- ADDENDA

HARRY THE HORSE (Featured Role)--(Some of these Gambler Roles may be doubled, split, combined, etc... depending on the number, quality and availability of male singers/actors.) Extra tough gambler, from Brooklyn (so needs an accent.....) SINGS. (same songs as male chorus). For audition, sing same as chorus.

LT. BRANNIGAN (Featured Role) - (does not really have to sing, but it'd help if he could..) Sharp, tough plain cloths Broadway area detective. Knows all, arrests only when necessary, wants a quiet street rather than full jail.
Officially sings only the curtain call song, but can sing others if a singer. Only in a few scenes...

BIG JULE (Featured Role)-- small but juicy non-singing role. Big, tough, taciturn, illiterate, wealthy, Chicago gangster. Funny. Slow-speaking, heavy-voiced. (If he can sing, so much the better, but doesn't have to......)

JOEY BILTMORE (offstage voice, so may be tape or a chorus member...) -- DUMB, BUT IN COMMAND. Has the garage where Nathan wants to hold crop game. Gouges for its use. TOUGH, GANGSTER TYPE.

FIG. 40. Audition Forms

Please Print: D

NAME:_____ AGE: _____

ADDRESS:_____ PHONE (S)_____

HEIGHT:_____ WEIGHT_____ HAIR COLOR_____

_____I do not anticipate any trouble with evening rehearsals.

or _____ I have some hard-to-reconcile conflicts, evenings, as stated below:

Do you sing? _____ If yes, please list briefly training and

experience:

Do you play any musical instruments _____ Which:_____

If you are cast, what role(s) would you accept?:

_____ Any part or parts you feel I could play,

or _____ I'd prefer only small role(s) as I haven't time, or would

prefer to begin small,

or _____ I'd prefer a larger role; if I must give up time, anyway, I'd

like it to be more worthwhile,

or _____ I will accept only the role(s) I have listed below, taken from

the above list of characters and from the script.

If I am not cast, or if I am cast in a small role, please consider me also
for the following NON-ACTING POSTS:

(Please list on the back all Theatre training & experience and be specific)

FIG. 40. Audition Forms

A, B, and C are the information sheets given the actors at the time of auditions. In this one session, we were casting two shows, to take advantage of the double thrust in bringing more men to try out. A was the basic sheet for both shows, meant to apprise the actors fully of what the work on each would entail, if they were cast; B went into detail as to what we were looking for in the female characters, and the two C pages listed the descriptions of the male roles. D is the form filled out by an applying actor for any play, giving you the information you need, partly to help you remember him, and partly to give you more than his reading to help you with casting. Is he deeply committed so many nights as to make a large role impossible for him to rehearse? Has he a large list of parts played? Just how tall is he? On this form (D) the director adds his own comments during the audition—immediate responses that will help him when the time for casting begins: "Blue dress"; "sang "It's All the Same"; "very nervous but obviously has talent"; "too short for Pat, but a possible for Mulleady?"; "didn't listen to directions"; "bright and vivacious—very stageworthy"; or a simple and direct: "NO!!!".

hear that actor again; if not, he dismisses the actor cordially.

Following the audition, the stage manager keeps the administrative paraphernalia with him and gives the director the cards he needs for referral in the time before the next audition.

The above audition routine refers mainly to straight plays. On a musical, this same regimen is followed, with obvious additions:

● The stage manager will arrange for a decent piano to be brought to the audition area and tuned. He will be sure the audition pianists are arranged for and given whatever they require.

● He will arrange a cleared space for dance auditions, and places for both men and women to change into audition clothing.

● He will have carbon copies of the audition cards made, one for each director: the choreographer, the musical director, and the overall director himself; or he will be sure that the single copy of the card reaches each director as the applicant is auditioning.

● He will keep his own roster of those auditioning, and be sure that each person auditions in each of three areas: singing, dancing, and reading. If someone leaves before auditioning in each area, the stage manager gets him back for the proper session.

CASTING

Following the last audition, the stage manager carries everything to the director's office, or wherever the actual casting will take place. He lines up the cards, by sex, and stands by to answer any questions for the director: Was Mary Smith the girl in the blue skirt or the one who sang "I Could Have Danced All Night"? This man seemed a little surly as he read; what was his demeanor in the lobby? (The stage manager will have the responsibility of running a happy company; a potential trouble-maker must be spotted by him early, or he will suffer with lateness, incompany friction, or prima-donna-ism as penance for his lack of observation before the play is cast.) As the director pencils in each potential cast member, the stage manager keeps his own list, double-checking for repetition. He will *not* offer casting suggestions from a creative standpoint, but will allow the director to cast his own play. However, in case of possible potential friction, as when both sides of a divorced pair have applied, or members of a romantic triangle, he should apprise the director, who will then determine whether the talent of such people requires

their being cast even beyond the possibility of tension in rehearsal or performance.

Once a full cast has been set, the stage manager telephones those who *have* been cast. (Remember the old show-business cliché: "Don't call us, we'll call you.") If the director likes to call those who have tried in vain, it's up to his public relations determination to do so himself; the stage manager can do little to soothe their hurt feelings. He should be given the task of phoning only those who *are* cast, to get a yes from them, and to notify them of first rehearsal, plus any instructions the director may have: Start letting your hair grow, start losing weight, bring a pencil, pick up your script and mark your role by first rehearsal. If an actor should refuse a role at this point (which can usually be prevented by including the *I will accept the following roles* section in your audition sheets as shown in Figure 40), the stage manager should stop his calling immediately and take the casting problem to the director to solve, before anyone else is notified. The whole play may have to be recast, necessitating some delicate phoning if the stage manager cavalierly continues to call at that point.

Precisely because of such eventualities as a part refused, the stage manager does not reveal to *anyone* any role cast until the actor involved has said yes. The director is not being well served if some actor finds that he was second choice for the role. (It goes without saying that all that passes between the director and stage manager remains absolutely confidential. Strong as the temptation may be to share an anecdote or a confidence, the stage manager must keep all casting—and subsequent—discussions to himself. Theatre is built on the emotions of the participants, and nonprofessional theatre, with its after-working-hours involvement of emotion, is wide open to hurt feelings especially in the offering of oneself at auditions.)

After all cast members have been notified —and have said yes—the stage manager posts the cast list at an agreed-upon central location, with copies (and phone numbers) for himself and for the costume designer. He goes over the audition sheets of those not cast, extracts from them names of those interested in nonacting assignments, and gets those names and phone numbers to the crew chiefs in whose areas the actors have expressed interest.

REHEARSALS

Here, again, the stage manager anticipates the director's needs and gives him freedom from administrative concern so as to put his mind completely onto the bringing to life of the script and the delicate handling of the many diverse human personalities he must deal with and meld into a creative unit.

The stage manager's duties in rehearsal fall into three areas: aiding the director with the a) environment, b) personnel, c) prompt script.

There are fuzzy lines between some of these jobs, of course, but a discussion of each separately should clarify any overlaps:

Environment

As with the audition room, the rehearsal space should be clean and usable before the director or cast get there. Toilets, water, warmth, light, and so on must all be seen to by the stage manager. Trash baskets and ashtrays prominently positioned will encourage their use by the cast.

The floor plan of the set must be taped to the floor in time for the first blocking rehearsal, by the designer or with him in attendance, to avoid errors in relationship of space to space. Adequate rehearsal furniture must be on hand to represent the set's chairs, sofas, and so forth, and, when needed, simple step units or platforms brought in to give the actors and the director a clear picture of the differences in height of the areas of the stage. Setup for the first scene to be rehearsed should be finished well before rehearsal time, and, with a multiset show, changes should be effected quickly during rehearsal. The stage manager must manage his stage, and he cannot do so without a thorough knowledge of the location of each door, window, stairway, and piece of furniture on every set of his play. He will keep the floor plans handy, but will not have to refer to them after the first rehearsal, so well will he know them.

The director will have a comfortable chair; the stage manager a large solid table for his prompt book, his watches (conventional and stopwatch), pencils for the actors who have forgotten to bring them, water, ashtray, rehearsal schedule, a portable doorbell/phonebell ringing device, clipboard to take notes from the director to other departments, and so forth.

Chairs or benches must be set up for visitors and offstage actors.

If the area is not clean when he gets there, the stage manager will clean it. If the space is used by other people at other hours of the day, the stage manager will restore it to its original setup before leaving, cleaning up all debris from his show and his cast, and being in every way a considerate visitor.

Personnel

In his assistance of the director, the stage manager will intercept anything that may disrupt the rehearsal or the director's concentration. This usually begins with late actors. The rehearsal call is the time rehearsals *begin,* not when actors are walking in the door. The stage manager, at a definite risk to his popularity, will insist on promptness. The first time someone is late, he should receive a gentle reminder that rehearsals begin *on time.* The second time, a real chewing-out is in order from the stage manager. By the third time, the director must be brought into the problem, if he is not already aware of it, and asked to add even stronger teeth to the stage manager's warnings. Volunteers' time is valuable and must be used properly. One late actor can misuse the time (and the tempers) of his fellow volunteers, and it's up to the stage manager to establish—and keep—the rule of promptness at rehearsals, or he will reap chaos on show nights with key actors arriving too late to prepare themselves properly for the rigors of performance.

If your rehearsal room is only part of a large building, getting the actors rounded up from other areas in time for a scene's rehearsal becomes an added problem. They should be conditioned to staying near for the stage manager's call, preventing his having to waste everyone's time looking all over the building. If someone has to go to the john or to telephone or to a costume fitting, he must always check with the stage manager before leaving the rehearsal area. Indeed, this check-in should become an established routine, upon arrival and departure from *every* rehearsal and every performance. On the Call Board, or on his desk, the stage manager should have an alphabetical listing of who is needed tonight, and at what times, with phone numbers handy. Actors arriving should check off their names, or give them verbally to the stage manager or his assistant; they should never leave rehearsal, either to go to another part of the building or to go home, without checking to see if they are needed by the director or by another department: music rehearsal, costume fitting, or publicity interview, for example. The Call Board is valuable in this sort of administration, and you should instill immediately in the entire company the professionalism of checking the Call Board upon arrival and before departure *every time they are in the building,* for messages, calls, and the like.

The stage manager's clipboard is his badge of office. On it go all notes to and from the director

—usually preceded in large letters by the name of the person for whom the note is intended. When that person enters the room, or when the stage manager goes to see him, a quick glance down the clipboard shows clearly what needs to be imparted. The clipboard, if constantly carried, reminds the stage manager of the constant need to *write everything down*. Especially in nonprofessional theatre, where every volunteer carries with him his day-long list of mind-filling data about his job, his family, his other life, he cannot expect himself to remember the myriad instructions he receives late at night at his avocation. It's not an admission of inadequacy to write everything down; it's a sign of high professionalism and is to be encouraged.

As soon as he arrives, the director should be given all his questions and notes (When do you want rehearsal props? Mary's going to be a half hour late; shall we start with scene 12 instead? The publicity chairman wants fifteen minutes with you sometime tonight; I suggest I run a line rehearsal of Act III at 9 o'clock, since they're very weak on lines, and you go at that time). At the same time the stage manager takes any notes from the director to other departments (PROPS—need the practical rocking chair by Thursday. PUBLICITY—may I see your newspaper ad layout before you leave tonight? COSTUMES—will you come find me at your earliest convenience tonight?).

Then, during the rehearsal, as the director adds a new prop, or cuts one, or tightens the time for a costume change, the stage manager should take these notes and pass them on to the proper person before the evening is over, by phone if necessary.

In all these exchanges, the stage manager should remember that he is not the director, and should not pass out *orders,* but make it clear that he is the messenger from the director, and if there is any question the director himself will defend his requests. At no time in the rehearsal should the stage manager set himself up as a loud-mouthed disrupter of good order, but as a strong representative of the director, making requests. Even with the actors, who will ultimately be beholden to him alone during performances, the stage manager must make it clear that the on-time rule is set by the director for productive, smoothly-flowing rehearsals; and with the other creative departments, he must gently convey changes and additions the director has decreed.

(When being interviewed for my first job as a Broadway assistant stage manager, the top stage manager quizzed me for a long time on my way of handling people. He never seemed satisfied, and finally asked outright: "How would you describe your way of work?" I thought for a minute and said "Firm, but gentle." He smiled a big smile, and said "That's just what I've been waiting to hear. That's my philosophy, too.")

The Prompt Book

Some directors preblock the entire play, and present the marked script to the stage manager; most, however, block only small sections where the positions are vital or where there are so many people onstage that some kind of predetermined traffic management is necessary. So most of the blocking—the movement and stage business of the actors—is set moment by moment in the rehearsals, and it's up to the stage manager to get it all into his master (prompt) book accurately and neatly, so that anyone can pick up the book and see the movement of a scene, check disputed blocking, or stage in an understudy quickly. Many theatres work with a variety of assistants to the director, called prompters, bookholders, show secretaries, and so on. But nothing has ever proven better than the professional use of one assistant—the stage manager. He will ultimately run the show, so he attends every rehearsal and keeps the prompt book day-to-day himself. He knows his play, he knows what the director wants from a given scene, and he anticipates trouble in lines and in timing and can solve problems before they happen, which he could not possibly do if he did not *both* keep the book in rehearsals and run the play himself. Do not split these jobs!

In a sort of shorthand (Figure 41), the stage manager enters every movement and the exact syllable on which it begins; occasionally he draws a little floor plan of the stage, inserting symbols for the characters to show their physical relationships. He will begin to add, rehearsal by rehearsal, all the director's instructions for physical and aural happenings—doorbells, knocks, light cues, offstage noises, an early entrance of an actor, placement of a special prop, and the like. When the director occasionally uses the same blocking as indicated in the printed script, the stage manager simply underlines those stage directions to indicate they are still used; if the director, being creative, does not slavishly follow the gospel according to Samuel French—since his set designer has not hewn dumbly to the trapezoidal floor plan in the back of the script—the stage manager strikes out all the italicized directions in his script, replacing them with accurate representations of what the director has blocked. At no time does the stage manager insert emotional direc-

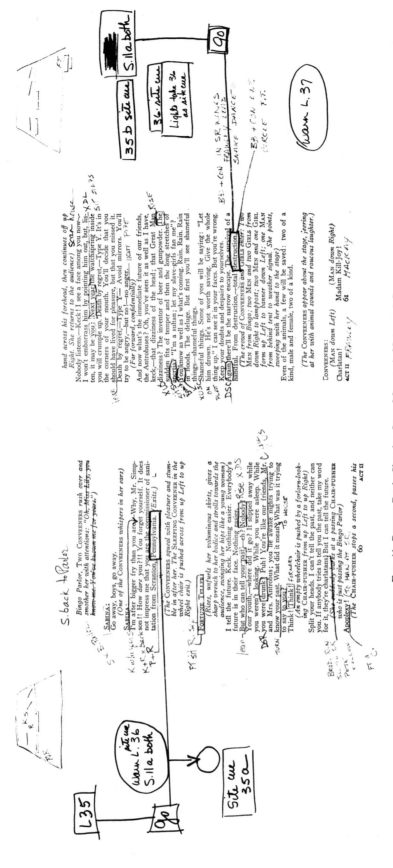

FIG. 41. Prompt Book, Showing Stage Manager's Notes and Cues

Note the specific way the stage manager has indicated blocking, showing the exact line on which each movement or piece of business occurs. The initials and abbreviations give, in small space, the information the stage manager, or his assistant, needs to keep the show to a pattern night by night in rehearsal. Warning cues for performance are written in a page ahead; Go cues begin toward the top of the page, and allow the stage manager to be sure all departments are ready before giving the Go on the actual word of dialogue or piece of business.

tions, unless physically manifest: (She cries. He yells.). His business is not to direct or redirect the actors in the interpretation of their roles, but to keep the physical and vocal pattern as set by the director.

Of course, the prompt book is also used for prompting by the stage manager. Even before the director has decreed *no more books on stage,* an actor may begin trying a scene off book, and the stage manager must ride with him, helping him all he can without being officious about it.

I again use the analogy to an operating-room nurse—as she *slaps* a scalpel into a surgeon's hand, so does the stage manager slap the actor with a prompted line—*loudly, clearly, unemotionally, giving only three or four words unless asked for the entire line.* No discussion, no chastisement, no extra words—just give the few words needed strongly and surely. I had a stage manager once who took it as a personal insult when lines were missed, and pouted when prompting. It's not helpful. Never give a line until an actor calls the word *line,* or unless the sequence is being disrupted by a bad cue or by jumping into a later speech. Then, again, with strength and sureness and no chastisement, state what you're correcting: "You jumped ahead, Bill. Take it back to: 'I don't love you any more!' That's where you went off." At no time repeat the error the actor has made. If he says, as he probably will: "What did I say that was wrong?," don't tell him. Say: "It doesn't matter. The correct line is . . ." and reaffirm the proper lines that he is garbling. The actor who says: "I know all my lines; it's the author's I'm having trouble with," is good for a laugh in rehearsal but doesn't contribute much to the disciplined pattern of the performance.

In a working rehearsal—one in which the director and the actors both stop occasionally to polish, to discuss, to rework, the stage manager may (must) correct erroneous lines or blocking. If the director—or the actor with the director's OK—wants to keep the new line or the new movement, the stage manager makes the change in his script, and the insert becomes law in the prompt book, which is the bible of the show. In a run-through, when no one stops, the stage manager keeps track of errors, either by little penciled crosses in the margin, or on his clipboard, and asks time at note-session to tell the actors of their omissions or mistakes. If the same error happens several times, the director should be reminded, as it is now becoming a pattern and should be broken for all time, or else accepted and identified as new and patterned business.

Whenever a scene is run—that is, without stopping—the stage manager should time it accurately with his stopwatch (making adjustments for any stopping for lines or discussion) and note it on a page of his book specifically for timings. This will be kept throughout the rehearsals and even into the performance, to give the director an exact statement of how long a scene is running, in comparison with previous run-throughs. In rehearsals, he gets a clear picture of how his show is tightening—or not—and can see about further cutting or perhaps the addition—or removal—of an intermission. There is no set limit on the time an audience will sit—though television viewing has conditioned most to frequent breaks—as some of the recent plays-without-intermission have proven. But the director must have the information as one more factor in his control of his show. Once the play has opened, the stage manager should inform him each night of any differences in the running time of an act. It can reinforce the feeling that the show is running too slowly, or too fast, and give him an impetus to call a line rehearsal, do further cutting, or just have a good talk with the cast or several members.

As dress rehearsal draws near, the director and stage manager will together insert all show cues into the prompt book.

THE DRESS REHEARSAL

The changeover in control of the show—from director to stage manager—is effected during the dress rehearsal. Going into the dress, the director is still kingpin of his show; by the end of the dress and the opening of the play, it's the stage manager's baby, and the director has no place backstage from before ringup until after curtain call.

In cooperation with the set designer, the costume designer, the lighting designer, and their preparation and running crews, the stage manager and director add the final notes to the prompt book, in special instructions for technical departments, mostly actual Cues and their Warnings.

It is at the first tech or dress rehearsal that the stage manager moves to his final position of authority backstage, at a desk or lectern or console, with access, preferably by intercommunication system, to all departments necessary to this play—lights, sound, flies. This is the control center of the play, and this is where he will be found from now through closing night.

Whether by intercom, voice, or hand cue, everything that happens during the performance —and, therefore, during technical and dress rehearsals—must be at the command of the stage manager, who by now knows the working of the show better than anyone. In a rare instance, such as a sight cue that the stage manager cannot see, a crewman may take his own cue, but this is the exception and should never be assumed to be a rule.

On the page in the prompt book before any cue is to happen, the stage manager will give a Warning to every department involved: lights, sound, flies, grips, and all. (See Figures 41 and 42.) It is written large and clearly in the prompt book, and when that page appears he says very simply to those involved: WARNING: LIGHT CUE 27, SOUND CUE 5, FLY CUE 12. The only answer to any such Warning is "Thank you." Any other answer means trouble, and all should look to its solution. Then, when the page is turned to the actual Cue, the stage manager begins immediately at the top of the page, by saying: LIGHT CUE 27 (to which the electrician repeats the words LIGHT CUE 27), SOUND CUE 5 (the soundman repeats SOUND CUE 5), FLY CUE 12 (the flyman repeats it)—then, *as the actor is saying the cue word, the stage manager says the operative word: GO.* And everyone involved in that cue goes. Not a second before, not a second after, but on the word *"GO."* If the timing is somehow wrong, this gives a specific point of departure from which to set it right. If the stage manager gives his *GO* a beat too early or late, or if the various departments take their cues on their own, there will be no clear pattern, and anarchy will result. If all are Going precisely on cue, and the timing isn't right, the stage manager, merely by asking one department to delay a second or to wait until the full blackout, can clear up the muddiness and reinstill a solid, repeatable pattern.

For set changes behind a closed curtain, the stage manager's position is down center with his back to the curtain, checking quickly and surely that everything is in its place *quietly,* with no omissions or additions. If he hasn't time to leave his desk, his assistant will station himself down center and report completion.

All these technical cue givings and takings should be rehearsed at the technical rehearsal, attended by the director, the stage manager, the lighting and set designers, and their running crews. (Costume changes, obviously, involve the actors and wait until the first dress rehearsal. But change booths, lights, mirrors, and everything for quick changes have been worked out by the stage manager and costume designer so that all physical necessities are in place at tech rehearsal, and time will not be wasted by rehearsing set changes without every possible impediment in place.)

Tech is a stop/start rehearsal, painstakingly coordinating every detail of the technical production into a pattern, so that when the actors are added the next day, they will lose none of the thrust of the play in having sloppy tech work going on around them. They must be warned, however, that the dress rehearsal is not for their developing of a character, which must have been long-since accomplished, so they will not be wasting the crew's time in dwelling on something they should have by now near-perfect.

At the dress rehearsal, the stage manager begins assuming authority over the entire company—actors, electricians, musicians, flymen, sound crew, prop crew, everyone—establishing firm check-in times, setup times, and curtain time. Each crew head reports to the stage manager when his department is ready to go, and the melding of the various elements of the play begins—the actors in character and in makeup and costume, carrying the props, surrounded by the set and the lighting and the sound. All departments, under the stage manager, now set about the final stages of bringing to life the original creation of the playwright, as interpreted by the director and his creative staff.

The director and designers stay in the auditorium, taking notes. The designers' assistants, the running crew, under the leadership of the director's assistant, the stage manager, run the production as they have been rehearsed, cued by the stage manager, for the creative staff to adjust and polish. All changes in timing are inserted into the prompt book (and into the cue sheets of each involved department), and from this pattern the performance will run, night by night, controlled by the stage manager.

The best dress rehearsal plan is to begin with a work-through of an act, stopping only and whenever there is a technical problem (here, again, characters' inner lives should have been solidified by now), solving it, and moving ahead. After the work-through, set for the top of the act and run it without stopping, for note-taking by the director and designers out front.

Several nights of run-through after the original work-through and the play should be ready to open, with all pertinent information having been added to the prompt book and rehearsed under the firm—but gentle—leadership of the stage manager.

LIGHTING—M B ELECTRA   A

AREAS TO BE CONTROLLED SEPARATELY: EACH ONE ON *DIMMER.*

1. EXTERIOR DAYLIGHT—(and *warming* for nighttime moonlight scenes)—entire down-stage area including entire apron, front porch and steps.

2. EXTERIOR MOONLIGHT—same area as above; cool, haunting moonlight, spilling all over the exterior drop.

3. INTERIOR DAYLIGHT—(and *warming* for the wharf scene).
   Entire platform area, all the way up to the sliding metal door, covering whole acting area, from blacks to blacks.

4. "INTERIOR" MOONLIGHT—same area as #3, to light the wharf scene, which is played on the House Interior platforms.

5. LOWER LEVEL OF SHIP—Warm interior. INCLUDES WALL LANTERN.

6. UPPER LEVEL OF SHIP, INCLUDING CYC—Nighttime—moonlight, with enough warmth for visibility and dimension. CYC very sea-like.

7. FRONT DOOR BACKING LIGHT—Warm; to illuminate front door backing flat and actors entering or exiting front door.

8. STUDY DOOR BACKING LIGHT—Warm; to illuminate backing flat behind study (up-stage) door, and actors entering or exiting.

9. SITTING ROOM DOOR BACKING—Warm; to merely give a light outside sitting room (left) door, so actors won't seem to be entering or exiting the black hole of Calcutta.

10. STUDY WINDOW BACKING LIGHT—Sundown. To come thru Study Window (Up Left) (((Could possibly be same light and gel and angle as #9??)))

11. LOWER LEFT WINDOW IN EXTERIOR DROP (kerosene light color).

12. LOWER RIGHT WINDOW IN EXTERIOR DROP ("   "   ")

13. UPPER RIGHT WINDOW IN EXTERIOR DROP ("   "   ")

14. Stage Right lamp plug—(For interior lamps-) Actually, we'd save set-changing time if we could have TWO plugs right, color coded. One for Study Lamp, one for Sitting Room lamp.

FIG. 42. Cue Sheets. Actual Sheets Given by the Director to Department Heads

A) *LIGHT CUES FOR* MOURNING BECOMES ELECTRA.
Includes a listing of each lighting area to be controlled individually, so the designer and electrician can set up the switchboard and patch panel with the ensuing cues in mind. The timings indicated are based on the director's feeling for each scene in the rehearsal situation, and give the lighting crew a point of departure for setting up their own actual Working Cue Sheets; many of the timings will change in tech and dress rehearsals, based on the effect the lights create, and the new timings will be made a final part of the Working Cue Sheets.

B) *SOUND CUES FOR* OH, WHAT A LOVELY WAR.
Indicates when each cue will begin, what it is, and a general statement on the volume. At tech rehearsal, actual volumes will be settled on, and their numbered intensities entered in the sound crew's Working Cue Sheets.

C) *FLY CUES FOR* GUYS AND DOLLS.
Indicates what should happen as each GO for each cue number is given over the headset to the locking rail fly crew. Each of the pieces of scenery to be flown will be hung on a numbered pipe; that pipe number will appear on the flyman's Working Cue Sheet in place of or in addition to the description of the set piece as given here.

LIGHT CUES—M B ELECTRA   A

PRESHOW CHECK—finish with House on.
— – – –
ON CUE: Lobby chimes.
          House to half.
          House Out.
– – – – – – –
ACT I

Cue 1—On a 5 count: Fade UP: (FRONT DOOR BACKING to standard reading.
                                (EXTERIOR DAYLIGHT—LATE SPRING AFTERNOON.
          THEN: Begin a *20 minute* Dim DOWN:
                                EXTERIOR DAYLIGHT—down to rosy sunset, with shadows of
                                                sundown and oncoming evening.

Cue 2—On a 3 count: Dim OUT: (FRONT DOOR BACKING
                                 (EXTERIOR DAYLIGHT
          THEN: Count 8 in dark.
          THEN: On a 5 count: Fade UP: (INTERIOR DAYLIGHT TO ¾
                                           (STUDY WINDOW BACKING
          THEN: Begin an *8 minute* dim DOWN:
                                (INTERIOR DAYLIGHT down to ½
                                (STUDY WINDOW BACKING out.

Cue 3—*SITE CUE:*   As Christine turns on lamp:

                  On a 3 count: Fade up: (INTERIOR DAYLIGHT to ¾ (brighter stage RIGHT).
                                             (STAGE RIGHT LAMP PLUG to ¾

Cue 4—On a 3 count: Dim OUT: (INTERIOR DAYLIGHT
                                 (LAMP PLUG

          THEN: Count 8 in the dark.
          THEN: On a 5 count: Fade up: (EXTERIOR DAYLIGHT to ¼
                                           (EXTERIOR MOONLIGHT to fill areas
                                           (FRONT DOOR BACKING to standard reading
                                           (LOWER LEFT WINDOW IN EXTERIOR DROP
                                           (LOWER RIGHT WINDOW IN EXTERIOR DROP
          THEN: On a 10 count: Dim down:
                                EXTERIOR DAYLIGHT almost to out.

Cue 5—On a 3 count: Fade UP: UPPER RIGHT WINDOW IN EXTERIOR DROP to full.

Cue 6—On a 3 count: Dim OUT: (EXTERIOR DAYLIGHT
                                 (EXTERIOR MOONLIGHT
                                 (FRONT DOOR BACKING
                                 (LOWER LEFT WINDOW
                                 (LOWER RIGHT WINDOW
                                 (UPPER RIGHT WINDOW

          THEN: Count 8 in dark.
          THEN: On a 3 count: Fade UP: INTERIOR MOONLIGHT to ¼.

FIG. 42. Cue Sheets. Actual Sheets Given by the Director to Department Heads

M B ELECTRA Light cue   page 2   A

ACT I continued

    Cue 7—*SITE CUE:* As Ezra lights match: Fade up: INTERIOR DAYLIGHT to ¼ (brighter stage
                                                                        RIGHT).

    Cue 8—On a 5 count: Dim OUT: (INTERIOR MOONLIGHT
                                    (INTERIOR DAYLIGHT
        THEN: On a 15 count: Fade up HOUSE LIGHTS, FULL.

INTERMISSION

ACT II
ON CUE: Chimes
          House to Half
          House Out.

    Cue 9—On a 5 count: Fade UP: (EXTERIOR DAYLIGHT to ¼
                                 (EXTERIOR MOONLIGHT to ¾
                                 (FRONT DOOR BACKING
                                 (*BOTH* LOWER WINDOWS IN EXTERIOR DROP

    Cue 10: On a 3 count: Dim OUT: (EXTERIOR DAYLIGHT—EXTERIOR MOONLIGHT—
                                    FRONT DOOR BACKING—BOTH LOWER WINDOWS)
        THEN: Count 8 in dark.
        THEN: On a 5 count: Fade UP: (INTERIOR DAYLIGHT to ¾—brighter stage RIGHT.
                                              (SITTING ROOM DOOR BACKING
                                          (LAMP PLUG

    Cue 11—On a 3 count: Dim OUT: (INTERIOR DAYLIGHT—SITTING ROOM BACKING—LAMP
                                      PLUG)
        THEN: Count 10 in dark:
        THEN: On a 5 count: Fade UP: (INTERIOR DAYLIGHT—brighter stage RIGHT.
                                              (LAMP PLUG

    Cue 12—On a 5 count: Dim OUT: (INTERIOR DAYLIGHT—LAMP PLUG)
        THEN: Count 10 in dark.
        THEN: On an 8 count: Fade UP: (INTERIOR DAYLIGHT to ¼
                                      (INTERIOR MOONLIGHT to ¾
                                      (UPPER LEVEL OF SHIP, including CYC to ½

    Cue 13—On a 10 count: Fade UP: LOWER LEVEL OF SHIP to ¾

    Cue 14—On a 15 count: Dim OUT: (UPPER LEVEL OF SHIP, including CYC—INTERIOR DAYLIGHT—
                                    INTERIOR MOONLIGHT)

    Cue 15—On a 5 count: Dim OUT: LOWER LEVEL OF SHIP.
        THEN: On a 15 count: Fade UP: HOUSE LIGHTS.

    INTERMISSION

FIG. 42. Cue Sheets. Actual Sheets Given by the Director to Department Heads

ELECTRA Lights   page 3   A

ACT III
On cue: Chimes
         House to half
         House Out:

Cue 16—On a 5 count: Fade UP: EXTERIOR DAYLIGHT—very late afternoon, sundown.

   THEN: START A *10 MINUTE* CHANGE: CROSS FADE: (EXTERIOR DAYLIGHT DOWN
                                                   to ¼
                                                   (EXTERIOR MOONLIGHT Up
                                                   to ½

Cue 17—On a 3 count: Fade UP: LOWER RIGHT WINDOW in exterior drop.

Cue 18—On a 3 count: Dim OUT: (EXTERIOR DAYLIGHT
                                (EXTERIOR MOONLIGHT
                                (RIGHT LOWER WINDOW

   THEN: Count 8 in dark.
   THEN: On a 5 count: Fade UP: (INTERIOR DAYLIGHT—brighter stage RIGHT
                                   (LAMP PLUG

Cue 19—On a 3 count: Dim OUT: (INTERIOR DAYLIGHT
                                (LAMP PLUG

   THEN: Count 10 in dark.
   THEN: On a 3 count: FADE UP: (INTERIOR DAYLIGHT to ½—brighter stage RIGHT.
                                   (LAMP PLUG

Cue 20—On a 3 count: Dim OUT: (INTERIOR DAYLIGHT
                                (LAMP PLUG

   THEN: Count 10 in dark.
   THEN: On a 3 count: Fade UP: (INTERIOR DAYLIGHT to ½—brighter stage RIGHT
                                   (LAMP PLUG

Cue 21—On a 3 count: Dim OUT: (INTERIOR DAYLIGHT
                                (LAMP PLUG

   THEN: Count 5 in dark.
   THEN: On a 5 count: Fade UP: (EXTERIOR DAYLIGHT, late afternoon.
                                   (FRONT DOOR BACKING.

   THEN: Begin a *10 minute* dim DOWN: EXTERIOR DAYLIGHT down to ¼.

Cue 22—CURTAIN CALL:

   As Curtain closes after show, fade up EXTERIOR DAYLIGHT to ¾ (5 count).

   THEN: As Stage Manager signals you LAST CALL:
          Next time curtain closes, Dim down: (EXTERIOR DAYLIGHT to OUT)
                                              (FRONT DOOR BACKING to OUT)   5 count
   THEN: IMMEDIATELY: On a 5 count: HOUSE LIGHTS UP FULL.

Fig. 42. Cue Sheets. Actual Sheets Given by the Director to Department Heads

SOUND CUES—Lovely War.   **B**

DANCE CLUB music is first band on tape.

READERS THEATRE Music (Donovan) is second band.

LOVELY WAR music and sound begins with the third band—but will be numbered from 1:

CUE	BAND #		WHAT IS IT?
Stage Manager will tell you to start show.	1	Overture.	Play to end; cue next quietly.
"Ever popular War Game!"	2	Circus Music.	Play to end; cue next band quietly.
"They've crossed into Belgium and all!"	3	"God Save The King."	Play to end; cue next band quietly.
WHISTLE BLOWS. "Britain Mobilizes"	4	"We Don't Want to Lose You"	Play to end; cue next band quietly.
"Angle of 60 degrees"	5	"Are We Downhearted" and "On Sunday I Walk Out"	(Lower volume) (Increase Volume) Play to end of both songs; then cue next band quietly.
"Able Bodied Man in the House"	6	EXPLOSION, followed by "Madeomoiselle from Armentieres"	(Increase volume) (Reduce volume) Play to end of both pieces—then cue next band quietly.
"He's marked for amputation"	7	"Goodbye-ee"	Play to end; cue next band quietly.
SIGHT CUE:: Slides: "Happy New Year That Will Bring Victory and Peace" (Following song, Goodbyee"	7-A	EXPLOSION, followed by Charity Ball music.	Play both to end; then cue next band quietly.
"my hairdresser at 10"	FADE *OUT* Band 7-A, the Charity Ball Music;		Cue up next band quietly.
"I know you will answer my prayer"	8	Machine guns.	Play to end; cue next band quietly.
"What, in shrouds? No—shirts"	9	"Sister Susie"	Play to end; cue next band QUICKLY.
"Sing it again— Sister Susie's sewing SHROUDS. . . ."	10	"Oh What A Lovely War."	Play to end; then turn off equipment.

FIG. 42. Cue Sheets. Actual Sheets Given by the Director to Department Heads

GUYS AND DOLLS—FLY CUES

Fly Cue 1: Drop in downstage street scrim simultaneously with tan traveler.

THEN fly out Broadway.

THEN as soon as mission is set, fly Broadway back in.

Fly Cue 2: Fly out downstage street drop and tan traveler.

Fly Cue 3: Fly in downstage street drop and tan traveler.
Fly in telephone   *ALL* simultaneously.
Fly out Broadway

THEN when unit is in place, fly in black drape and fly in Hotbox drop.

Fly Cue 4: Fly out telephone. Simultaneously fly out tan traveler.

Fly Cue 5: Fly out Downstage streetdrop.
(NOTE: This is in view of the audience, so make it smooth.)

Fly Cue 6: Downstage street scrim and tan traveler fly in.

THEN immediately fly out Black and Hotbox Drop.

THEN when mission is set, fly in Black.

Fly Cue 7: Fly out street scrim and tan traveler.

Fly Cue 8: When Mission clears, fly in upstage street drop.

THEN fly out Black

THEN fly in Havana Drop.

Fly Cue 9: Fly out upstage streetdrop.

Fly Cue 10: Fly out Havana drop. Fly in black as soon as mission is set.

PAUSE—INTERMISSION 15 MINS.

During intermission, fly out black.

THEN when Hotbox is set, fly in Hotbox drop and black.

Fly Cue 11: Fly out Black and Hotbox drop.

THEN when Hotbox furniture is struck, fly in upstage street drop and Black.

Fly Cue 12: Fly out upstage street drop. Fly in sewer drop.

Fly Cue 13: Fly in Downstage street scrim and tan traveler.

THEN fly out Sewer drop and Black

THEN as mission unit rolls downstage, fly in Broadway drop.

Fly Cue 14: Fly out downstage street scrim and tan traveler.

Fly Cue 15: Immediately drop in street scrim

THEN fly in wedding cake and Broadway drop as soon as mission furniture
is cleared.

Fly Cue 16: Fly out downstage street scrim.

Fly Cue 17: Fly out wedding cake.

FIG. 42. Cue Sheets. Actual Sheets Given by the Director to Department Heads

PERFORMANCES

Promptness on show nights is still the stage manager's first cry, for the entire cast and crew. He will get them to the theatre on time, make sure the actors start immediately into costume and makeup, see the crews checking their areas of responsibility and reporting themselves to him as ready for curtain, solving any last-minute problems by his sure knowledge of the play and the production, assemble the company for a talk by the director, call ONE HOUR, HALF HOUR, FIFTEEN MINUTES, FIVE MINUTES, and then PLACES (all prewritten into his prompt book and followed).

Apart from unexpected problems, everything now is just a matter of the stage manager's following his prompt book, as amended through tech and dress rehearsals, and staying one full scene, or about ten minutes, ahead of the action, keeping his antennae out for possible trouble—an actor not yet in the wings, something blocking a doorway, a prop knocked to the floor of the set and not picked up, a light burned out—and solving it immediately.

If the dress rehearsals have been well run, the performances are a pleasure for a good stage manager, who will finally see all his administrative work produce a smooth-running show. And, sadly, the better his work, the less likely it is that anyone in the audience will know he even exists. The only stage management that shows is sloppy stage management that calls attention to errors. The well-run performance will earn applause, which the stage manager (sometimes alone) will know is for him, too.

To conclude as we began, the stage manager must be the director's good right hand at every step, and make life as easy for the leader of the creative team as he can, reflecting his approach to the play, spotting trouble before it develops, and staying well ahead of the cast and the director in bringing people, furniture, and props to the ready. Much of what I have said, and what Gruver says, may lead you to think that the stage manager is a glorified pack horse and list maker; he's not, if he approaches his job as the ultimate in the Art of Organization and Management. If he knows that nothing can be created without his managerial mind and determination at their sharpest, he will *make* an art of his support of his director and his handling of his responsibilities. He is not just a doer of routine, menial duties—he is the proudest man in the theatre when his organization and management result in a happy company, a solid piece of theatre art, and a knowledge that he has done his task well—he has managed his stage.

Chapter XI

ORGANIZATION OF A STRIKE

One theatre I know of used to have what it called Strike Parties. On closing night, after the final curtain, everyone in the cast and crew put on work clothes and took down the sets and put away the props and costumes. This is true of nearly every theatre. But this one included a twist—a band set up at center stage, the audience joined in, everyone pulled out his bottle as well as his ratchet, and a bar materialized on the apron of the stage. The set was then well and truly struck, with some elements of it never to be seen again. Not recommended.

* * *

A show is never truly over; the joys and terrors live in the memories of the participants well beyond final curtain. And in a nonprofessional company, a community theatre or a school, final curtain isn't even the end of the tangible show—there is still the strike, the removal and disposal or storage of everything pertaining to sets, costumes, props, lights, front-of-house—in short, everything not to be used in the same place immediately again. Until the physical properties of the play have been put to bed, the show is not over—and it behooves everyone involved with the production, from director and cast through every department head through every crew, to participate fully in the strike, to complete the one final ensemble task they can perform on their show.

The strike, like everything else, must be organized and managed, generally by the designers and/or the technical director. They know best what is salvageable and what is junk; how to dismantle things, and where to put the dismantled elements; and most importantly, how to arrange for the safety of both the personnel and the equipment.

Figure 43 shows a highly organized strike sheet of a nonprofessional summer theatre. The best use of the personnel was included in the planning for the strike with the best use of time and equipment, the inclusion of all departments and each person by name, and the safety of everyone and everything concerned.

Your own TD will know best how he wants his shop used, but here are a few general rules for your guidance:

All furniture, props, and set dressing should be struck from the stage first, and put somewhere safely out of the way of falling scenery, dropped tools, and dirty hands. The aisles or the lobby are good repositories. A special crew (preferably the ones who did the gathering) have the responsibility of returning each prop to its proper place—the theatre storage area, a private home, a department store, or wherever—as soon as possible. The next day. Each piece should be checked for its condition and cleaned or repaired if necessary. Honest junk should be honestly junked. Every prop room in the world is crammed with nostalgic and unusable pieces that were ingeniously built for a show and served well and faithfully, but that have no reuse value at all. Don't give them space. Some theatres have fun, make a little money, and rid their prop rooms of potential spacetakers by holding an auction, attended by the cast and crew, immediately before strike or on the first break during the strike. Children's plays, especially, and musicals garner many props, set pieces, and costumes that are colorful, fun to have around, and of utterly no use to the theatre after that show. Get your chief comedian, give him carte blanche—with a suggested beginning price for each piece—and start the bittersweet strike period off joyously with an auction, all proceeds of which go to the Building Fund or some such.

Moving alongside the prop crew in clearing the stage is the electrical crew, ridding the scenery of all wiring, backing lights, practical onstage lamps, bells, and buzzers. Then all lighting instruments are taken down, stacked and inventoried (three lighting instruments always seem to end up in an aisle or hidden under an unfurled drop, and are found only the next day), their gel frames emptied, cable coiled and stacked, top hats, barn doors, and such lined up for counting and putting away.

In striking the set itself, nothing should be put

144

STRIKE PROCEDURE - Odd Couple

3rd Quad SET CREW (Corky, Don, Bruce.....):

Before Minstrels, bring rolling tool cabinet from Change Booth to Shop.

At 8:30 (Marcia & Noonie at 9:30):

PUT ON STRIKE CLOTHING RIGHT AWAY.

Noonie with one helper - Change 2 Lab Theatre signboards from ODD to THURBER;

re-set Tues-Sat sign on same signboards in a more readable way.)

Organize shop:
All passageways open -- coke cases out of the way.
2 hammers and one each of all other tools remain in shop - in view.
All other tools into rolling cabinet.
Straighten lumber & sort miscellaneous hardware.
Refill nail & screw bins in shop and in rolling cabinet.
Stack non-Thurber flats in order, in scene dock.
Organize lumber rack.
Total cleanup of shop and painting area.

+ As ODD is ending: Don drive truck to tent, carrying:
Rolling tool cabinet,
All green sawhorses.

++ After ODD ends (1050/55):
Above 3rd Quad SET CREW continue to run shop for strike.
ACTORS out of costume and makeup IMMEDIATELY. Hang costumes neatly.

Move all ODD furniture not belonging to us
to Chapin stage; tag for returning to owners;
THEN:
Roll ODD carpets, taking all tacks out; tag for
returning (Linda knows where all belong):::

Linda	Graham
Taube	Gary
Sarah	Dick
Springer	

Sweep basement floors (dressing rooms &
rehearsal room.)
Wash all tables; clean mirrors; empty
wastebaskets):

Kathy	Constance

Clean all Tent booths:
CAROL& RORY

Thorough clean-up of Green Room
Lobby
1st Floor Hall
Sweep, vacuum, mop, empty ashstands:
MARCIA   JOHNSON

On Lab stage, complete THURBER painting:
Noonie   Paul

Costume strike:
Mary   Laverne   Ann   Judy   Larrabee

Strike all hand props to Radio Room;
tag for returning to proper owners;
return Lab things to Prop Room (neatly):
Jenny   Sandy
Constance will quickly advise disposition
of props, after makeup off & before cleanup.

Clean Dorm (Fontaine, Lewis & Constance
will determine just which area(s) - check
with them early in the evening as to what
is to be done; get materials ready early:
Bruce   Lin   Beth
(Return to tent as soon as finished)

* Strike all ODD doors - in their frames -
nailed shut. Stack neatly on Chapin stage.
* Clean ODD standard flats of all nails (not
corner blocks) - return to shop.
* Clear stage of EVERYTHING except revolve;
sweep stage thoroughly. Lift revolve onto
green horses.
* IF TIME: Carry THURBER set pieces up to
tent. (Check with Paul):::

SARAH	GARY	DICK	SPRINGER
JOHNG	LEWIS	LINDA	MICHAEL
KEVIN	TAUBE	RAY	JOHNC
GRAHAM			

FIG. 43. Schedule of a Strike

This detailed strike sheet refers to a nonprofessional summer theatre in a tent and involves cleaning of living quarters, the setup of a new show immediately upon the completion of strike, etc. But the specific assignments, the fullness of the instructions, and the naming of names are recommended in any strike in any theatre.

ODD STRIKE   Pg 2

ODD totally struck and stage cleared by 12:30.
VOLUNTEER will then Fog The Tent.
Pizza and coke on Chapin stage for everyone.   (((NO FOOD anywhere except on Chapin stage -
                                                       not in the House, nor in the tent.....)))
After food break, clean up Chapin::: SANDY & SPRINGER.

After food break:

PAUL - supervise THURBER set up.

MARCIA, JENNY, SARAH - make backstage black legs.

JOHNG, MICHAEL, RAY, LEWIS - set in THURBER false proscenium.

EVERYONE NOT STILL WORKING AT LAB THEATRE JOBS (should be all through by now):
     Paint Floor of stage, and cover revolve: PREPARE ELMERS GLUE AND MUSLIN FOR COVER."
   NOONIE - supervise sign changeovers - AESOP & ODD out; POOH, THURBER & CACTUS in;
LIGHT SET-UP CREW BEGIN.   COMING SIGNS up....

When Thurber fully in and Odd fully out, when all cleanup of dorm, tent and Lab complete,
Bill or Doug will dismiss the company. NO ONE LEAVE UNTIL THIS OFFICIAL COMPLETION.
Light setup crew (PAUL, JOHNC, BETH, LINDA) will stay, with STAGE MANAGEMENT & DIRECTORS
(Laverne and Dick). (Judy and Fontaine may stay or not, as they choose).

Remember: HASTE MAKES WASTE.
            Work efficiently but please - no sledge hammer techniques on any work for
            strike.

            Jim, Bill or Doug will answer any questions regarding strike.

            Please don't moan and groan: "I don't have a hammer".... If you need a
            tool, wait until one is free or go on to something else.   Try - Think -
            Help.

                 Good luck -
                 Only 204 Quadrants left this summer....

                                                                     Bill

FIG. 43. Schedule of a Strike

away until it has been completely cleaned—down to the bare lumber or bare flat. All hardware (except used nails, which are thrown away) should be taken off the set and set pieces and put into strike buckets placed strategically around the stage and shop area for salvage. Lumber of three-foot lengths and longer should be cleaned of all nails, staples, and screws and stacked according to type of board and length. Anything smaller is scrapped. Flats should be left intact but cleared of all random toggles, all profile pieces, everything except the bare wood and canvas that made the basic piece, and stacked neatly—face to face and back to back—in the scene dock. (If a dry pigment scene paint was used, you will want to wash the flats before stacking them.) Reusable pieces and material of all kinds must be kept in usable condition—plywood, composition board, cardboard, whatever you use for masking, facing, covering, can generally be saved for 90 percent reuse. This is where the frugality of the TD is manifest—he must carefully instruct each striking group on what is good and what is junk in each unit, and show how to save the good and dump the bad. And he should be handy for questions from even the most experienced theatre person, who may not know precisely what should be saved from certain pieces.

Most theatres have too few tools for an average strike. Avoid this unnecessary omission. Straight-claw hammers, pliers, screwdrivers, wrecking bars are not expensive and should be kept on hand, if not for the building of the set, then at least for its strike. Each cast and crew member should be encouraged to bring personal tools on closing night to beef up the supply. Name or initials should be painted on each personal tool (as the theatre should have its brand on all its equipment) to prevent honest—or dishonest —walking away with the wrong tools at strike's end.

Costumes, too, must be struck carefully, with all borrowed items carefully cleaned before being returned. In fact, nothing should be put away dirty. Stage use, because of makeup, perspiration, physical business, and so on, is ten times as hard on ordinary clothing as normal street use, and if put away dirty, costumes probably will never be of any use to anyone again for anything. If you have an available washing machine, wash what you can during the strike; get everything else to a professional laundry or cleaner the next day, and then charge the costume designer or her crew chief with the storage as soon as everything is returned from laundering.

The front of the house must be struck, too. Have you a lobby display set up for this play alone? Get it down and its pieces returned to proper places or people. Keep the programs needed for the archives and throw away the rest; get rid of everything that won't be needed again, so that the staff of the next show (or the owners of the building) won't have to clean up your mess when they come to occupy the space.

Friends and relatives should certainly be allowed to help with the strike—perhaps it's the only chance some husbands and wives will have to work side by side on the show. Welcome them. But close the door to booze. Have your big party the previous night, or, if it's a simple strike, immediately following; but liquor and electrical tools, flown scenery, and expensive equipment do not mix. The rule of *no liquor in the theatre* should be most carefully stressed on this night,

especially to newcomers who have not been greeted with your no-liquor rule throughout the preproduction period.

This last joint effort must be shared by everyone. Make it mandatory that the entire company stay, and make it fun for them to stay. Organize the whole strike well, using everyone equally and in the best areas for his strength and experience. Consider dismissing the majority early, keeping only a few experienced technicians for a late crew, when the large-scale bulk work has been done, and only a few intricate jobs remain. Provide free refreshments—pizza or sandwiches, and nonalcoholic drinks—just after the peak of the work has been accomplished. Getting them back to the strike after a break isn't easy, but with cajolery and an announcement that the end is in sight, you can get the last bits done more easily after a relaxed and food-filled change of pace.

When everything has been struck to its proper place, or by the loading door awaiting pickup on the next working day, the entire area—the stage, shop, costume area, lobby, green room, dressing rooms, and all—must be swept with sweeping compound to get rid of the dirt that accumulates only on a stage, and then, probably, wet-mopped, to leave it as clean as possible. You can do no less for the next occupants; they may even happen to be you.

You have now been through the entire show, from organization of the basic group into the reason for the group's forming—the show—to the striking of the show. Step back, and at a special meeting review all the steps you have taken, evaluating each one honestly and fully, and accepting suggestions, from those involved and those observing, for more efficient, more artistic, more economical use of your personnel and your group on the next play. Don't accept a first-time success as your due, or assume it's the way things automatically happen. Don't accept a failure as inevitable. Build on your right moves, eliminate the wrong, organize better and continually, manage with friendliness and strength, and you will have an exciting, producing theatre, as sure as anyone ever can be of not flopping.

In following the premise, Manage or Flop, I have tried to point specifically and positively toward means of achieving the former, and have asked that you apply these collections of thoughts to your individual problems and needs. A few areas touched on lightly are expanded here:

Volunteers. They must be actively sought, by honest and frequent advertising, and by personal appeal from current satisfied members. One method of finding them is by forms inserted into the program of the most popular show of the year (see Figure 44), with colorful, easy-to-find deposit boxes in the lobby for their collection. Just getting the sheets filled out and turned in is not enough; you must follow through and *use* the volunteers in the jobs in which they have expressed interest. Applying for volunteer work for which he is never called will soon turn your potential member's interest off or elsewhere.

Once brought into the fold, your volunteers must be well treated and given interesting and exciting work, gone about in a professional manner under the leadership of department heads who will teach, make the work pleasant and even fun, and demonstrate specifically how each piece of volunteeer work fits into the production. Volunteers must be kept; their participation is one of your chief reasons for being. Their presence makes your theatre a community enterprise. Their work must be acknowledged in the program, and they must be thanked personally.

Thank You's. The value of a Thank You is enormous, in a special column in the program, by a personal letter from the president or crew head, and by a sincere handshake on opening night or at the end of that crew's assignment. However small the donation, the work period, the value of the lent object, or the amount of advice, you cannot survive by *expecting* the community to support you with gifts, loans, and man-hours. You must actively and cordially thank each person and each firm who has helped you in any way, on a specific show or just by a service to the theatre as an organization. Forgetting this

courtesy just a few times will convince the doubters that you're a self-seeking group of artsy-craftsy dreamers, and it may even sow doubt in the hearts of former believers. And they may be right. If you appreciate the help, show it. If you don't, or can't, don't ask for it in the first place. So I shall practice what I preach and take this chance to give my very grateful thanks to those whose help and encouragement have made this book possible. I will always be grateful to Fontaine Syer, Taubey Shedden, and Ibby Lang, co-workers and former students, whose editorial help, suggestions, and moral support kept me going; and to Alison Buck Cook, for deciphering my rough drafts and interminable emendations to type the clean copy of this manuscript.

Rehearsal Schedules. Some nonprofessional theatres rehearse a three-act play for three months. If you can sustain the interest, the artistic growth, and (especially) the attendance of amateur actors for this long a time, I can't argue. But it seems to me that six weeks is long enough, and four and a half to five weeks should be plenty for any straight play, with a few weeks added for a musical or a Shakespearean play.

To set up a proper schedule for rehearsals (and a schedule *must* be set, not just allowed to float along week to week, seeing who can come when) I use the system of Commitment Sheets. (See Figure 45.)

When I know the nights and weekends that each actor can rehearse, and when I have broken down the script into proper-length scenes for each rehearsal, I am able to make up a schedule for the entire month. (See Figure 46.) I take into consideration the difficulty of each role and each scene, the technical necessities for the production, and the availability of the actual stage we shall be using. I add to this the exact dates each person can come, and, taking many hours—many well-spent hours—draw up a full rehearsal schedule that hits each scene the number of times I feel it should be hit, rehearsing each specific scene at times when *everyone* necessary to that

TO OUR AUDIENCE:

As a Community Theatre, one of our chief reasons for being in to INVOLVE THE COMMUNITY (That's you and all your friends.)

BUT - if we don't know which areas of Theatre you are interested in, we can't involve you. So we're asking you to fill out this form and drop it in the Suggestion Box in our Lobby, or Mail it to: Jim Cavanaugh
The Omaha Playhouse
6915 Cass St.
Omaha, Nebraska   68132

We will call you when we have activity going on in the area(s) you have checked. If you can come then, fine....we'll have a good time working together on a show. If you can't come then, that's perfectly ok; we'll call you again next time and hope that we'll find a time when we can involve you in one of the most rewarding, most creative and most enjoyable civic-cultural pursuits in town: The Omaha Playhouse.

EVEN IF YOU HAVE ALREADY FILLED OUT A SIMILAR SHEET WEEKS OR MONTHS AGO, FILL THIS OUT, TOO. PERHAPS YOU HAVE DEVELOPED AN INTEREST IN A FEW MORE ASPECTS OF OUR THEATRE SINCE THEN.....

- -

Check as many or as few as you like. All are fun, and the more you indicate an interest in the better your chance of working a show. And we want you with us!

DEPARTMENT	I DO NOT HAVE ANY EXPERIENCE IN THIS DEPARTMENT, BUT WANT TO GAIN SOME WITH YOU.	I DO HAVE SOME EXPERIENCE IN THIS LINE, AND WANT TO USE IT AT THE PLAYHOUSE
Stage Management		
Assistant Stage Management		
Scenery Building		
Scenery Painting		
Prop & Furniture Making (as for a Shakespeare show.)		
Prop Gathering (before a show opens)		
Prop Crew (during a show).		
Gathering Props and Working Prop Crew on the same show.		
Electrician		
Lighting Switchboard Operator		
Sound Equipment Operator (Mostly Tape Recorder)		
Costume Sewing		
Costume Seeking		
Scenery Shifting the nights of a show		
Make-Up and/or Hairdressing		
Usher		
Volunteer Office Work (Typing)		
Volunteer Office Work (Telephoning)		
Host (Hostess) in lobby once per show		
Box Office Volunteer		
Acting (I am NOT a Season Ticket holder, so please put me on mailing list for tryouts.)		

NAME: _____ ADDRESS _____

PHONE: _____

FIG. 44. Form for Soliciting Volunteer Help

A simple mimeographed appeal, with specifics and a place for name, address, and phone, will bring in volunteer help that you need: need for getting the shows on, and need for making yours truly a community theatre. When someone indicates an interest, through a form like this or by stopping by and telling you, USE HIM.

<u>COMMITMENT SHEET</u> - <u>Lab Theatre</u> - <u>Mount Holyoke College</u>

We will make up Rehearsal Schedules based on your ability to come to rehearsal (whenever possible) so you'll have your exact schedule for the entire rehearsal period.

To do this, we need to know when you <u>ARE</u> <u>NOT</u> available. Please write in below the <u>dates</u> (and <u>times</u> - often a half-evening is better than none) when you know you CANNOT ATTEND REHEARSAL AT MOUNT HOLYOKE

<u>MONDAY THRU FRIDAY EVENINGS</u> (<u>7:30-11:00 p.m.</u>) between <u>Now</u> and <u>Opening</u>:

<u>SATURDAY AFTERNOONS</u> (<u>1-5:00 p.m.</u>)   <u>SATURDAY EVENINGS</u> (<u>7:30-11:00 p.m.</u>)

<u>SUNDAY AFTERNOONS</u> (<u>2-6:00 p.m.</u>)   <u>SUNDAY EVENING</u> (<u>7:30-11:00 p.m.</u>)

When listing Conflicts, be sure it <u>is</u> a conflict, and not something that could be dropped for a week or two, in the interest of a better play...............

If anything above needs clarification, or if you have special requests as to when you'd prefer to rehearse, or not to rehearse, please use the space below:

PLEASE RETURN TO LAB THEATRE WITHIN 24 HOURS. THANKS

YOUR NAME_____PHONE_____

FIG. 45. Commitment Sheet

Hand one to each actor when he picks up his script, or at first rehearsal. Get it back within twenty-four hours and make up your rehearsal schedule based on these sheets without demanding time the cast can't give, but using the actors when they are available. The word "commitment" does not represent their commitment to the show, but to outside activities that cannot be circumvented.

Rehearsal Schedule ~   SKIN OF OUR TEETH ~ Mt. Holyoke College

WHO'S IN WHICH SCENE ~ - please circle your character(s) right away - and then mark the scenes
on succeeding pages involving your characters:

ACT I

Sc 11~ Pgs 7-9
Announcer
Non-speaking: Stetson, Simpson, Moriarity,
Pateslewski, Sabina, Henry,
Gladys, Mr & Mrs Antrobus

Sc 12 ~ Pgs 10-14
Sabina   Fitz (2 lines)   Dinosaur (no)

Sc 13 - Pgs 14-18
Mrs Antrobus   Sabina   Dinosaur (1 line)

Sc 14 - Pgs 18-23
Mrs Antrobus   Sabina   Telegraph Boy
Dinosaur & Mammoth (important biz)

Sc 15 - Pgs 24-34
Mrs Antrobus   Sabina   Gladys Henry
Mr Antrobus   Dino & Mamm(important biz)

Sc 16 - Pgs 34-50
Mrs Antrobus   Sabina   Gladys   Henry
Mr Antrobus   MUSES   REFUGEES
Homer   Doctor   Professor   Judge
Dino & Fitz (1 line ea.) Mamm (no)

ACT II

Sc 21 - Pgs 51-52
Announcer
Non-speaking: Mr & Mrs Antrobus

Sc 22 - Pgs 52-56
Mrs Antrobus   Mr Antrobus   Announcer

Sc 23 - Pgs 56-60
Sabina   Fortune Teller
CONVEENERS   BATHING BEAUTIES

Sc 24 - Pgs 60-62
Fortune Teller   CONVEENERS   B. BEAUTIES

Sc 25 - Pgs 63-73
Mrs Antrobus   Gladys   Henry   Mr Antrobus
CONVEENERS   BATHING BEAUTIES
Sabina (no lines)   Fortune T. (1 line)

ACT II cont:

Sc 26:- Pgs 73-75
Sabina   Mr Antrobus   Fortune Teller

Sc 27 - Pgs 75-78
Sabina   Mr Antrobus   Fitz   Crying Woman (no)
ENTIRE CAST (No lines)

Sc 28 - Pgs 78-79
Sabina   Mr Antrobus.

Sc 29 - Pgs 79-92
Sabina   Mrs Antrobus   Mr Antrobus   Gladys
Broadcast Official   Asst Broadcast Official
Fortune Teller   CONVEENERS   BATHING BEAUTIES
Henry (2 lines)

ACT III

Sc 31 - Pgs 93-100
Sabina   Mr Antrobus   Fitz   Tremayne   Ivy
Hester   Florence Bailey   ENTIRE CAST (No lines)

Sc 32 - Pgs 200-105
Mrs Antrobus   Sabina   Gladys

Sc 33 - Pgs 105-111
Mrs Antrobus   Sabina   Gladys   Henry

Sc 34 - Pgs 111-116
Mrs Antrobus   Sabina   Henry   Mr Antrobus

Sc 35 - Pgs 116-119
Mrs Antrobus   Sabina   Mr Antrobus

Sc 36 - Pgs 119-122
Mr Antrobus   Florence Bailey   Ivy   Hester
Tremayne   Mrs Antrobus(no)   Gladys (no)
Henry (no)

Sc 37 - Pg 122 -   Sabina

If anything in this schedule is unclear to you,
ask about it NOW; not after you've missed a
rehearsal . . . . .

ON THE FOLLOWING PAGES ARE YOUR REHEARSAL DAYS FOR THE ENTIRE REHEARSAL PERIOD - - please mark
carefully, and FOLLOW WHAT YOU HAVE MARKED. Do not come late, do not be absent. If through some
calamity you must be late or absent, PHONE US AS SOON AHEAD OF TIME AS YOU KNOW.   But be with
us, on time, and ready to work. Always.

Bring a pencil to EVERY rehearsal.   Bring your script to every rehearsal, even after you know
your lines (for review, changes, notes, etc. . .)

NO LIQUOR, NO DRUGS - in the building or in your bloodstream (no partaking 4 hours before any
rehearsal or performance.)

FIG. 46. Rehearsal Schedule

Note, again, the specificity of what is needed from whom, and when. The cast will work better knowing when they must be in attendance, and when they may stay away or leave early. Be thoughtful of their time, but be sure their time is used well. The earlier you can provide them with such a schedule, the more sure you are of their being able to adjust any conflicts and provide you with everyone needed on time for a certain scene. Who's in Which Scene, on page 1 of the schedule, is the arbitrary breakdown by the director of logical stopping and starting places for the best use of his people in the best rehearsal situation.

SKIN Rehearsal Schedule   page 2

WED Sept 30   7:30 Sc 15 Work   8:30 Sc 21 Block (including Mr & Mrs A.)   9:00 Sc 22 Block
10:00 Sc 12 Work (NO Fitz or Dinosaur)   10:30 Sc 13 Work (NO Dinosaur)

THUR October 1 - NO REHEARSAL. See CHARLIE BROWN, if you like.

FRI Oct 2   7:30 Sc 11 (Announcer only)   8:30 Sc 21 (Announcer only)
9:00 Sc 22 Work.   10:00 Sc 24 Block (Fortune Teller only)

SAT Oct 3
SUN Oct 4   NO REHEARSALS - learn lines!!

MON Oct 5   7:30 Sc 16 (REFUGEE Scene) - Block.   9:30 Sc 14 Block.
10:30 - Sc 11 (Announcer only) Work.

TUES Oct 6   7:30 Sc 14 Work.   8:15 Sc 16 (Family & Sabina only) work
9:00 Sc 23 (Sabina & Fortune Teller only) Block.   9:30 Sc 24 Work (F.T.only)
10:00 Sc 25 Block. (NO conveeners or beauties).   10:30 Sc 26 Block.

WED Oct 7   7:30 ACT I ENTIRE, EVERYONE WHO APPEARS, SPEAKS OR EVEN BREATHES. No books.
9:30 Sc 26 Work.   10:00 Sc 27 Block (Sabina, Antrobus, Fitz only).
10:30 Sc 28 Block.

THUR Oct 8   With Corky:) 7:30 Sc 32   8:15 Sc 33   9:00 Sc 34
Blocking:) 9:30 Sc 35   10:00 Sc 36 (NO hours.)

FRI Oct 9   NO REHEARSAL   - Most of the show has been blocked; learn all lines.
SAT Oct 10   NO REHEARSAL.

SUN Oct 11   7:00 ((NOTE EARLIER TIME.....)) ACT I, EVERYONE; No Books. Twice, with notes.
9:00 Sc 21 & 22 NO BOOKS.
10:00 Sc 23 Work. No Conveeners or beauties.   10:30 Sc 25 Work. No Conveeners
or beauties.

MON Oct 12   7:30 Block Bathing Beauties & Conveeners (and everyone else) into ACT II.
EVERYONE (Except Announcer) who speaks, runs, peeks or stands there in II,
be here at 7:30 ready to work.

TUE Oct 13   7:30 Sc 23 - NO BOOKS. (Speaking parts only).
8:15 Sc 24   "   "   "   "   "
8:45 Sc 25   "   "   "   "   "
9:30 Sc 26   "   "   "   "   "
10:00 Sc 27 WORK.   "   "   "
10:30 Sc 28   "   "   "   "

WED Oct 14   7:30 Block Sc 29 Speaking Parts only.
9:30 "   " 31   "   "   "   10:30: Block Sc 36 & 37.

THUR Oct 15   NO REHEARSAL. LEARN SHOW.

FRI Oct 16   Alumnae Council making special trip to watch rehearsal - even tho it's Friday,
there wasn't a very large list of Commitments, so I hope you'll all be here
- a rehearsal with people missing won't make much sense to the Alumnae Council
WORK ACT III Scenes: 7:30 Sc 32   8:00 Sc 33   8:30 Sc 34   9:00 Sc 35
9:30 Sc 36 (Antrobus only)   10:00 Sc 37

SATURDAY Oct 17   NO REHEARSAL.   Learn.
SUNDAY Oct 18   "   "   " " " " " .

WE HAVE DONE OUR BEST TO AVOID YOUR COMMITMENTS, IN MAKING OUT THIS SCHEDULE. OBVIOUSLY, WITH
THIS HUGE CAST, WE COULDN'T AVOID ALL; PLEASE WILL YOU TRY TO CONFORM TO THIS SCHEDULE, ALWAYS.

FIG. 46. Rehearsal Schedule

SKIN Rehearsals   page 3

Mon Oct 19	7:30 Sc 31 Work. Speaking Parts only. 8:30 Sc 36 Work. 9:00 – ACT III ENTIRE (Speaking Parts Only). TRY WITH NO BOOKS.

TUES Oct 20	7 pm (NOTE EARLIER TIME). Dress Parade for pictures. Get dressed:
	    All Bathing Beauties.
	    Sabina, Gladys, Henry, Mr & Mrs Antrobus, F.T.
	7:45p.m. ACT I Complete Runthru EVERYONE.
	9:00 – ACT II Complete. Workthru. EVERYONE.

WED Oct 21	7:30 ACT II Complete. EVERYONE. No books. FROM NOW ON, NO BOOKS 9:00 ACT III Complete, EVERYONE. No books. ON STAGE; but bring them.

THUR Oct 22	PUBLICITY PHOTOS TONIGHT. 7 p.m.: Those who dress paraded on Tuesday, wear
	                those same costumes for pix.
	7:30 – ACT III (Everyone in it) – No books. FROM NOW ON, YOU MUST BE HERE
	9:00 – ACT I " " " FOR EACH REHEARSAL OF SCENES YOU
	                ARE IN. MUST. MUST.

FRIDAY, OCT 23 **SATURDAY , OCT 24**	No rehearsals – – entire play is off books now; refine character, business; double-check lines for accuracy.
SUN Oct 25	7:00 (Note early time) –– ACT I, everyone. TWICE THRU, WITH NOTES.
MON Oct 26	7:00 " " " ACT II " " " " "
TUE Oct 27	7:00 " " " ACT III " " " " " "

NOTE::	This is Recess Week at Mt. Holyoke. If a scene, an act, or the show is
	    in trouble, we'll schedule daytime rehearsals, too. At this point,
	    every evening seems sufficient, but we'll see how the show goes.

WED Oct 28	7:00 Note early time. ENTIRE PLAY. ENTIRE CAST HERE ON TIME. Once thru with notes.
THUR Oct 29	NO REHEARSAL. Rest, prepare for tough weekend.

FRI Oct 30	Afternoon (time to be set) – Scene shifting crew (includes a lot of cast
	    members) – Rehearse scene shifts.
	7:30 pm – TECH REHEARSAL (Scenery, Prop, Stage Management crews . . .
	    This involves many actors; Lights only if called).

SAT Oct 31	9 a.m. LIGHTING CREW and Stage Management.
	1 p.m. FULL DRESS OF ACTS I & II. (Act I people check in, get dressed. 1pm)
	    (No Makeup) All running crews check
	                    in at 1 p.m.)
	3 p.m. – ACT II People check in.
	    We will work ACT I Twice, Act II Once – will work into evening with a
	        dinner break.

SUN Nov 1 –	1 p.m. FULL DRESS OF ACTS II & III – (Act II People, check in, get dressed 1pm
	    (No makeup) All running crews check in, 1 p.m.)
	1:45 p.m. – ACT III People check in.
	We will work ACT II once, and ACT III Twice. Will work into evening with a
	        dinner break.

FIG. 46. Rehearsal Schedule

SKIN Rehearsals   Page 4

MON Nov 2	FULL DRESS OF ENTIRE PLAY - (No makeup)	7 p.m. - ENTIRE CREW and ACT I Cast check in. 7:30 p.m. ACT II & III Cast check in. 7:30 - Cast & crew meet in House for opening remarks. Begin FULL DRESS ENTIRE PLAY.
We may work until after 11 p.m. all week.		

TUES Nov 3   ELECTION DAY. No rehearsals - - but, if show is in trouble, we WILL call a rehearsal for everyone, and set up TV sets backstage.

WED Nov 4   FULL DRESS OF ENTIRE PLAY, With Makeup.

7:00 - Entire Crew and Act I people check in, get set and MADE-UP.
7:20 - ACT II People check in, get made up.
8:00 - ACT III People check in, sit in house.

THUR Nov 5   INVITATIONAL DRESS OF ENTIRE PLAY. With audience. Battle conditions.

7:00 - Entire Crew & ACT I people check in, get set and made up.
7:30 - ACT II People check in, get made up.
8:00 - ACT III People check in, stand by for director's remarks - get made up after play begins.

8:30 8:15 p.m. - CURTAIN.

FRI Nov 6
SAT Nov 7
SUN Nov 8   PERFORMANCES OF YOUR PLAY.   8:15 p.m. Curtain.

Nov 12, Thur   Check in times: Every Night: Running Crew (including
Nov 13, Fri   actors on crew) and
Nov 14, Sat   ACT I Actors: 7:15 pm
Nov 15, Sun
                                                     ACT II Actors: 7:30 pm
                                                     ACT III Actors: 7:45 pm

Exercises at 7:55 pm each night.
Entire Cast.

There should be several Company parties during the run - Cavanaugh will have one.
Host should furnish the house, glasses (paper cups?) ice and a happy smile.
Company should chip in for food, and should bring own potables.
Company party should include: Cast, Running Crew, Faculty
working on this play.
+ One date of the opposite sex for each.

FIG. 46. Rehearsal Schedule

scene is available to rehearse. No scene in your play is unimportant, so rehearsing *any* scene without the presence and full concentration of each actor who appears in it is foolish and a waste of everyone's time. Pass out and follow Commitment Sheets; draft and follow a workable rehearsal schedule; you will be best serving your actors, and those other important masters, the playwright and the audience.

Liquor—or beer or drugs. They're all part of the culture of some part of your membership, and it's not your business to judge how time is spent away from the theatre. But it is certainly your job to be sure that the artistic product is prepared and presented clearheadedly, and with no offense to other volunteers whose mores spring from a different culture. At parties away from the theatre, set what key you like (see below), but legislate and uphold the rule of no booze, tranquilizers, or even 3.2 beer in the building ever, or in anyone's bloodstream within four hours of any rehearsal or performance. At the grand opening of a new theatre, or of a season, a reception in the building with something festive, in small amounts, might be especially decreed by the Board, but only on the rarest occasion. When an actor or crewman shows up under the influence of, or with breath or eyes betraying the presence of, artificial stimulants, have a few words with him and send him home. He can do you no good, and your condoning his failure to meet your standards will open the door for others to break the rule as well.

Parties. A gathering of theatre people after rehearsal, set-building, or performance is another story. Good work, done in communion with other volunteers, should be celebrated—after the night's work is finished—and the nature of the party is up to you, so long as it's outside the theatre building. At someone's home or at a local restaurant, enjoy-enjoy.

Be sure everyone from that crew or that show is invited (selective parties will kill the volunteer system and the theatre) and that it is made clear what will be served. A teetotaling party may not be to the taste of a hard drinker. Fine, he knows what to expect and can stay away if he chooses. The same is true of a wide-open, free-flowing party. Students under the legal drinking age should not be invited, and adults with no interest in this way of celebrating are fairly warned.

If the party is held in a public place, remind everyone that he is representing the theatre in the eyes of the community, and keep an eye out for a noise level or a display of abandon that will bring on the traditional comment: "Those theatre people again!!"

Some theatres pay for all refreshments at cast parties; some provide only the food; some follow a routine that I encourage: Have the party at someone's house, and have everyone bring his own beverage (whether soft drink or something stronger) and a snack for the common board. Whether a box of pretzels or the specialty of one of your amateur chefs, the price of admission should be some sort of party food, which even a bachelor can pick up inexpensively at the supermarket. This provides a variety and enough to go around and takes the onus of buying and preparing off the host, whose contribution should be only ice, paper cups, the premises, and understanding neighbors.

In another party routine, everyone contributes a dollar to the host, who then buys the snacks himself. This adds to his work, but is the best system at schools or army camps, where not everyone has easy access to a store.

Mutual Need. I have stated several times in preceeding chapters that a theatre not supported by the community is probably not needed by the community. *You* need *them,* certainly, to survive; if the box-office returns and the turnout at auditions are small, perhaps they don't really need your theatre. Sell yourself, using all the methods described here and plenty of your own, and if the community still doesn't need you, close up. Art is not art in the doing but in the receiving, I believe. No matter how artistic your show may be, if there is no one to see it and be moved by it, it's not art.

The same is true of personnel, whether volunteer or staff, who are hurting your theatre by really bad work or by giving the theatre a bad reputation in their contacts with the public in the theatre's name. However much good they find in the theatre, however they need the theatre, you don't need them. I caused a stir at a recent state community theatre convention when a member of the audience asked what to do about a really bad volunteer director who produced such consistently bad shows that good actors wouldn't try out for him, and audiences were diminishing, but who was "the only director in town." I said: "Train new directors, or find trained people through the local colleges or by tapping newcomers to town with previous experience." No possibility, they answered. My reply was simple: Close the theatre. If your top man is inept and there is no way to replace him or to help him improve, why compound the error by keeping open on poor shows? Close down. The audience does not need bad work, and your theatre does not need bad work. Give your efforts to an organization that serves the community and that needs you.

A misunderstood, unhappy person often finds a home in the theatre. And often the happiness of mounting a show side-by-side with people from all over the community with this common goal will temper the sourest, most ill-adjusted person and make him productive. It's a valid use of your facilities. But you do not need someone who hides out there, does not contribute anything but more sourness, and stamps your theatre as a disturber of the community. Help anyone who will be helped by theatre work, but don't let the theatre die in the process.

Open Auditions, Open Books, Open Everything. The word clique has almost passed from our vocabulary, except in nonprofessional theatres. There it still hangs on, and in the truest sense of its meaning. A few people who mutually appreciate one another run everything, alternating directing one another in plays they themselves have chosen, creating and maintaining the illusion that they are indispensable. They are not (see *Mutual Need,* above). Your surest way to succeed is to manage an open theatre—open auditions at which it can truly be said that no one has been precast, open rehearsals for potential actors to see the fairness and fun that pervades, open books for anyone interested in how the theatre handles the public funds that come across the ticket window. Annual meetings should be open to the public, as should more frequent special meetings of the membership. Even Board meetings should be open to anyone who wants to be present. Open elections, certainly, with nominations by mail or from the floor legitimatized by the constitution. A regularly-changing board and committee structure, and new faces on the stage frequently, can dispel any clique feeling that exists in the community and can open your doors to new ideas, new blood, and growth.

Theatre Organizations. No matter what problem your theatre faces today, you are not alone. Chances are that the same problem is currently on the agenda or the director's desk at a dozen theatres in your state or around the country. The way to find solutions and to share the satisfactory solutions you have found to other troubles, is through theatre organizations. If you're in a large enough city with a number of nonprofessional theatres, there may be such a group already established. If not, establish one. Many states have theatre groups covering all theatre from professional organizations through community, college, and even high schools. Write your State Arts Council for addresses. On the national and regional level, several very fine organizations exist. The American Theatre Association (formerly American Educational Theatre Association) has a permanent staff, many committees studying problems and ways to improve and grow, and divisions covering nearly every form of theatre:

    American Community Theatre Association
    Children's Theatre Association
    Secondary School Theatre Conference
    National Association of Schools of Theatre
    University and College Theatre Association

The ATA also has an excellent placement service, through which you can find a one-show director or designer or someone to guide you for many seasons.

The American National Theatre and Academy (ANTA) has long had the development of the regional theatre as its chief cause, and it can help you with many of your problems, whether you're just organizing or having fifth-season-plateau pains. They, too, have a fine placement service for theatre leaders, and a script service.

National conventions of theatre organizations give you the opportunity to exchange ideas on a face-to-face basis with your counterparts, volunteers and professionals, from all over the country, and to ask the advice of people who have already been through your current problems. And nothing is so thrilling as the realization that *you* can help another theatre by sharing some of the knowledge you have acquired in the formation and growth of your own organization. The speakers, the panels, the displays, the shows to be seen, the dinner-table conversations, the very atmosphere of theatre conventions make them valuable to everyone who attends and to all at home with whom he can share his feelings and new knowledge. Most regions have their own theatre conferences, providing speakers, demonstrators, and panelists, some with big names, others with merely talent and skill.

Addresses of many of these groups are in the Appendix. Any of them would be pleased to hear from you with questions, problems, or requests. Most are staffed with volunteer experts, who have been through a situation just like yours, and who enjoy sharing their knowledge and their experience.

And you are always welcome to write to me.

Touring Shows. Providing your actors with a new and different audience that doesn't *have* to love them is a magnificent experience for them and helps to spread your fame farther afield. Troupe to prisons, hospitals, any institutions whose residents can't afford or aren't allowed to get out and travel. Enter regional competitions or festivals where you can see other theatres' work as they see yours.

Talk to theatres similar to yours in other towns and exchange shows, working out a financial arrangement so that neither theatre loses money in the project. Perhaps an annual exchange could stimulate both auditions and the box office at both theatres. Anything that can add a challenge to your organization and a new boost to your attendees is to be sought and worked for.

Workshops. In addition to the main offering of your theatre, consider Workshops. Or Studio Shows. Or whatever name you wish to give them (Directors' Bonus Shows; Poco Mas; Underground Mondays). These are shows worth doing but not considered to fit into the regular season because they are unsalable to the largest percentage of your audience. Prudence has kept them off the main boards, but they must be available to those who want to see them and those who want to direct, design, and play in them. New styles, new techniques, perhaps a classic or an original play must be offered by your theatre, unless you're just an entertainment machine. A shorter run in a smaller theatre—or just a big empty room—is the hallmark of the Workshop. Keep the creative juices of your best members flowing by allowing them to work on—or to see—theatre of all kinds, not just Broadway's best.

Workshop also connotes theatre activities of an instructional nature—classes, demonstrations, panels, sessions in the scene or costume shop—through which new members or those not skilled in some areas of theatre can be taught by doing. Peer-teaching is big in education today; so should it be in your theatre. Fine actors may be waiting among your ushers, or in the costume room, right now; potential costume designers may be carrying spears. Give them a chance to expand their abilities, and use your theatre and its personnel to their fullest extent.

Assembly Programs. Although nearly every area in this book can and does apply equally to high-school theatre groups, one activity of such theatres that has not been touched on enough is assembly programs. The budget may be smaller, the run shorter, the audience more captive, but the organization and management of such shows must be as clearly drawn and as specifically guided as with a production of *Hamlet* by the Old Vic. Organize and manage with an eye to solid, stageworthy, quality productions, whether skits or plays or speeches, or publicity previews of Thespian Club plays to come. Make them fun, of course, but don't have fun at the audience's expense, and don't, please, treat them as a pure lark or something just to be lived through. Assign department heads, give them deadlines, insist on promptness at rehearsals, coordinate the scenery and costumes within the overall concept of the director. Use the facilities tenderly, be good guests of the auditorium, clean up after rehearsals and strike the sets totally after performances. You are of the theatre, and as such represent a disciplined, structured, communicative art form. Be proud of what you present, and make every member of the cast and of the production team equally proud of their work. Accept criticism and direction from faculty advisers, and make each program build from the errors and the right choices of the last.

Children's Theatre. No audience is so satisfying to play to as children, no show as much fun to present from every angle as a kid show; and there is no activity your theatre can engage in that will so convince the community of your seriousness in adding to its cultural life. And where are tomorrow's audiences and tomorrow's actors

and crewmen and administrators coming from? Obviously, from today's children's theatre audiences and young theatre participants. It is not enough merely to say: "Get them away from the TV set." Whether you decide to use all-adult or all-teen-aged or all preteen-aged actors, or some combination of these, get your community's young people into the magical, beautiful world of children's theatre, and produce enough plays for them to satisfy the hunger that will develop. If you have your own building, schedule major plays so as to allow time and space for rehearsal and performance of kid shows, too. If you use a rented auditorium for your main stage plays, see about another location for children's plays. Set up an entire arm of your theatre organization, with a decent budget, and go into the frequent production of this sort of happy, productive theatre. If a children's theatre already exists in town, talk with its staff about joining forces, sharing scenery and costume materials, using common publicity media, and working under the organizational umbrella of a common Board.

Foundation money will come more easily for youth activities; volunteers who don't care about theatre itself will find themselves becoming interested as they work on a children's show strictly because it *is* for children; and the community will be better served, which is why you are there.

Your Own Building. Set your sights early on owning your own building. Start a Building Fund from the first day. Have all your members constantly looking for suitable locations, existing theatres going out of business, empty buildings that could be converted, local philanthropists with a need for the giving of land, structure, or money. It may take years—the perfect building certainly will—but getting there is half the fun, and the dreams and plans and the lists of optimum requirements you would actually accept, and the field trips to look at other theatres in nearby communities, and the meetings with architects and real estate brokers and possible donors will involve many members of your theatre and your community.

Even starting with a converted roadhouse, or sporting goods store, or bottling plant, or firehouse, as some theatres have done, will give you your location, where your sets are built and stored, your shows are auditioned and rehearsed and presented, your box office is located, your meetings are held, and your classes are given. Your home. Where everyone can find every theatre activity, and each department can set up shop and function within sight and sound of everyone else. Where an ensemble may develop and a community organization come together and thrive. A few years in an adapted building will tell you better what you ultimately want in a theatre designed for your specific needs. But be prepared. After you're in that beautiful new theatre, whose years of dreaming and planning and building have brought more sweat and tears and revamping of plans than your own residence, you'll wistfully think back to the old days. You'll recall hauling sets into the high-school auditorium, or the night the furnace in your converted church went on the blink, or getting rid of the bats in the attic . . . and you will agree that all you really needed all along for the best theatre was a platform and a passion or two. But when it's your own platform, in your own building, you can settle in, disturbing no one, finding everything in its proper place when you need it. Aim early for your own building, of whatever nature, and work constantly toward its realization.

Communication. Theatre is communication. Organization and management depend on communication. And when a show or a theatre flops, communication failure is probably the cause.

From the first meeting of the first nucleus of your theatre, on through the years to your fiftieth anniversary production, *talk to people.* Within the group, keep the chain of command true and flowing—let department heads communicate with the producer and their crews; let the director be specific on what he wants from each designer and from his actors; let the audiences be heard as to what they really want to see, and let the theatre advise them in return why you're attempting some new styles. When you hire a professional director, listen to his ideas and, in turn, tell him precisely what you want from him. *Do not assume anything. Anytime. With anyone.* Write everything down, get it to the proper people on time, and follow through on all you are asked to do. Don't elide steps on the chain of command; don't eschew responsibility because you aren't really sure what you're supposed to do. *Ask questions. Constantly. Of everyone above you and below you on the chain.* Clarify, specify, take time to be sure everyone understands, repeat when necessary, demand that deadlines be met, fulfill all leadership responsibilities, and require that everyone down the chain fulfill his.

Talk to your community about your plans, talk to your membership about your needs, talk to your Board about its duties, talk to your crews about their importance, talk to your actors about the burden on them in carrying the show to the audience, and you are communicating. You are organized, and you are managing well, and you cannot flop.

COMMITTEES OF A COMMUNITY THEATRE
(Currently in use, and working beautifully)

I. EDUCATION AND SERVICE COMMITTEE

A. The Playhouse Theater Guild.

1. Provides through its informative and entertaining monthly programs an opportunity for broadening one's knowledge of Theatre and the related arts.

2. Provides assistance for the Board of Trustees in membership drives, box-office work, social affairs, First Night dinners or parties, tours of the Playhouse, a pamphlet on Playhouse history, and so on.

B. Educational Activities.

Theatre classes, taught by staff members and skilled members of the organization. Offered at a small cost, with a discount to members.

C. History, Memorials, and Courtesies.

1. Keeps the Playhouse scrapbooks up to date.

2. Binds the programs of each play.

3. Keeps a record of all memorial gifts and duly acknowledges them.

4. Extends such courtesies as seem advisable—notes, gifts, and the like—in addition to the Memorial notes—to express the appreciation or thoughtfulness of the Board of Trustees.

D. Social Committee.

Responsible for arrangements for social functions, excluding those already assumed by the Playhouse Guild.

II. STUDIO THEATRE COMMITTEE

A small, flexible studio theatre in the Playhouse basement presents approximately three plays a year, deliberately less commercial than the normal main stage season.

The Studio Theatre Committee functions for the Studio Theatre in much the same manner as the Board of Trustees does for the main stage. The Associate Director of the Playhouse directs the play productions; all other activities are handled by volunteers. The financial management is in the hands of the regular Playhouse treasurer.

III. PRODUCTION COMMITTEE

A. Awards Committee.

To see that the volunteer service to the Playhouse is given proper recognition. This is done mainly by the presentation, at a gala annual Awards Night, of plaques, statuettes, commendations, and the like. The committee is in charge of the evening and its preparation. Awards fall into these general categories:

Excellence in Acting.

Excellence in Front-of-House activities.

Excellence Backstage.

In addition to selecting the above award-winners, the committee may also recommend people for theatre scholarships at accredited schools.

B. Playreading Committee.

Selects the plays and musicals to be produced during the regular season and the summer season. Final approval of this committee's selections is made by a majority vote of the Board of Trustees, or the Executive Committee during an emergency.

C. Recruiting Committee.

Assists the director in recruiting talent for the plays, and the designer in recruiting volunteers for backstage work. Sends out notices of tryouts and organizes the mechanics of the audition sessions.

D. Costume Committee.

Assists the costumer in any way possible, including keeping a file on and recruiting volunteers for costume work on a play. Assists in the maintenance of the Playhouse costume stock.

E. Makeup Committee.

Assists the director and costumer in achieving desired makeup for all actors. Trains crew. Maintains makeup supply, ordering new stock when necessary.

members, subject to the will of the membership.

Section 2. The Board of Directors shall have control of the property and management of the organization, subject to the will of the membership. Funds of the organization shall be withdrawn from the bank with which they are on deposit by the joint signature of the Treasurer and/or Secretary or President.

Section 3. Vacancies on the Board of Directors or in any office shall be filled by vote of the Board of Directors; such appointee is to serve for the duration of the term of the individual being replaced.

ARTICLE IV

Section 1. Not less than thirty (30) days prior to the annual election of officers and directors, the President shall appoint, with the approval of the Board of Directors, a nominating committee of not less than five members.

Section 2. The nominating committee shall, at the April meeting, decide upon and make recommendations to the members the names of the candidates for election and the committee shall secure consent of candidate so selected. Annual election will be held at this meeting.

Section 3. No member of the nominating committee shall be eligible to any office by action of the nominating committee.

Section 4. In addition to nominations from the nominating committee, nominations for officers and directors may be made by any member from the floor at the time of the annual election.

Section 5. At the annual election, there shall be elected a president, vice-president, a secretary, and a treasurer, all of whom shall constitute the Officers of this organization. To complete the Board of Directors, there shall be elected three directors, one to serve for a period of one year, one to serve for a period of two years, and one to serve for a period of three years. Committee Chairmen shall be elected for a period of one year and will serve as ex officio members of the Board of Directors.

Section 6. Voting shall be by individuals, and no person shall cast more than one ballot, and no proxy votes will be recognized.

Section 7. Officers and Directors shall take office at the annual May meeting, which shall begin the organization's fiscal year.

ARTICLE V

Section 1. Regular organization meeting shall be the first Monday in each month.

Section 2. The Annual Meeting, including the installation of officers, shall be held in May of each year, and notice will be published prior to this meeting.

Section 3. Special meetings may be called by the President, or Vice-President in the absence of the President, or by majority vote of the Board of Directors, without meeting in regular session.

ARTICLE VI

Section 1. Regular meeting of the Board of Directors shall be held one week prior to the regular organization meeting.

Section 2. Special meeting may be called by any member of the Board of Directors by notifying every other member. No proxy votes will be recognized.

Section 3. The Board of Directors shall have the power, by a two-thirds vote of its entire membership, to strike from the roll the name of any member who is no longer deemed acceptable to the organization. Such offending member may, by written request, appeal to the Board for reinstatement herein. Notice of such action shall be given to such offending member by the Secretary.

ARTICLE VII

Section 1. The President, as chief executive officer of the organization, shall supervise the organization's affairs and activities and shall make an annual report thereon to the members.

Section 2. The Vice-President shall preside at membership and Board of Directors meetings in the absence of the President. He shall further act as business manager of the organization and be in charge of procurement of advertisement.

Section 3. The Secretary shall give all notices of meetings as herein provided; he shall issue notices of the dues payable and be responsible for the collection thereof; he shall keep a permanent record of the minutes of all such meetings; he shall issue membership cards and keep a permanent record of the membership, and he shall be the custodian of all official records of the organization. He shall further carry on all correspondence ordered by the membership and shall perform all other duties herein provided.

Section 4. The Treasurer shall keep the financial books of the organization; he shall disburse funds at the direction of the Board of Directors and he shall report in detail, at the Annual Meeting or such other times as directed, on the financial condition of the organization.

Section 5. The Corresponding Secretary shall be in charge of intertheatre correspondence and assist the Secretary in the intertheatre correspondence.

Section 6. The House Manager shall be in charge of maintenance, repair, heating, and cleaning.

Section 7. Two (2) junior board members shall have full floor rights at meetings of the Board of Directors with the exception of voting powers.

Section 8. The organizational chart shall be the guide to the duties and responsibilities of the officers and committees and shall be controlling in cases of conflict with it and the preceding sections.

ARTICLE VIII

Section 1. The Board of Directors shall appoint a Director of Production at a salary fixed by the Board of Directors and for the purpose of directing productions and presentations of the organization. Such director shall be an ex officio member of the Board of Directors and all committees.

Section 2. Each year the President, with the approval of the Board of Directors, shall appoint a Director of Art whose job it shall be to design the set for each production of the organization. Such design shall be subject to the approval of the Director of Production concerning the workability of same and subject to the approval of the Board of Directors concerning the financial feasibility of same.

ARTICLE IX

Section 1. The President shall appoint a reading committee consisting of not less than two (2) members, to review plays recommended by the Director of Production, and to present them to the Board of Directors for their approval.

Section 2. The President, for each production, shall appoint a casting committee, consisting of four (4) members and, in addition thereto, the President shall also be a member of said committee. The casting committee must read and be familiar with the play being cast and it will be their duty to contact and interest old and new members best suited for the parts. The casting committee shall select person or persons who are to be cast in the respective parts, and any conflict in the action of the casting committee shall be resolved upon the majority vote of the entire committee. The chosen cast is to be subject to the approval of the Director of Production.

Section 3. Any member of the general public is eligible to try out for a part in a production of this organization, and the selection of him to enact a part therein automatically allows him to become a member of this organization with all the duties, rights, and privileges of every other member.

Section 4. Any person who is cast in a part in a production of this organization will forfeit such part for any unexcused absence from rehearsal of said production.

Section 5. All rehearsals of the productions presented by this organization shall be closed to everyone except members of this organization except by invitation and approval of the Director of Production.

Section 6. "Sides" for any part in any production of this organization will not be issued until the time of the first reading of the play to be presented.

Section 7. For each production of this organization, the President shall appoint all committees. The number of committees and number of persons of each committee shall be at the discretion of the President, except as herein otherwise provided. Only the chairman of each committee shall have the authority to confer with the Director of Production concerning the work of his respective committee.

ARTICLE X

Section 1. Robert's Rules of Order shall govern the proceedings of all meetings of this organization and its constituent parts except as herein otherwise provided. These Bylaws may be amended by presentation of said proposed amendments at any regular organization meeting and to be followed by a majority vote of members present at the following regular organization meeting.

This Constitution and these Bylaws were unanimously adopted by 100 percent vote of the prospective members of this organization at a meeting held for that purpose in ———, Ohio, on the 18th day of February in the year of our Lord, nineteen hundred and fifty-two.

———————————
President

CONSTITUTION OF A SCHOOL THEATRE
(Taken verbatim from an existing high school theatre)

I. Purpose.

The purpose of the ——— is to develop an active interest in theatre and to expand its members' knowledge about various technical and performing aspects of the theatre.

II. Membership.

Membership in ——— is limited so that individual accomplishment and participation can be fully developed. Membership is contingent upon the active and continuous involvement in plays. It can be rewarding to those who conscientiously devote their time and effort to school productions.

Requirements for membership:

One should have been in two plays with a speaking part, or should have been a student director on one play, or on the stage crew for three productions.

If a candidate has had a major speaking role in one production and worked on crew for another he is eligible.

A candidate who meets eligibility standards may be voted in by a two-thirds majority of the entire active membership.

If a member misses three meetings without justifiable cause he is expelled.

III. Duties of Officers.

President: The President's job is to conduct meetings, prepare agenda, and organize extracurricular activities, e. g., workshops, trips, plays. He should serve as a channel of communication for the adviser and the club members. He should be aware of the financial and social condition of the club.

Treasurer: The duties of the Treasurer are to keep an accurate record and give up-to-date reports on the financial status of the club. He is to attend to such matters as royalties, tickets, and collecting money for trips.

Secretary: The duties of the Secretary are to promptly handle all correspondence. This includes ordering scripts, keeping an active file on all available plays, and keeping the club memorial. The Secretary should keep the notes of all formal meetings and be prepared to give a report of the previous meeting at all formally announced meetings.

Student Director: The Student Director should be the choice of the club adviser. He may be voted a member of the club after one play. His duties are to assist the director in any way he can. He is a temporary officer during the period of his first production.

ARTICLES OF INCORPORATION OF A COMMUNITY THEATRE

(Taken verbatim from an existing community theatre)

We, —— as President, and ——, as Secretary, of the ———— Theatre, Inc., a nonprofit corporation, do hereby certify that at a monthly meeting of the members of said corporation held at 8 P.M. on the 16th day of December, 1962, at the registered office of the corporation, in the city of ————, Minnesota, which said meeting was legally held pursuant to proper notice given to all of the members containing the time, place, and purpose of such meeting, the following resolution was proposed by the Board of Directors of said corporation and passed by more than a majority vote of the members of said corporation then and there present and voting, to wit:

"RESOLVED that the Articles of Incorporation of —— Theatre, Inc., as heretofore adopted, be and the same are hereby amended so that said Articles of Incorporation shall read as follows, to wit:

"ARTICLE I

"The name of this corporation shall be —— Theatre, Inc. The registered office of the corporation shall be located in ——, Minnesota. Its corporate existence shall be perpetual.

"ARTICLE II

"The purpose of this corporation shall be to promote interest in and enjoyment of the dramatic arts in the community of ——, Minnesota, including the surrounding area, providing both educational and recreational facilities and stimuli in that field, and, from time to time, to produce and offer to the public various dramatic productions. For such purpose, this corporation shall have the power to receive, own, administer, encumber and dispose of, in any way whatsoever, funds and properties of all kinds, whether received by gift, bequest, legacy, purchase, or otherwise, and to borrow money and to secure the same by mortgage or other hypothecation of its assets, and to acquire assets subject to and charged with the payment of obligations. The corporation shall also have all of the powers afforded to it by the provisions of the Minnesota Non-Profit Corporation Act and all acts amendatory and supplementary thereof. No part of the properties or income of the corporation shall ever be used or employed directly by the corporation for the purpose of carrying on propaganda or otherwise attempting to influence legislation.

"ARTICLE III

"There shall be no capital stock in this corporation, and the corporation shall not afford pecuniary gain, incidentally or otherwise, to its members.

"ARTICLE IV

"The government of this corporation and the management if its affairs shall be vested in a Board of Directors consisting of the President, Vice-President, Secretary, Treasurer, and not less than five, nor more than fourteen, additional directors. The directors shall be elected by the membership as the Bylaws provide, and the four above-named officers shall be elected by the Board of Directors from its membership. The four directors who are also officers of the corporation shall have all of the rights, privileges, duties and authority of directors generally and shall serve as such officers for the period of one (1) year and until their successors are elected and qualified. All directors shall serve for such period, not exceeding three (3) years, as the Bylaws may pro vide. Vacancies of officers and directors shall be filled for the unexpired term of the person whose position is vacated.

"ARTICLE V

"The members, directors, and officers of the corporation shall have no personal liability for corporate obligations."

IN WITNESS WHEREOF, we have hereunto set our hands this 17th day of January, 1963.

_____
President

_____
Secretary

STATE OF MINNESOTA)
) SS
COUNTY OF _ _ _ _ _ _ _)

On this 17th day of January, 1963, before me, a Notary Public within and for said County, personally appeared ——— and ———, to me known, who, being by me first duly sworn did say that they are respectively the President and Secretary of the ——— Theatre, Inc., the nonprofit corporation named in the foregoing instrument; that said corporation has no corporate seal; and that they executed the foregoing certificate by authority of the Board of Directors and Members of said nonprofit corporation; and the said ——— and ——— acknowledged the foregoing instrument to be the free act and deed of said nonprofit corporation.
(NOTARIAL SEAL)

_____
Notary Public, ——— County, Minn.
My commission expires
Sept. 12, 1967

BYLAWS OF ——— THEATRE, INC.

ARTICLE I
Corporate Seal

The corporation shall have no corporate seal, and all instruments executed on behalf of the corporation shall be attested simply by the signature or signatures of one or more officers who may certify that the corporation had adopted no seal.

ARTICLE II
Membership

Section 1. Membership in the ——— Theatre, Inc., shall be open to every person who applies therefor and whose application is approved by the Board of Directors and who maintains the periodic contributions required of members of his class as the same become due. Membership shall be divided into the following classes:

A. Subscription members, who shall be entitled to regular season tickets as an incident of their membership dues.

B. Patron members, who shall be entitled to patron's season tickets as an incident to their membership dues.

C. Active members, who shall be otherwise qualified as either subscription members or patron members (thereby being entitled to the season ticket incident to their membership dues) or who have paid annual membership dues.

The Board of Directors shall by resolution from time to time fix and determine the amount of the annual dues or contributions to be assessed each member, according to his classification as a subscription member, a patron member, or other active member.

ARTICLE III
Meetings of Members

Section 1. An annual meeting for the election of directors and the transaction of other business shall be held upon due notice once each year at such day and at such time and place as the Board of Directors may determine.

Section 2. When the annual meeting has not been held, or directors have not been elected thereat, directors may be elected at a special meeting held for that purpose. Upon demand of any member, the President, Vice-President, or Secretary shall call the special meeting.

Section 3. In addition to the annual meeting of the members, special meetings of the members may be called by the Board of Directors. The Board of Directors shall also call a special meeting when requested in writing to do so by ten or more active members of the ——— Theatre.

Section 4. All active members whose annual contributions for the current year are paid at the time of any meeting shall be entitled to vote at such meeting. Representation at any meeting of the members shall be in person only.

Section 5. Notices of meetings, when required,

may be given orally or in writing, by telephone, by announcement or delivery to the members present at a regular meeting, by mail, in person, or by publication in any newspaper of general circulation in —— County, not less than two (2) nor more than forty-two (42) days prior to the time of the meeting. No notice shall be required to be given to members not entitled to vote at such meeting, determined as of the time notice is given. It shall not invalidate any action or proceeding at any meeting otherwise regularly constituted, that notice was not actually received by any member or members.

Section 6. The presence of fifteen (15) active members, including four (4) directors, at any meeting shall constitute a quorum.

ARTICLE IV
Officers

Section 1. The officers of the corporation shall consist of a President, a Vice-President, a Secretary, and a Treasurer, but only one office shall be held by any one individual at any one time. The terms of office of the officers shall be for one year from June 15th and until their successors are elected and enter upon their duties.

Section 2. The President shall preside at all meetings of the members and of the Directors and shall have such other duties as the members or the Directors may prescribe.

Section 3. The Vice-President shall temporarily perform the duties of the President during the absence or disability of the latter and shall have such other duties as the members or the Directors may prescribe.

Section 4. The Secretary shall attend and act as clerk of all meetings of the members and of the Board of Directors, keeping a record of all of the proceedings thereof in the minute book of the corporation, and shall have such other duties as the members or the Directors shall prescribe.

Section 5. The Treasurer shall keep an accurate record of all monies and other assets of the corporation and render accounts thereof to the directors and the members whenever required. He shall deposit all monies of the corporation in its name and to its credit in such banks as the Board of Directors shall from time to time designate. He shall have power to endorse for deposit all notes, checks, and drafts received by the corporation. He shall disburse the funds of the corporation, and shall have power to draw checks and drafts on the corporate bank accounts over his own signature alone. In the absence or disability of both the President and the Vice-President, he shall temporarily perform the duties of the President, and he shall have such other duties as the members or the directors may prescribe.

In the absence or inability of the Treasurer to perform the duties of his office, the power to draw checks and disburse the funds of the corporation shall vest in such other officer as the Board of Directors may, by resolution, have designated. A copy of such resolution shall be kept in the files of the bank or banks designated as the corporation's depository or depositories.

It shall be the duty of the Board of Directors to provide for an annual audit of the books and records of the Treasurer.

Section 6. Vacancies among the officers of the corporation shall be filled by the Board of Directors at the meeting of the Board of Directors immediately following such vacancy.

ARTICLE V
Directors

Section 1. The operation of this corporation shall be controlled by a Board of Directors consisting of twelve (12) directors and such additonal directors not to exceed four (4) as the members may approve upon the recommendation of the directors, who shall be elected from the membership of the corporation for a term of three (3) years. One third of the total number of directors shall be elected annually so that of the first Board of Directors to take office subsequent to the approval of the within amended Bylaws, one third of them shall have a one (1)-year term, one third of them a two (2)-year term, and one third of them a three (3)-year term, but in each case as the term of office of each said group of directors expires they shall be replaced by directors who shall serve for a full term of three (3) years, so that each year approximately one third of the directors' terms of office shall expire.

Section 2. The officers of the corporation shall include a President, a Vice-President, a Secretary, and a Treasurer, to be elected by the Board of Directors from its membership.

Section 3. A majority of the Board of Directors, if one officer be present, shall constitute a quorum for the transaction of business by the Board; provided, however, that if any vacancies exist by reason of death, resignation, or other inability to act, a majority of the remaining directors shall constitute a quorum for the filling of such vacancies.

Section 4. The Board of Directors shall meet at

such times and places as the President or any three directors may by notice direct.

ARTICLE VI
Nomination and Election of Board of Directors

Section 1. Prior to each meeting of the members at which directors are to be elected, other than the annual meeting, the Board of Directors shall meet and nominate one or more persons for each vacancy to be filled. These nominations shall be presented to the meeting of the members where they shall be subject to additional nominations from the floor. Upon the close of nominations, elections for each vacancy for which more than one nomination has been made shall be by secret ballot, with a simple majority required to elect. Election to all other vacancies shall be by voice vote, subject to the call of any member for a standing vote. Procedure following the failure of any vote to elect shall be determined by motion from the floor, duly carried.

Prior to the last regular meeting of the members held before the annual meeting, the Board of Directors shall meet and appoint a Nominating Committee for the directorships to be filled by election at the annual meeting. Said Nominating Committee shall be composed of the last three past presidents of the corporation who are still residing in —— County, Minnesota.

Prior to the annual meeting of the corporation, the Nominating Committee shall meet and nominate one or more persons for each directorship to be filled by election at the annual meeting. These nominations shall be presented at the annual meeting of the members where they shall be subject to additional nominations from the floor.

Elections of such directors shall be conducted at the annual meeting in the manner above provided for all other elections.

Section 2. Officers of the corporation shall be elected as provided in Article V, Section 2, above.

Section 3. All directors may be chosen from among all of the persons who are active members in good standing.

ARTICLE VII
Amendment of Bylaws, Publication

Section 1. These amended Bylaws may be further amended, in whole or in part, by the vote of a simple majority of all active members present at any meeting of the members, but only after due notice of the substance of the proposed amendment or amendments.

Section 2. It shall be the duty of the Secretary to cause the Amended Articles of Incorporation and these Amended Bylaws and further amendments thereto to be published as directed by the Board of Directors.

IN WITNESS WHEREOF, we, being all of the officers of —— Theatre, Inc., do hereby certify that the foregoing amendments to the Bylaws were adopted at a duly constituted meeting of the members of the corporation on the 16th day of December, 1962.

S/ _____
　　　　President
S/ _____
　　　　Vice-President
S/ _____
　　　　Secretary
S/ _____
　　　　Treasurer

ORGANIZATIONS OF VALUE TO THE NONPROFESSIONAL THEATRE

(Most have publications, conventions, festivals, memberships. Write to them for full information.)

NATIONAL AND INTERNATIONAL

American Community Theatre Association (ACTA), a division of ATA, 815 17th Street N.W., Washington, D.C. 20006.

American National Theatre and Academy (ANTA), 245 W. 52nd Street, New York, N.Y. 10019.

American Theatre Association (ATA) (formerly American Educational Theatre Association), 815 17th Street N.W., Washington, D.C. 20006.

Assn. Canadienne du Théâtre d'Amateurs, Centre Culturel, Cité des Jeunes, Vaudreuil, Quebec, Canada.

Canadian Child and Youth Drama Association, 2250 W. 356th Street, Vancouver 13, British Columbia, Canada.

Children's Theatre Association, a divison of ATA, 815 17th Street N.W., Washington, D.C. 20006.

Children's Theatre International, c/o Mrs. Vera Stilling, President, 79 Eton Road, Bronxville, New York 10708.

Dominion Drama Festival, 170 Metcalf Street, Ottawa 4, Ontario, Canada.

International Theatre Institute (ITI), 245 W. 52nd Street, New York, N.Y. 10019.

International Thespian Society, 1610 Marlowe Avenue, Cincinnati, Ohio 45224.

National Association of Dramatic and Speech Arts, c/o Joseph Adkins, Executive Secretary, Fort Valley State College, Georgia 31030.

National Association of Schools of Theatre, a division of ATA, 815 17th Street N.W., Washington, D.C. 20006.

National Collegiate Players, c/o Howard Morgan, Executive Secretary, 4645 E. Granada Road, Phoenix, Arizona 85008.

National Theatre Arts Conference (formerly National Catholic Theatre Conference), c/o The Reverend Roger A. Emmert, Executive Director, 3333 Chippewa Street, Columbus, Ohio 43204.

National Theatre Conference (closed membership, but some fine publications), c/o Paul Meyers, Secretary, Library for the Performing Arts, Lincoln Center, New York, N.Y. 10023.

Phi Beta (music and speech fraternity), c/o Mrs. Harry J. Lumby, Secretary, 4950 W. Walton Street, Chicago, Illinois 60651.

Puppeteers of America, c/o Olga Stevens, Executive Secretary, Box 1061, Ojai, California 93023.

Secondary School Theatre Conference (SSTC), a division of ATA, 815 17th Street N.W., Washington, D.C. 20006.

Society of Stage Directors and Choreographers (a possible source of applicants for a paid director's position), 1619 Broadway, New York, N.Y. 10019.

Speech Communication Association (formerly Speech Association of America), c/o William Work, Executive Secretary, Statler Hilton Hotel, New York, N.Y. 10001.

Theta Alpha Phi (honorary drama fraternity), c/o Joel Climenhaga, President, 1010 Vattier Street, Manhattan, Kansas 66502

United States Institute for Theatre Technology (USITT), c/o Charles Levy, Secretary, 245 W. 52nd Street, New York, N.Y. 10019.

University and College Theatre Association, a division of ATA, 815 17th Street N.W., Washington, D.C. 20006.

University Resident Theatre Association (URTA), c/o Robert Schnitzer, Executive Director, Mendelssohn Theatre, University of Michigan, Ann Arbor, Michigan 48104.

Zeta Phi Eta (speech sorority), c/o Mary C. Wheeler, Executive Secretary, P. O. Box 1236, Seattle, Washington 98111.

REGIONAL AND STATE

American Community Theatre Regional Offices (for current names and addresses write ATA, 815 17th Street N.W., Washington, D.C. 20006).

American Theatre Association Regional Offices (for current names and addresses write ATA, 815 17th Street N.W., Washington, D.C. 20006).

Arkansas Community Theatre Association, c/o Dan McCraw, Meyer Building, Hot Springs, Arkansas 71901.

Carolina Dramatic Association, c/o Clark M. Rogers, Graham Memorial, University of North Carolina, Chapel Hill, North Carolina 27514.

Central States Speech Association, c/o Kenneth E. Anderson, Secretary, Department of Speech, University of Michigan, Ann Arbor, Michigan 48104.

Children's Theatre Association Regional Offices (for current names and addresses write to ATA, 815 17th Street N.W., Washington, D.C. 20006).

Community Theatre Association of Michigan, c/o Sydell Teachout, Secretary, #3, Portland, Michigan 48867.

Delaware Dramatic Association, c/o Mrs. William A. Hoffman, 3334 Centerville Road, Wilmington, Delaware 19807.

Eastern States Theatre Association, c/o John F. Havens, Secretary, 5 Hazelwood Drive, Jericho, New York 11753.

Florida Theatre Conference, c/o Clay S. Davis, 35 Flynn Drive, Pensacola, Florida 32507.

Georgia Theatre Conference, c/o Mrs. Sally Schatz, Secretary, P. O. Box 552, Albany, Georgia 31702.

Illinois Community Theatre Association, c/o H. Olendorf, 1103 Hillcrest Avenue, Highland Park, Illinois 60035.

Indiana Theatre League, c/o A. L. Bowlsby, President, 1935 Fairhaven Drive, Indianapolis, Indiana 46229.

Iowa Community Theatre Association, 1434 Idaho Street, Des Moines, Iowa 50300.

Kansas Community Theatre Conference, c/o Mrs. Amber Rebein, 1016 1/2 Baker, Great Bend, Kansas 67530.

Kentucky Theatre Association, c/o Bill Parsons, Western Kentucky University, Bowling Green, Kentucky 42101.

Midwest Theatre Conference, c/o Drama Advisory Council, 320 Westbrook Hall, University of Minnesota, Minneapolis, Minnesota 55455.

Mississippi Theatre Association, c/o Dr. Ray Graves, President, 833 S. Main Street, Greenville, Mississippi 38701.

New England Theatre Conference, c/o Miss Marie Philips, Executive Secretary, 50 Exchange Street, Waltham, Massachusetts 02154.

New Jersey Theatre League, Inc., c/o Mrs. Betty Mueller, Secretary, 54 Westro Road, West Orange, New Jersey 07052.

New York State Community Theatre Association, c/o Mrs. Catherine Gericke, Secretary, 42 Garfield Street, Glens Falls, New York 12801.

New York State Speech Association, c/o John J. Carney, Jr., President, Administration Building, State University of New York, Oneonta, New York 13820.

North Carolina Theatre Conference, c/o Marian A. Smith, 310 Irving Place, Greensboro, North Carolina 27408.

Northwest Drama Conference, c/o Horace Robinson, University of Oregon, Eugene, Oregon 97403.

Ohio Community Theatre Association, c/o Mrs. J. J. Lane, Secretary, 6672 Mallard Court, Orient, Ohio 43145.

Oklahoma Community Theatre Association, c/o Mrs. Jody Williams, 1622 7th Avenue S. W., Ardmore, Oklahoma 73401.

Puppetry Guild of Greater New York, c/o Rod Young, President, 93 Perry Street, New York, N.Y. 10014.

Rocky Mountain Theatre Conference, c/o Ron Willis, President, Colorado State College, Fort Collins, Colorado 80521.

South Carolina Theatre Association, c/o Mrs. Aileen Lau, Greenwood Little Theatre, Greenwood, South Carolina 29646.

South Dakota Theatre Association, c/o Carolyn Margulies, Community Playhouse, West 33rd Street, Sioux Falls, South Dakota 57105.

Southeastern Theatre Conference (SETC), c/o Philip G. Hill, Executive Secretary, Department of Drama, Furman University, Greenville, South Carolina 29613.

Southern Speech Association, c/o Julian C. Burroughs, Jr., Executive Secretary, Wake Forest University, Winston-Salem, North Carolina 27109.

Southwest Theatre Conference, c/o Mrs. Margaret Glen, Secretary, 106 Fairfield Oaks, Shreveport, Louisiana 71104.

Speech Association of Eastern States, c/o Thomas D. Houchin, Executive Secretary, Department of Speech, St. John's University, Jamaica, New York 11432.

Tennessee Theatre Association, c/o Fred Fields, T-101 McClung Tower, Knoxville, Tennessee 37916.

Theatre Association of Pennsylvania (TAP), c/o Ann Folke Wells, Secretary, P. O. Box M, Pleasant Gap, Pennsylvania, 16823.

Western Speech Association, c/o Robert Vogelsang, Executive Secretary, Department of Speech, Washington State University, Pullman, Washington 99163.

Wisconsin Community Theatre Association, c/o Mrs. William Bollow, Secretary, 314 W. Sugar Lane, Milwaukee, Wisconsin 53217.

STATE AND TERRITORIAL ARTS COUNCILS

(Your state council is a marvelous source of information, of disseminating your schedules, and possibly of funding one of your projects. Contact them, get to know their Boards and their permanent employees, especially those concerned with the performing arts.)

Alabama State Council on the Arts and Humanities. M. J. Zakrzewski, Executive Director, 513 Madison Avenue, Montgomery, Alabama 36104.

Alaska State Council on the Arts. A. James Bravar, Executive Director, 338 Denali, Anchorage, Alaska 99501

American Samoa Arts Council. Mrs. John M. Haydon, Chairman, Government House, Pago Pago, American Samoa 96920

Arizona Commission on the Arts and Humanities. Mrs. Floyd J. Tester, Executive Director, 6330 N. 7 Street, Phoenix, Arizona 85014

Arkansas State Council on the Arts and Humanities. Sandra Perry, Coordinator, Arkansas Planning Commission, Game and Fish Commission Building, Little Rock, Arkansas 72201.

California Arts Commission. Albert Gallo, Executive Secretary, 1020 O Street, Sacramento, California 95814.

Colorado Council on the Arts and Humanities. Robert N. Sheets, Executive Director, 1550 Lincoln Street, Denver, Colorado 80203.

Connecticut Commission on the Arts. Anthony S. Keller, Executive Director, 340 Capitol Avenue, Hartford, Connecticut 06106.

Delaware State Arts Council. Sophie Conagra, Executive Director, 601 Delaware Avenue, Wilmington, Delaware 19801.

District of Columbia Commission on the Arts. Leroy Washington III, Executive Director, Munsey Building, Room 543, 1329 E Street N.W., Washington, D.C. 20004.

Fine Arts Council of Florida. Beverly Dozier, Director, Division of Cultural Affairs, The Capitol Building, Tallahassee, Florida 32304.

Georgia Commission on the Arts. George Beattie, Jr., Executive Director, 225 Peachtree Street, N.E., Atlanta, Georgia 30303.

Guam—Insular Arts Council. Louise Hotaling, Director, University of Guam, Box EK, Agana, Guam 96910.

Hawaii—The State Foundation on Culture and the Arts. Alfred Preis, Executive Director, 250 King Street, Room 310, Honolulu, Hawaii 96813

Idaho State Commission on the Arts and Humanities. Suzanne D. Taylor, Executive Director, P. O. Box 577, Boise, Idaho 83701.

Illinois Arts Council. S. Leonard Pas, Jr., Executive Director, 111 N. Wabash Avenue, Suite 1610, Chicago, Illinois 60602.

Indiana State Arts Commission. Michael F. Warlum, Executive Director, Thomas Building, Room 815, 15 E. Washington Street, Indianapolis, Indiana 46204.

Iowa State Arts Council. Jack E. Olds, Executive Director, State Capitol Building, Des Moines, Iowa 50319.

Kansas Cultural Arts Commission. Robert A. Moon, Executive Director, 352 North Broadway, Suite 204, Wichita, Kansas 67202.

Kentucky Arts Commission. James Edgy, Executive Director, 400 Wapping Street, Frankfort, Kentucky 40601.

Louisiana Council for Music and the Performing Arts. Mrs. Edwin H. Blum, President, Suite 912, International Building, 611 Gravier Street, New Orleans, Louisiana 70130

Maine State Commission on the Arts and Humanities. Richard D. Collins, Executive Director, State House, Augusta, Maine 04330.

Maryland Arts Council. Donald Mintz, Executive Director, 15 W. Mulberry Street, Baltimore, Maryland 21201.

Massachusetts Council on the Arts and Humanities. Louise G. Tate, Executive Director, 14 Beacon Street, Boston, Massachusetts 02108.

Michigan Council for the Arts. E. Ray Scott, Executive Director, 10125 East Jefferson Avenue, Detroit, Michigan 48214.

Minnesota State Arts Council. Dean A. Myhr, Executive Director, 100 E. 22nd Street, Minneapolis, Minnesota 55404.

Mississippi Arts Commission. Mrs. Shelby R. Rogers, Executive Director, P. O. Box 1341, Jackson, Mississippi 39205.

Missouri State Council on the Arts. Mrs. Frances T. Poteet, Executive Director, Room 410, 111 South Bemiston, St. Louis, Missouri 63105

Montana Arts Council. David E. Nelson, Executive Director, Fine Arts Building, Room 310, University of Montana, Missoula, Montana 59801.

Nebraska Arts Council. Leonard Thiessen, Executive Secretary, P. O. Box 1536, Omaha, Nebraska 68101.

Nevada State Council on the Arts. Merle L. Snider, Chairman/Acting Director, 124 West Taylor, P. O. Box 208, Reno, Nevada 89504.

New Hampshire Commission on the Arts. John G. Coe, Executive Director, 3 Capitol Street, Concord, New Hampshire 03301.

New Jersey State Council on the Arts. Byron R. Kelley, Executive Director, The Douglass House, John Fitch Way, Trenton, New Jersey 08608.

New Mexico Arts Commission. Mrs. Josephine Cudney, Secretary, Lew Wallace Building, State Capitol, Santa Fe, New Mexico 87501.

New York State Council on the Arts. Eric Larrabee, Administrator for the Executive Committee, 250 West 57th Street, New York, N.Y. 10019.

North Carolina Arts Council. Edgar B. Marston III, Executive Director, 101 North Person Street, Room 245, Raleigh, North Carolina 27601.

North Dakota Council on the Arts and Humanities. John Hove, Chairman, North Dakota State University, Fargo, North Dakota 58102.

Ohio Arts Council. Donald R. Streibig, Executive Director, 50 West Broad Street, Room 2840, Columbus, Ohio 43215.

Oklahoma Arts and Humanities Council. Donald W. Dillon, Executive Director, 1426 Northeast Expressway, Oklahoma City, Oklahoma 73111.

Oregon Arts Commission, Terry R. Melton, Executive Secretary, 494 State Street, Salem, Oregon 97301.

Pennsylvania Council on the Arts. Gregory C. Gibson, Executive Director, 503 North Front Street, Harrisburg, Pennsylvania 17101.

Institute of Puerto Rican Culture. Ricardo E. Alegría, Executive Director, Apartado Postal 4184, San Juan, Puerto Rico 00905

Rhode Island State Council on the Arts. Hugo Leckey, Executive Director, 4365 Post Road, East Greenwich, Rhode Island 02818.

South Carolina Arts Commission. Wesley O. Brustad, Executive Director, 1001 Main Street, Room 202-A, Columbia, South Carolina 29201.

South Dakota State Fine Arts Council. Mrs. Charlotte Carver, Executive Director, 233 South Phillips Avenue, Sioux Falls, South Dakota 57102.

Tennessee Arts Commission. Norman Worrell, Executive Director, 507 State Office Building, 500 Charlotte Avenue, Nashville, Tennessee 37219.

Texas Commission on the Arts and Humanities. Maurice D. Coats, Executive Director, 818 Brown Building, Austin, Texas 78701.

Utah State Institute of Fine Arts. Wilburn C. West, Executive Director, 609 East South Temple Street, Salt Lake City, Utah 84102.

Vermont Council on the Arts. Frank G. Hensel, Executive Director, 136 State Street, Montpelier, Vermont 05602.

Virginia Commission on the Arts and Humanities. Frank R. Dunham, Executive Director, 932 Ninth Street Office Building, Richmond, Virginia 23219.

Virgin Islands Council on the Arts. Stephen J. Bostic, Executive Director, Caravelle Arcade, Christiansted, Saint Croix, United States Virgin Islands 00820.

Washington State Arts Commission. James L. Hazeltine, Executive Director, 4800 Capitol Boulevard, Olympia, Washington 98504.

West Virginia Arts and Humanities Council. Ewel Cornett, Executive Director, State Office Building #6, 1900 Washington Street East, Charleston, West Virginia 25305.

Wisconsin Arts Council. Oscar Louik, Executive Director, P. O. Box 3356, Madison, Wisconsin 53704.

Wyoming Council on the Arts. Mrs. Frances Forrister, Executive Director, P. O. Box 3033, Casper, Wyoming 82601.

BIBLIOGRAPHY

ANTA, ed. *Play Publishers and Distributors.* New York (245 W. 52nd Street).

———. *Pre-Sales Plan for Selling Blocks of Theatre Tickets.* New York (245 W. 52nd Street).

Aronson, Joseph. *The Encyclopedia of Furniture.* New York: Crown, 1938.

Association of Junior Leagues of America. *Catalogue of Children's Theatre Plays.* New York. (Write Junior League, Waldorf-Astoria, Park Avenue and 50th Street, New York, N.Y. 10022.)

Bailey, Howard. *The A.B.C.'s of Play Producing.* New York: David McKay Company, 1955.

Baumol, William J. and William G. Bowen. *Performing Arts—The Economic Dilemma.* Cambridge: The M.I.T. Press, 1966.

Bavely, Ernest, ed. *Dramatics Director's Handbook.* (Write National Thespian Society, College Hill Station, Cincinnati, Ohio 45224.)

Bernheim, Alfred L. *The Business of the Theatre.* New York: Little, Brown, 1929.

Bilowit, Ira J. *How to Organize and Operate a Community Theatre.* New York: American National Theatre and Academy (245 W. 52nd Street), 1964.

Bongar, Emmet. *Practical Stage Lighting* (The Theatre Student Series). New York: Richards Rosen Press, 1971.

Bruder, Karl C. *Properties and Dressing the Stage* (The Theatre Student Series). New York: Richards Rosen Press, 1971.

Buerki, Frederick. *Stage Lighting Simplified.* (Write Wisconsin Idea Theatre, Room 3026, Stadium, University of Wisconsin, Madison 53706.)

———. *Stagecraft for Non-Professionals.* Wisconsin Idea Theatre, Room 3026, Stadium, University of Wisconsin, Madison 53706.

Burris-Meyer, Harold and Edward C. Cole. *Scenery for the Theatre.* New York: Little, Brown, 1938.

———. *Theatres and Auditoriums.* New York: Reinhold, 1949.

Chalmers, Helena. *The Art of Make-Up.* New York: Appleton, 1935.

Chinoy, Helen and Toby Cole. *Actors on Acting.* New York: Crown, 1949.

Ciaccio, Mary Eleanor. *Prologue to Production.* (Write Association of Junior Leagues of America, Inc., Waldorf-Astoria Hotel, Park Avenue and 50th Street, New York, N.Y. 10022.)

Cotes, Peter. *Handbook for the Amateur Theatre.* New York: Philosophical Library, 1957.

Crafton, Allen. *Play Direction.* Madison, Wisconsin. (Write Wisconsin Idea Theatre, Room 3026, Stadium, University of Wisconsin, Madison 53706.)

Dean, Alexander. *Little Theatre Organization and Management.* New York: Duell, Sloan & Pearce, 1959.

Drummond, Alexander M. *Manual of Play Production.* (Write Cornell Cooperative Society, Cornell University, Ithaca, New York 14850).

Dusenberg, Delwin B. *Elements of Play Direction.* (Write National Thespian Society, College Hill Station, Cincinnati, Ohio 45224).

Fuchs, Theodore. *Stage Lighting.* New York: Little, Brown, 1929.

Gabriel, Ellen W. *Public Relations—and Your Box Office.* New York State Community

Theatre Association, 233 Warren Hall, Cornell University, Ithaca, New York 14850.

Gard, Robert E., and Gertrude S. Burley. *Community Theatre, Idea and Achievement.* New York: Duell, Sloan & Pearce, 1959.

Gassner, John. *Producing the Play* (Includes *The New Scene Technician's Handbook* by Phillip Barber). (rev.) New York: Holt, Rinehart & Winston, 1953.

Gillette, A. S. *Designing Scenery for the Stage.* Wisconsin Idea Theatre, Room 3026, Stadium, University of Wisconsin, Madison, 53706.

———. *Stage Scenery, Its Construction and Rigging.* New York: Harper and Brothers, 1959.

Green, Michael. *Downwind of Upstage, The Art of Coarse Acting.* New York: Hawthorn Books, 1966.

Gruver, Bert. *The Stage Manager's Handbook.* New York: Harper and Brothers, 1953.

Halstead, William P., *Stage Management for the Amateur Theatre.* New York: Crofts, 1937.

Hopkins, Arthur. *Reference Point.* New York: Samuel French, 1948.

Houghton, Norris. *Advance from Broadway; 19,000 Miles of American Theatre.* New York: Harcourt Brace, 1941.

Hovious, Jeanlee, ed. *A Guide to Community Theatre Organization and Management.* New York: ANTA (245 W. 52nd Street) 1967.

Jones, Margo. *Theatre in the Round.* New York: Holt, Rinehart, 1951.

Jones, Robert Edmond. *The Dramatic Imagination.* New York: Theatre Arts Books, 1941.

Kleckner, Donald C., ed. *The Ohio Community Theatre Association (OCTA) Manual.* Bowling Green, Ohio: State University Press, 1961.

Krows, Arthur Edwin. *Play Production in America.* New York: Henry Holt, 1916.

McCleery, Albert and Carl Glick. *Curtains Going Up.* Chicago and New York: Pitman, 1939.

McGaw, Charles J. *Acting Is Believing.* New York: Rinehart and Company, 1956.

Macgowan, Kenneth and William Melnitz. *The Living Stage.* Englewood Cliffs, New Jersey: Prentice-Hall Inc., 1955.

Messenger, A. Carl. *How to Build an Audience.* ANTA (245 W. 52nd Street, New York).

Miller, James Hull, *et al. Initial Factors in Theatre Planning.* ANTA (245 W. 52nd Street, New York).

Morison, Bradley G., and Kay Fliehr. *In Search of an Audience.* New York: Pitman, 1968.

National Information Bureau, Inc. *The Volunteer Board Member in Philanthropy.* New York (305 E. 45th Street).

National Recreation Association. *Community Theatre in the Recreation Program.* New York (8 W. Eighth Street).

———. *How to Produce a Play.* New York (8 W. Eighth Street).

National Thespian Society. *Rehearsal Techniques.* (Write National Thespian Society, College Hill Station, Cincinnati, Ohio 45224.)

———. *Theatre Publicity and Public Relations.* (Write National Thespian Society, College Hill Station, Cincinnati, Ohio 45224).

Nelms, Henning. *Lighting the Amateur Stage.* New York: Putnam, 1932.

New York State Community Theatre Association. *Notes for the Play Director.* (Write 233 Warren Hall, Cornell University, Ithaca, New York 14850).

Ommannay, Katherine Anne and G. Pierce. *The Stage and the School.* New York: Harpers, 1950 (rev.).

Oxenford, Lynn. *Playing Period Plays.* Chicago: Coach House Press, 1957.

Pearson, Talbot. *Encores on Main Street: Successful Community Theatre Leadership.* Pittsburgh: Carnegie Institute of Technology Press, 1948.

Plette, W. Frederic, ed. *Directory of Stage Equipment and Supply Houses.* (Write National Thespian Society, College Hill Station, Cincinnati, Ohio 45224).

Prickett, Charles F. *Aids for the Formation and Management of Little Theatres.* Pasadena, California: Pasadena Playhouse (39 S. El Molino).

Province of Ontario, Council for the Arts. *The Awkward Stage.* Toronto, 1970.

Publitex International Corporation. *Tested Methods in Fund Raising.* King of Prussia, Pennsylvania (P. O. Box 247).

Rappel, William J. and John R. Winnie. *Community Theatre Handbook.* Iowa City: Institute of Public Affairs, University of Iowa, 1961.

Rubin, Joel E., ed. *Basic Technical Bibliography.* New York: ANTA (245 W. 52nd Street).

——. *Stage Lighting for High School Theatres.* (Write National Thespian Society, College Hill Station, Cincinnati, Ohio 45224.)

——. and Leland H. Watson. *Theatrical Lighting Practice.* New York: Theatre Arts Books, 1955.

Seattle Junior Programs. *Children's Theatre Manual.* Anchorage, Kentucky: Children's Theatre Press.

Selden, Samuel, ed. *Organizing a Community Theatre.* New York: Theatre Arts Books, 1945.

——. *The Stage in Action.* New York: Crofts, 1941.

Simon, Bernard, ed. *Simon's Directory of Theatrical Materials, Services and Information.* (Write 247 W. 46th Street, New York, N.Y. 10036.)

Simon, Harry M. *Summary of Basic Insurances to Cover Production Operation by a Resident Theatre.* New York: ANTA (245 W. 52nd Street).

Stanton, Sanford E. *Theatre Management.* New York: Appleton-Century, 1929.

Stell, W. Joseph. *Scenery* (The Theatre Student Series). New York: Richards Rosen Press, 1971.

Taylor, John Russell. *The Penguin Dictionary of the Theatre.* Baltimore: Penguin Books, 1966.

Terry, Ellen and Lynne Anderson. *Makeup and Masks* (The Theatre Student Series). New York: Richards Rosen Press, 1971.

Theatre Architecture Project of the American Theatre Association. *Suggested Readings in Theatre Architecture.* ANTA (245 W. 52nd Street, New York).

Thompson, Helen M. *Handbook for Symphony Orchestra Women's Associations.* Vienna, Virginia: American Symphony Orchestra League Inc., Symphony Hill, 1963.

Ver Becke, W. Edwin. *Community Theatre Structure.* New York: ANTA (245 W. 52nd Street), 1953.

Walkup, Fairfax Proudfit. *Dressing the Part.* New York: Crofts, 1938.

Weiss, David W., Jr. *Low Budget Lighting.* Wisconsin Idea Theatre (Room 3026, Stadium, University of Wisconsin, Madison 53706).

Whiting, Frank M. *An Introduction to the Theatre.* New York: Harper & Row, 1961.

Whorf, Richard B. and Roger Wheeler. *Runnin' the Show.* Boston: Baker, 1930.

Wright, Edward A. *Understanding Today's Theatre.* Englewood Cliffs, New Jersey: Prentice-Hall, Inc., 1959.

Young, John Wray. *The Community Theatre—and How it Works.* New York: Harper and Brothers, 1957.